mountain people in a flat land

mountain people in a flat land

*a popular history of appalachian migration
to northeast ohio, 1940–1965*

Carl E. Feather

OHIO UNIVERSITY PRESS   ATHENS

Ohio University Press, Athens, Ohio 45701
© 1998 by Carl E. Feather
Printed in the United States of America
All rights reserved

Ohio University Press books are printed on acid-free paper ∞ ™

05 04 03 02 01 00 99 98   5 4 3 2 1

Portions of the text have appeared in different form in the *Ashtabula Star Beacon* and in *The Best Newspaper Stories of the Year/2* (Thomson Newspapers, 1995).

Frontispiece: John Fetters. *Photo by Carl E. Feather*
Front cover: David Alley harvesting ginseng in the floodplains of the Ashtabula River. *Photo by Carl E. Feather*
Back cover: Arvin Rumer. *Photo by Carl E. Feather*

Library of Congress Cataloging-in-Publication Data

Feather, Carl E.
    Mountain people in a flat land : a popular history of Appalachian migration to northeast Ohio, 1940–1965 / by Carl E. Feather.
        p.   cm.
    Includes bibliographical references and index.
    ISBN 0-8214-1229-9 (cloth : alk. paper). — ISBN 0-8214-1230-2 (paper : alk. paper)
    1. Appalachian Region, Southern—Biography. 2. Mountain whites (Southern States)—Appalachian Region, Southern—Biography. 3. Mountain whites (Southern States)—Ohio—Ashtabula County—Biography. 4. Rural-urban migration—Ohio—Ashtabula County—History—20th century. I. Title.
F217.A65F43 1998
977.1′34—dc21   97-46493

To my parents,
Carl Junior and Cossette Feather,
who left their mountain homes in 1956
to come to Ashtabula County and create
a better life—and, in the process, history.
This book is dedicated to them in appreciation
for all the sacrifices they made
in building that life in the flat land.

contents

illustrations

Kedron Apple Butter Reunion

foreword

From the mid-1800s to the mid-1900s, a great migration transformed the United States. During that time, the nation changed from largely rural in its population to largely urban. Some of the new urbanites migrated to the city from other countries, but a large proportion came from the rural hinterlands. Ohio was no exception, as rural migrants streamed into the cities, especially in the years after the Civil War. By the 1920s a majority of Ohioans and Americans in general lived in cities, and still the rural migration continued, making the urban population an overwhelming majority by late in the century. One of the last great rural-to-urban migrations in the United States was that from the Southern Appalachian Highlands, which began in the early twentieth century, but reached its peak in the decades after World War II.[1]

Because of its proximity to the mountains, Ohio became a major destination of these Appalachian migrants. Between 1940 and 1970, up to seven million people moved out of the mountains, about one million of them to Ohio. The vast majority were white, though about fifty thousand of those who came to Ohio were African Americans.[2] Most of these mountaineers moved to Ohio's large cities. They followed the highways: Kentuckians to Cincinnati and Dayton, West Virginians to Akron and Cleveland. Columbus received a share from both states.

A relatively smaller number took the highway from West Virginia to Ohio's northeastern tip on the shores of Lake Erie in Ashtabula County. It is the story of these newcomers to Ohio that Carl E. Feather relates in this book. While Ashtabula County was not a leading destination for Appalachians, it is a wonderful vantage point for surveying the migration. For the experiences of Ashtabula Appalachians provide a picture in miniature of the thousands of their fellows in Ohio's urban centers. Highlanders in Ohio all faced challenges of adjusting to factory work, strange customs, and a stranger landscape. They experienced prejudice because of their accents, and they earned the respect of their neighbors through their hard work and strong family bonds. They enriched Ohio by adding their music and religious traditions to the migrant and immigrant mix of Ohio culture.

The importance of the Appalachian migration to Ohio is finally being recognized. I am glad to have been a part of this through my work for the Ohio Historical Society. In 1996 the Society opened a new exhibit, "Paradise Found and Lost: Migration in the Ohio Valley, 1850–1970," in which the story of the move from the Appalachian highlands to Ohio is told. The exhibit is located at the Society's Campus Martius: The Museum of the Northwest Territory in Marietta, Ohio. Carl Feather's book is another valuable form of recognition of this migration.

The Appalachian Range extends from Canada to the southern United States. Only in the late nineteenth century did writers and reformers identify a section of the southern Appalachians in eight states as a separate region of the country, distinguished by a peculiar set of cultural characteristics. The discovery of Appalachia was primarily a literary phenomenon, the work of writers who mined Appalachia for "local color." One of the earliest images central to this literary construct was that Appalachia represented America's pioneer past, a vestige of the life Americans had lived a century before. What the writers described was poverty, but the grinding reality of being poor does not sell as many magazines as does the picturesque. As time went on, however, reformers and missionaries saw Appalachian otherness less as a colorful remnant of a bygone time and more as a social problem to be solved. Missionaries and social workers came to the Appalachia of literature and strove to solve real social problems in the mountains. Appalachia came to mean to many Americans backwardness, ignorance, and poverty. Almost a century of social construction culminated in 1965 with the creation of the Appalachian Regional Commission and a program to end Appalachian poverty.[3]

In fact, Appalachia is a diverse region, one that contains cities and towns as well as isolated rural farmsteads. Its culture is more a subset of southern culture than a distinct pioneer holdover. But many of its residents did experience poverty and hardship. Lack of jobs at home and opportunity in the North were the economic pushes and pulls for the great migration. The Appalachian economy was based on subsistence farming and characterized by social and economic isolation. In the 1870s the mountain economic and social system began to change when railroads extended their lines into the region. The railroads opened the rugged and previously (for the most part) inaccessible region to commercial development, in particular logging and coal mining.[4]

These industries offered cash wages, and people left farms to work in them. Many also sold land. Thus, by 1900, 90 percent of Mingo and Logan Counties and 60 percent of Boone and McDowell Counties, all in West Virginia, were owned by absentee landlords, mostly in New York, Boston, Baltimore, and London. Mountaineers began to abandon their old ways of life. Hog production, for example, a mainstay of the traditional economy, declined by 60 percent in the years immediately before World War I.

Coal mining was hard, dangerous work, and notoriously underpaid. Many workers turned to unions to improve wages and safety. In the 1920s and 1930s strikes rocked the Appalachian coal country. These confrontations often pitted miners against guards or private detectives hired by the mine companies. Mine owners had other ways of retaliating against workers sympathetic to unions. When a group of West Virginia miners joined the United Mine Workers Union, they and their families were thrown out of their company housing by the Liberty Fuel Company.

Although employment figures for coal miners in West Virginia continued to rise in the 1930s and 1940s, they reached their peak in the early 1950s, and fell drastically thereafter as the increased use of alternative fuels and mining mechanization threw thousands of mountaineers out of work. Thus 1950–60 was the major decade of migration from West Virginia coal field communities.

The timber boom went bust in the early 1920s. The nation was oversupplied with timber, and this overproduction led to a sharp fall in prices. The large logging companies laid off workers and the industry collapsed, leaving thousands of men out of work. Unemployed miners and loggers returned to their farms in the hollows. But industry had caused a great deal of damage to the Appalachian environment. Water pumped out of mines polluted streams and rivers. Mines at least were underground; logging devastated the hillsides. Rainwater runoff from ridge tops denuded of trees washed away thousands of acres of soil, ruined creek bottoms, and even changed the course of streams.

Appalachians had grown accustomed to the cash economy. The nearby towns had changed, becoming more like towns in other parts of the country, with beauty parlors, jukeboxes, movie theaters, daily newspapers, and local distribution of national magazines. Grocery stores had fresh meat, fresh vegetables, even citrus fruits—all items that were unavailable a few years before. The mountain people could not go back to their isolated ways. They turned to cash crops, especially tobacco, but also corn. But good cropland was limited. It was hard to make a living on the marginal land available on ridge tops and hillsides. Furthermore, most farms were overpopulated.

Between 1900 and 1930, the population of mountain counties grew by 55 percent. This compares with a 33 percent growth rate in non-mountain areas of the same states. Consider, for example, Russell County in southwest Virginia. In 1830 the population of Russell County was 6,714. There was plenty of land on which to grow crops and raise livestock. By 1930 the population had reached almost 26,000 and there were only about 2 to 2.5 tillable acres per person. Farms became too small to support the population. In the 1930s there was virtually no work, and a New Deal investigator described poverty as "chronic."[5]

In short, an area characterized by a subsistence economy had become moderately industrialized and partially integrated into the cash economy. Then the region had deindustrialized. The result was an area of poverty and limited opportunities. As a Kentucky mountaineer remembered, "There was nothing to do all around—no jobs. Maybe a farmer might have an odd job for you to do, but then he'd only pay you a quarter. So, I decided to go to Cincinnati."[6]

In the 1910s and 1920s, the northern states experienced a labor shortage. This shortage would have a profound effect on the Appalachian region. Industrial states such as Ohio, Michigan, and Illinois depended on two major sources of labor: migrants from farms and migrants from abroad. The major source for unskilled and semi-skilled factory labor had been European immigrants. Although the outbreak of World War I in Europe in 1914 stopped that migration stream, in 1919 and 1920, with the war over, immigration began to revive. But many Americans feared that too many immigrants would have a negative effect on national culture. In the 1920s, therefore, the United States Congress passed laws restricting immigration. European workers were no longer available in large numbers for American manufacturers to hire, just when the population decline in rural areas in the 1920s caused migration from that source to slow down as well.

Industry turned to Appalachia for laborers. Companies such as Goodyear

Tire and Rubber of Akron, Buckeye Steel of Columbus, Champion Paper of Hamilton, and Armco Steel of Middleton advertised for workers in West Virginia and Kentucky newspapers. Mountain recruitment had begun during World War I. In March of 1918, for example, Goodyear advertised in the *Wheeling Intelligencer*: "We need a large number of skilled and unskilled people between the ages of 18 and 45, both male and female. . . . We are doing an enormous business both in government and regular commercial lines, necessitating exceptional demand for labor." In the 1920s, industrialists hired labor recruiters to spread the word about opportunities in Ohio using handbills and personal contacts. Firms also sent special trains into the mountains in search of workers. The process slowed down during the Depression of the 1930s, but picked up again during and after World War II. In the 1950s, Buckeye Steel, for example, used chartered buses to bring in Appalachian workers to its Columbus factory.[7]

West Virginians and Kentuckians heard about opportunities in the north from sources other than advertisements and handbills. Kinship networks played a large role in Appalachian migration. The relocation of one family member to an Ohio city created a beachhead, as it were, and others followed. Migrants wrote back home about their jobs. Some returned to the mountains for visits, full of stories of their new life in Ohio. One West Virginia woman remembered that "my mama's sister and her husband came up to Cincinnati about '35. When they left, they left with nothing—caught a bus to the city. When they came back, he was driving his own car, he had a nice suit on, and he had *money.*" Once the migration stream started, it was just this sort of personal, family contact that kept it going, and, indeed, increased the flow. "Yes, I had a lot of relatives helping me," remembered one Kentuckian. "I . . . [had] a sister in Cincinnati and another one in Dayton. . . . I went up to Cincinnati with my cousin." Migrants moved to areas where relatives already lived. These relatives typically gave them a place to sleep, and helped them find a job and a permanent place to live.[8]

Once migration started, it grew steadily. But who migrated? Most of the migrants were young men or young families with children. The average age of an adult migrant was the early twenties. The majority of migrants had an eighth-grade education; about a third had a high school diploma or higher. The Appalachian migrants tended to be from the better-off families in their community. This fact may seem surprising, but this characteristic is generally true of all migrations, whether from farm to city or from one country to another. The poorest in any community are the last to leave, if ever. Of course, "better-off" is relative. The most fortunate family in a Kentucky hollow in the 1940s would seem destitute when compared to even a moderately well-off resident of Cleveland. Appalachians of higher status had enough resources to send their children to school longer. These young people could read: read the advertisements for jobs in Ohio, read the letters from kin that told of jobs. They had the resources to move: to afford a car or at least bus fare. And they had the foresight to recognize, painful as it often was, that there were no longer opportunities in the mountains.[9]

Appalachians migrated for reasons other than economic concerns. Mountaineers moved to take advantage of the better housing and schools that cities offered or to experience more interesting professional or leisure opportunities. Many migrants saw the cities of Ohio as the best place to raise their children. One mountaineer commented, "It's better for my children up here. In a city you can get some money. . . . I don't make much, but . . . I make enough to feed my family." A Kentucky mother living in Cleveland wanted her "boys to go through school here and get a first-class city education for themselves." And there were more things to do. A young man in Ohio concluded: "I like Dayton. . . . You can live it up here. You can take a girl out on the town. You can have a good supper, any kind you want, then go to a movie, almost any kind you want. You can go bowling and you can go play pool and you can hear a good singer in a club and have a few drinks. It's not bad living in a city." Moving to Columbus made a Kentucky woman realize how closed and isolated her home had been: until she moved, she said, "I had never been in a city this big. I had never ridden on an escalator. I had never been in a big department store. I had never been to a really nice restaurant. I had never eaten seafood."[10]

Moving was not easy. It meant leaving the familiar mountains, family, and friends. It meant taking a chance in a world that could be frightening as well as appealing. As one West Virginia mother said: "I am worried about my children moving to the city because I hear every day of children being destroyed, being . . . run over by cars, . . . being on dope. One dose of it calls for another, and they go from bad to worse. A lot of them wind up in prison, and a lot of them wind up dead." The city posed dangers, yes. But what was the alternative? "You don't want to leave the mountains because of the strangeness ahead of you," said one migrant. "But you know you leave or you near die." This migrant implicitly recognized that a cultural divide would be crossed making the move. The Appalachian migrant was much closer to the immigrant experience than were the participants in earlier farm-to-city migrations.[11]

Language provides one analog between the immigrant and mountain migrant experience. The accent of the migrants often at best caused them embarrassment, and at worst resulted in harassment. Hazel Dickens recalled that "People were always putting down my accent," and that she "felt terribly inferior when I came to the city." As Jim Hammitte, who migrated from Kentucky in 1942, remembered, "There was a lot of discrimination on the job or in the city. . . . You had a constant be on your toes, have your guard up for southern language you used because if you spilled some of it out and it wasn't according to Hoyle, why some northern person grab it and poke fun at you immediately. . . . [T]he ones that could cope with it and roll and joke back come through all [right]."[12]

The migrants retained other cultural touchstones as a way of bringing the warmth of home to cold northern cities. Country music was one of these. Country music combines traditional balladry and instrumentation with the institutions of commercial popular music. It developed as a largely regional phenomenon. The migration of southerners, including Appalachians, made the music a part of the national culture. Migrant and singer Hazel Dickens remembered that "If I mentioned anybody that I liked or respected in the music field, nobody knew who I was talking about, unless I was talking to somebody who came from back home." For the Kentuckians and West Virginians, going out and listening to country music was an important recreation. As Dickens remembered, "they'd get all dressed up and come and listen to the music and dance all night." Live performances and jukeboxes in bars brought the music to Ohio cities. From there, local radio stations picked it up, adding the music to their other offerings in programs such as "Midwestern Hayride" on WLW in Cincinnati. This program made the transition to television in the 1950s, becoming one of the earliest country broadcasts in that medium. Eventually, in the 1970s, some radio stations adopted all–country music formats. This reflected the large audience of first- and second-generation migrants in Ohio cities and the growing taste for the music among other Ohioans.[13]

To take one example, the influence of the migration and of Ohio shows clearly in the career of singer Dwight Yoakam. Born in 1956 in Pikeville,

Kentucky, he moved with his family to Columbus in the late 1950s, graduated from high school in Columbus, and studied history and philosophy at Ohio State University, while playing in a rockabilly band at gigs around southern Ohio. Initially unsuccessful at breaking into the Nashville country music scene, Yoakam moved to Los Angeles, working as a truck driver by day and singer by night before finally launching his recording career in 1986. He was one of several younger performers credited by music critics with reviving country music from a stagnant period. In January 1992 Yoakam made his debut at Nashville's Grand Ole Opry. Several of his songs touch on migration themes, most notably "Readin', Rightin', Rt. 23"—Route 23 being the highway that took migrants from Kentucky to Columbus. Yoakam sings of the hope of migrants for greater opportunity in the north, their loneliness, and the sadness of failed dreams.[14]

Religious institutions also constituted a way for migrants to retain their cultural identity. Most Appalachian migrants to Ohio did not feel at home in the Protestant and Roman Catholic churches they found in the state. These churches typically did not reflect Appalachian religious belief or style of worship. Appalachians tended to belong to Baptist or Pentecostal religious traditions rooted in nineteenth-century revivalism. They focused on individual salvation and a literal interpretation of the Bible. The Pentecostal tradition featured an emotional worship style, including speaking in tongues.[15]

Whether they constituted a small storefront or a large congregation, migrant churches often served as the center of members' community life. At prayer meetings, members supported one another through the problems they faced at work, with family or with their health. Social programs included suppers, picnics, gospel singing nights, and other activities for young people and adults. Churches often helped to maintain members' ties to the hills through mountain summer camps for young people or arranging for "back home" burials for members.[16]

One example of this new religious culture was Dallas Franklin Billington's Akron Baptist Temple. Born in Kentucky in 1903, Billington moved to Akron in 1925 to work in a rubber factory. He wrote to his fiancée that Akron was "the wickedest place this side of hell." Not finding a church to his liking, he started preaching at storefront missions and on the local radio. In 1934 he founded the Akron Baptist Temple with just six families. In six months more than two hundred attended, mostly Appalachians working in the rubber factories, the group that was always the core of the Temple's ministry. By 1949 the church had 15,000 members, claimed to have the largest Sunday school in the world, and was described in *Life* magazine as the country's "biggest Baptist Church."[17]

Besides independent churches, the migration brought new denominations to Ohio. The most important of these was the Southern Baptist Convention. Kentucky migrants established the first Southern Baptist churches in the state in Cincinnati and nearby Hamilton in the 1930s. In the 1950s, as migration increased, Southern Baptist leaders began aggressive efforts at church planting. One motivation was that churches such as Billington's represented a more fundamentalist theology than that of most Southern Baptists at the time. Another motivation was the change of the Northern Baptist Convention's name to American Baptist. This declaration of continental rather than regional status encouraged Southern Baptist leaders to look beyond the South. Ohio was one of the first places they looked. The Rev. Ray E. Roberts, a native of Kentucky, was instrumental in this expansion, serving as a missionary planting churches in Ohio in the early 1950s and as executive secretary of the Ohio Southern Baptist Convention from 1954 to 1979. During Roberts's tenure the convention grew from a half-dozen or so churches to more than four hundred congregations located in all parts of the state.[18]

The Appalachian migrants, in their search for opportunity, changed the culture of Ohio and the nation. Their efforts to maintain their culture, especially through churches and musical traditions, spread their southern values. This movement added diversity to Ohio and the other states to which they moved and at the same time made the South less regionally distinct and more a part of the whole culture. Migration to Ohio cities proved a benefit for most Appalachian migrants and for Ohioans as well. Appalachians provided a major part of the industrial workforce needed for the economic expansion of the 1950s and 1960s. Most migrants had steady work and better houses, and were able to send their children through high school and often to college.[19]

But the move took a heavy toll. Though not great in miles, the highlanders' journey took them across a cultural divide that was almost as great as that encountered by immigrants from Europe or Asia. Indeed, in our modern, urban, mass media-dominated culture, the Appalachian migrants may have been the last internal migrants to cross a divide comparable to that experienced by foreign immigrants. The story of West Virginians and Kentuckians in northeast Ohio is a moving one, and a very American story. Carl Feather has looked to one small corner of Ohio and found stories of mountain dreams fulfilled in a flat land.

Dr. Stuart D. Hobbs
Historian, Ohio Historical Society

Notes

1. Eric H. Monkkonen, *America Becomes Urban: The Development of United States Cities and Towns* (Berkeley: University of California Press, 1988), 5–6. For bibliographical introductions to these migrations, see Howard P. Chudacoff, "A Reconsideration of Geographical Mobility in American Urban History," *The Virginia Magazine of History and Biography* 102 (1994): 501–18, and Jack Temple Kirby, "The Southern Exodus, 1910–1960: A Primer for Historians," *The Journal of Southern History* 49 (1983): 585–600, especially 595–600.

2. Estimates for the number of migrants can vary widely for a variety of technical reasons, most related to the way census data has been tabulated. These figures come from the Appalachian Regional Commission as cited in the *Columbus Dispatch*, 31 August 1997, 2A. For other estimates, see Dan M. McKee and Phillip J. Obermiller, *From Mountain to Metropolis: Urban Appalachians in Ohio* (Cincinnati: Ohio Urban Appalachian Project, Urban Appalachian Council, 1978), [1]; William Philliber, "Introduction," in Philliber and Clyde B. McCoy, eds., *The Invisible Minority: Urban Appalachians* (Lexington: University of Kentucky Press, 1981), 1. For a broad introduction to the migration, see James S. Brown and George A. Hillery, "The Great Migration, 1940–1960" in Thomas R. Ford, ed., *The Southern Appalachian Region: A Survey* (Lexington: University of Kentucky, 1967), 54–78.

3. Henry S. Shapiro, "Appalachia and the Idea of America: The Problem of the Persisting Frontier," in Bruce Ergood and Bruce E. Kuhre, eds., *Appalachia: Social Context Past and Present*, 2nd ed. (Dubuque, Iowa: Kendall/Hunt Publishing Company, 1983), 71–76. For a fuller treatment, see Shapiro's *Appalachia on Our Mind: The Southern Mountains and Mountaineers in the American Consciousness, 1870–1920* (Chapel Hill: University of North Carolina Press, 1970), and also Allen W. Batteau, *The Invention of Appalachia* (Tucson: University of Arizona Press, 1990).

4. This discussion of the Appalachian economy draws on Jack Temple Kirby, *Rural Worlds Lost: 1920–1960* (Baton Rouge: Louisiana State University Press, 1987), 80–111; Ronald D. Eller, *Miners, Millhands, and Mountaineers: Industrialization of the Appalachian South, 1880–1930* (Knoxville: University of Tennessee Press, 1982);

and Stephen Douglas Wilson, "The Adjustment Process of Southern Appalachian Whites in Cincinnati, 1940–1979" (Ph.D. diss., University of Kentucky, 1983), 11.

5. Kirby, *Rural Worlds Lost*, 99.

6. Wilson, "The Adjustment Process of Southern Appalachian Whites," 11.

7. *Wheeling Intelligencer*, 20 March 1918, 12. Similar ads were also placed in the *Wheeling Register* during this same period. Daniel Nelson, *American Rubber Workers and Organized Labor, 1900–1941* (Princeton: Princeton University Press, 1988), 52–54. John L. Thompson, "Industrialization in the Miami Valley: A Case Study of Inter-regional Labor Migration," (Ph.D. diss., University of Wisconsin, 1956), 136–39. Mansel A. Blackford, *A Portrait Cast in Steel: Buckeye International and Columbus, Ohio, 1881–1980* (Westport, Conn.: Greenwood, 1982), 130.

8. Shackelford and Weinberg, *Our Appalachia*, 328; Wilson, "Adjustment Process of Southern Appalachian Whites," 29. William L. Hamilton, et al., *The Causes of Rural to Urban Migration among the Poor* (Cambridge, Mass.: Abt Associates, Inc., 1970), 15–30. Jesus Rico-Valasco, "Immigrants from the Appalachian Region to the City of Columbus, Ohio: A Case Study" (M.A. thesis, Ohio State University, 1969).

9. Harry K. Schwarzweller, James S. Brown, and J. J. Mangalam, *Mountain Families in Transition: A Case Study of Appalachian Migration* (University Park: Pennsylvania State University Press, 1971). Clyde B. McCoy and James S. Brown, "Appalachian Migration to Midwestern Cities," in Philliber and McCoy, *Invisible Minority*, 35–78.

10. Robert Coles, *The South Goes North*, vol. 3, *Children of Crisis* (Boston: Little, Brown, 1972), 619, 324–25, 358; Ohio Urban Appalachian Awareness Project, *Report on Appalachians in Columbus* (Cincinnati: Urban Appalachian Council, 1978), 26.

11. Shackelford, *Our Appalachia*, 310; Coles, *South Goes North*, 618.

12. Guy and Candie Carawan, *Voices from the Mountains* (New York: Alfred A. Knopf, 1975), 69. Jim Hammitte Interview, Samford Oral History Program, Department of Special Collections, Samford University Library, Samford University, 2.

13. Bill C. Malone, *Country Music, USA*, rev. ed. (Austin: University of Texas Press, 1985), 171, 181–82, 208. Carawan, *Voices from the Mountains*, 69. Wilson, "Adjustment Process of Southern Appalachian Whites," 111–26. See also D. K. Wilgus, "Country-Western Music and the Urban Hillbilly," *Journal of American Folklore*, 83 (April–June 1970): 157–79; Paula Grundy, "'We Always Tried to Be Good People': Respectability, Crazy Water Crystals, and Hillbilly Music on the Air, 1933–1935," *Journal of American History* 81 (1995): 1591–1620; and Cecelia Tichi, *High Lonesome: The American Culture of Country Music* (Chapel Hill: University of North Carolina Press, 1994).

14. Joe Flint and Judy Nelson, *The Insiders Country Music Handbook* (Salt Lake City, Utah: Gibbs Smith Publisher, 1993), 368–69. *The Comprehensive Country Music Encyclopedia* (New York: Times Books, 1994), 445–46. *Hillbilly Deluxe*, Reprise Records, CD 25567-2.

15. Deborah Vansau McCauley, *Appalachian Mountain Religion: A History* (Urbana: University of Illinois Press, 1995). John D. Photiadis, ed., *Religion in Appalachia* (Morgantown: West Virginia University Press, 1978).

16. Wilson, "Adjustment Process of Southern Appalachian Whites," 92–101. William David Worley, "Social Characteristics and Participation Patterns of Rural Migrants in an Industrial Community" (M.A. thesis, Miami University, 1961), 82–84.

17. Billington quoted in "Biggest Baptist Church," *Life,* 25 July 1949, 59. See also *Colliers,* 18 November 1950, 32–33 and *Newsweek,* 11 April 1949, 76. Dallas Franklin Billington, *God Is Real* (New York: McKay, 1962). *Akron Baptist Temple: 50 Golden Years* (Akron: Akron Baptist Temple, 1984).

18. L. H. Morre, *The History of the Southern Baptists in Ohio* (Columbus: State Convention of Baptists in Ohio, 1979).

19. Gene B. Peterson, Laure M. Sharp, and Thomas F. Drury, *Southern Newcomers to Northern Cities: Work and Social Adjustment in Cleveland* (New York: Praeger Publishers, 1977), 232–35.

acknowledgments

This book belongs to the mountaineers, for I am but a weaver working with borrowed yarn. Their sweat, heartaches, and labors created the history that I have spun into words. I thank each one of them for the many hours spent around kitchen tables as they recalled the past, bared their hearts, and shared their dreams with the stranger with a pen. I pray that this work honors their lives and the contributions they gave not just Ashtabula County, but Ohio and the United States in those incredible postwar years.

My wife Barbara and son Aaron had the misfortune of living with me during these years of writing. This is my gift to you, a package of weekends and evenings lost, now recovered in what I hope you will regard as a significant investment of our sacrifices.

Gillian Berchowitz, senior editor for Ohio University Press, saw the merit in the cumbersome original manuscript and became a champion for its revision. Nancy Basmajian, manuscript editor, was the director of that revision. Her expertise and sharp eye for detail instilled harmony, style, and authority to the work. Thank you both; your encouragement sent me over the finish line running rather than crawling.

Jean Holden, a historian and fellow writer from Pierpont, reviewed the section on farm migration and was an encouragement throughout the writing process. Thanks, Jean; I hope to possess a modicum of your wisdom and vast knowledge by the time I, too, am an octogenarian.

Thanks to the librarians at Ashtabula County District Library and Kingsville Public Library, who helped track down books, obituaries, old city directories, clippings, and all the other details that go into a book like this.

Dave and Paula Bennear and Howard and Virginia Cosner reviewed the Thomas chapter and pointed out several potentially embarrassing errors. Thanks for your concern, interest, and friendship.

Neil Frieder, *Star Beacon* editor, allowed me to do the initial series and transfer the title of that newspaper piece to my book. Thanks for your support and encouragement as a writer. This book would probably never have happened if that first series had not been given print and received such a strong response. Accordingly, I am indebted to the many readers who called and gave their praise of the series and asked, "When are you going to put it in a book?"

Ron Lewis of the West Virginia University Department of History provided coal mining statistics and background for the original series. The staff at the West Virginia Collection of West Virginia University in Morgantown was also extremely helpful in tracking down scholarly material on the migration and local history background. The Appalachian Collection of that university was also a valuable resource.

Finally, thanks to my parents, who gave me a story to tell, a life to live, and the wherewithal to make it happen. Thank you for a childhood when I, too, was a migrant. I love you.

mountain people in a flat land

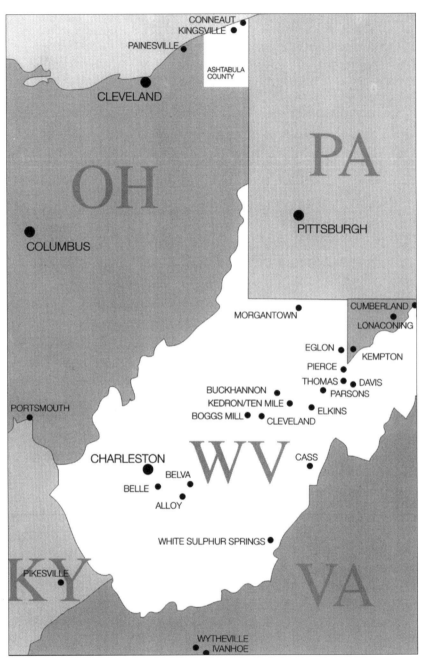

A few of the many Appalachian communities that provided Ashtabula County industries with workers from 1940 to 1965. *Illustration by Ed Freska*

introduction

looking for work

"If you took the hillbillies out of Ashtabula County, you wouldn't have anyone left here." That's the assessment of Halley Hamrick, who, like hundreds of other mountaineers from West Virginia, Kentucky, Virginia, southern Ohio, and southwest Pennsylvania, came to Ashtabula County in search of work from 1940 to 1965. A few found the labor too hard, the industrial work schedule too structured, or the workplace walls too confining, and returned home. Another small percentage found the locals unfriendly, aloof, or downright biased and returned to the familiarity and warmth of kin. And for some, the pace of urban life was too quick, the neighborhoods too large, or the temptations of liquor, city women, and easy credit too hard to resist for an honest country boy in search of work.

But most stayed. Taking advantage of the wide variety of blue-collar jobs that could be had for the asking, they built new lives, started families, bought homes, raised children, sent them to college, and took active leadership roles in their places of employment, worship, recreation, and community service. Names common in Appalachia were interwoven with the surnames of Western Reserve pioneers[1] and Italian, Irish, Swedish, and Finnish immigrants who defined the typical Ashtabula County resident prior to 1940.

It was not a migration of great distance. Most of the Appalachian migrants to the Western Reserve traveled less than five hundred miles and for many it was only three hundred. But differences in the culture and landscape were significant. Most obvious was the contrast in the physical environment: Ashtabula County has no mountains or valleys to speak of.[2] The region's relative flatness amazed the mountaineer motorist accustomed to being able to see no more than a few hundred yards of the road ahead. For this convenience he sacrificed the mountaintop vistas of cascading peaks extending to the horizon and most likely into another state. In return he got Lake Erie, which gave the mountaineer a "fishing hole" unlike any he'd ever seen in the mountains. There were woodlands for hunting, too, and some of them yielded the familiar ginseng, yellowroot, and other herbs that were essential items in the mountaineer's medicine chest.

There was a price to pay in culture, as well. The migrants' cultural traditions had been preserved in isolated hollows and hamlets since the Scotch-Irish began to settle the backwoods of Appalachia in the mid-1700s.[3] This traditional culture was destined to clash with the more progressive outlook of the North. In time, traditions became diluted or, especially in the case of music, assimilated and expanded. But in the first years of the mountaineers' arrival, there were cultural differences to be reckoned with and worked through.

Traditionalism in Culture

Mountain Families in Transition, a case study of Appalachian migration from Beech Creek, Kentucky, to industrial cities of the Ohio Valley, identifies three basic traits of Appalachian culture: familism, meaning that all social relationships and institutions are "permeated by and stamped with the characteristics of the family"; puritanism, the foundation of the mountaineer's faith and outlook on life; and individualism, which views every individual as a child of God and places high value on the self-made man.[4]

Familism was a key to the success of the migration. The Beech Creek study demonstrated that strong kin relationships provided the link for entire families to pack up and move north. It took only one migrant to establish a beachhead in the new community; others soon followed. This closeness and cooperation of family made it possible for many of the migrants to survive and succeed in a culture that was opposed to their own: they had a local circle of family and neighbors from back home to which they could withdraw in times of crisis, need, or loneliness. A 1968 comparative social study of more than five hundred West Virginians who migrated to and remained in Cleveland showed that 26 percent of the suburban migrants no longer had relatives in West Virginia; the researcher, John D. Photiadis of West Virginia University, speculated that those who were well established in the Cleveland suburbs had attracted their relatives to the city.[5] And a 1969 study of Columbus Appalachian migrants, done by Jesus Antonio Rico-Velasco, showed that 40 percent of the migrants interviewed cited the presence of kin already living in Columbus as their reason for settling there. Economics was the only factor cited by more migrants (51 percent) as a significant reason for coming to Columbus. "For Appalachian migrants, it was found that the area of destination is not randomly selected," according to Rico-Velasco. "Family structure and kinship ties played a very important role in the decision to migrate and in the selection of a place of destination."[6]

The other side of this familism was that the migrant did not sever ties with the family back in the mountains. While work, house, and conjugal family were in the North, the migrant's "home" remained in the mountains. This love of ancestral homeplace drove the migrant to practice a rite of return for weekends, holidays, vacations, funerals, reunions, hunting seasons, and whatever other excuse he could devise. One of the first purchases the transplanted mountaineer made was a car so he could make the trip back to kin and homeplace, if only for a few precious hours on a weekend. John Photiadis's study showed that up to 11 percent of the West Virginia migrants interviewed went back for visits more than ten times a year and only 7 percent of West Virginians who had migrated to the Cleveland suburbs never visited their home state. In the course of my interviews for this book, one migrant told me that he wondered if his move to the North had actually netted him an economic gain after subtracting all the money he had spent on cars, gasoline, and maintenance associated with these frequent trips back home.

The mountaineer's love of homeplace did not go unnoticed by his northern neighbors. Merlin Mead was a union president and treasurer for Electromet during the era that the Ashtabula Township factory hired many migrant workers. Merlin said Electromet workers could get a four-day weekend by working ten days straight. The Appalachian workers loved this arrangement and came to work with their cars packed for the trip. As soon as they were done working, they drove by the house, picked up the wife and children, and headed south.

This love of homeplace was expressed in a joke that a mountaineer shared with Merlin. A man died, went to heaven, and was getting the introductory tour from St. Peter. He pointed out sections reserved for each denomination as they toured the valley. Then he came to a hillside with a fence around it, and the new arrival asked who lived there. "Oh, these are all our West Virginia people," St. Peter said. "They still think they have to go home every weekend."

The Cold North

Another aspect of familism is the high value it places on neighborliness and hospitality. This value was often found wanting in the new culture, and the migrant could not understand why his Yankee neighbor did not open up his house or make available his resources as neighbors in his home hamlet would have done. Flavia Myers Cole migrated to Ashtabula County from near Charleston, West Virginia, in 1949. One of the differences she noticed between the two cultures was the northern attitude toward someone dropping in to visit. In the north, if the host was preparing dinner, the visit was viewed as an intrusion. A formal invitation was required for dinner, whereas in the Appalachian culture a visitor could expect his host to set another place at the table and insist he eat with them. This practice remains today in the homes of migrant families, where a visitor, no matter how casual, can hardly get away without eating a meal, or at the very least, having a beverage and snack with the family.

Industrial recruiters made the mistake of underestimating the strength of kinship when they scoured the mountains for out-of-work and underemployed Appalachian men. The industrialists expected to find desperate workers who would eschew the unity of the labor union and be thankful to have a good-paying job. This worked to a certain extent; as the Beech Creek researchers discovered, most of their subjects were not good "joiners."[7] But the tie of kinship imposed a unity that supervisors had not considered. If a relative, no matter how distant, fell ill or needed help back home, it was not unusual for the plant to see a substantial number of workers take off and head south to meet their kin's need.[8] But more distressing to the industrialists was the kinship of workers in time of strike. Ralph Ware, a West Virginia migrant, worked for Union Carbide thirty-nine and a half years, counting the strikes that periodically interrupted the work. Ralph said the worst strike came in 1967 and lasted seven and a half months. He said the workers as a whole exhibited solidarity during strikes, but for the migrants the struggle to do better and help each other extended beyond the union card to kin and community ties.

Merlin Mead was union president during the 1967 strike. He said moun-

Dave Bennear from Thomas, West Virginia, who found his first job in Ashtabula County at Lake City Malleable. The plant, shown in the background, has changed substantially since it was bought and renovated by RMI. *Photo by Carl E. Feather*

taineers showed a commitment to the cause that was not demonstrated by many of the other workers when it came time to pull picket duty or hold out for better benefits and higher wages. "The number one picketers I loved were the hillbillies," he said. "You bet your boots they were good people. Them, followed by the blacks. You give me a handful of mountaineers any time, and they'll do it for you."

The male migrant became assimilated into the new culture rather quickly by virtue of the workplace. His friendly, laid-back, honest personality helped him make friends with co-workers while his industrious work ethic won his supervisors' support.[9] For the migrant's wife, however, assimilation was a slower process. Many of the women did not have a driver's license. Further, most migrant families arrived in the North with only the clothes on their back, a few dollars in their pocket, a bed, and perhaps a piece of heirloom furniture. A migrant family getting established in a new community could barely afford one car (and its associated costs of operation with the frequent trips back home), much less a second vehicle for the wife to run errands. The migrant's wife and young children were stuck at home during the day; their neighborhood was only as wide as their feet could take them. Many of them lived in fear of their neighbors and the fast pace of the industrialized communities. Until friends and interests were established in the new community, the migrant housewife's life was frequently one of boredom and fear broken by the periodic joy of a trip back home.[10]

The northerner had been trained to be suspicious or contemptuous of the migrants by way of stereotypes perpetuated in media sources such as Lum and Abner radio shows, Snuffy Smith cartoons, Ma and Pa Kettle films, and —in the 1960s—the *Beverly Hillbillies* television situation comedy. Many northerners were thus surprised when their migrant neighbors didn't wear bib overalls, carry a "little brown jug," have a still in the backyard and chickens running loose in the house, or drive a red junker with a Confederate flag painted on the hood. Emma Bonham, a West Virginia migrant, tells of her daughter, Pauletta Ann, coming home from school shortly after migrating in 1955. Pauletta was puzzled that the teacher had asked her if she really wore shoes and if she knew how to make moonshine. "Pauletta didn't even realize what moonshining was," Emma said. "She said she thought it was something you did under the moon."

Perhaps the ultimate stereotype of a mountain person is a barefoot, bearded man lying on the front porch of a cabin, moonshine jug and shotgun next to him, pregnant wife rocking in a rickety chair, and hunting dog snapping at flies. Harry Gillespie, a White Sulphur Springs native, said that's a hillbilly, and he never saw one when he lived in West Virginia—although he's been called as much in Ohio. "I was a sophisticated hillbilly. . . . I'm a *West Virginia hillbilly mountaineer*," he said proudly.

Regardless of how thoroughly the mountaineer adapted to the culture and ways of the North, his dialect remained an articulated disclosure of his origins. Jean Hornbeck, a West Virginia migrant, said some landlords didn't trust the Appalachian migrants and turned them down over the phone on the basis of their dialect. Some mountaineers, desperate for housing, disguised their voices when inquiring about apartments. Other migrants found it was their unique vocabulary that caused problems. "I asked this clerk in a store to give me a poke," Jean Wilfong said. "They called them 'bags' up here." "She came home and told me what had happened," Jean's husband Loye said. "I told her, 'You better keep your mouth shut or you *are* going to get poked.'"

Maurice Osburn and his sister Jean Hornbeck with the model Maurice made of the family's home in Kedron, West Virginia, a farmhouse their father bought in 1944 after losing his job with the lumber company. *Photo by Carl E. Feather*

Ultimately what helped many mountaineers become assimilated into the new community was their strong religious background, which forced the migrant to find a place where the God of his childhood and mountains could be worshiped.[11] Some northeast Ohio churches took on a strong Appalachian flavor as the mountaineers brought their faith and music to worship. First Baptist Church in Ashtabula became a magnet for many of the West Virginia families after Harry and Ruby Gillespie came to faith there. So strong was the presence of West Virginians in the church that adult members put on "Hillbilly Nights" for those of mountain heritage. Dozens attended the gatherings, which featured down-home storytelling, music, and food.

The Appalachian migrants felt that God was with them as they came north, and that helped them weather the inevitable storms of settling in a new region. Further, the Beech Creek researchers concluded that the puritanical component of the culture gave the migrant a strong sense of right and wrong. Specifically, the mountaineer defined right as "self-discipline, hard work, keeping away from sensual pleasures, marital fidelity, thrift, and sacrificing for future goals."[12] These are welcome traits in any society, traits that contribute to industry, strong families, neighborhoods, and futures.

Individualism, the third of the cultural traits identified by the Beech Creek researchers, is an outgrowth of that puritanical outlook. The mountaineer believes in the ultimate strength of democracy. He does not like to be told what to do, yet his attitude is not flippant, for the mountaineer knows freedom must be tempered with responsibility. This attitude produced a clash with the structured society of the North on more than one occasion.

The story is told of a migrant who came to Ashtabula in the early 1950s and rented an apartment on Center Street. Back in his West Virginia home the man had a habit of building a fire in his backyard, sitting by it and drinking beer late into the evening. He transferred that habit to the city, much to consternation of an elderly neighbor, who reported his barbecue to the fire department. The migrant insisted he wasn't causing any harm and even showed the firefighters the garden hose he kept near the fire. But the firefighters insisted the fire had to be put out, and—grudgingly—the mountaineer obliged. "Fine," he said. "But you'll have to use YOUR hose to put it out with!"[13]

On a more positive note, this individualism and sense of right and wrong made the mountaineer a good worker and, combined with his kinship social structure, contributed to his success and adaptation in the North. The Appalachian culture places a high value on the self-made man, and urban communities like Ashtabula provided the migrant with channels for attaining that status. The mountaineer's culture and surroundings demand hard work for survival; in an environment of opportunity, that value blossoms into success.

The mountaineer is an individualist, but not a specialist. Out of the necessity to maintain an isolated lifestyle far from a service economy, he had to be a jack of all trades. The mountaineer continued to be a pioneer long after the rest of the country was settled. He is used to working hard and can do many different jobs, yet is modest about his accomplishments. Employers found these qualities desirable. Further, the mountaineer is a true self-starter who can take on and accomplish many different tasks with minimal supervision. Merlin Mead said the mountaineers who worked at Electromet possessed a keen ability with anything mechanical. "A lot of them weren't real educated, but, by gosh, they had mechanical ability," he said. "They could tear anything down, put it back together and make it work. They could keep the place running and do a good job."

First-Generation Sources

The story of these migrants is the saga of any group forced to leave home for that once-in-a-lifetime chance at success in the world. They were no different than the Italian and Irish immigrants who had arrived at Ellis Island some fifty to seventy years before and ended up laying railroad track and mining coal in the mountains of West Virginia. They, too, had stories to tell, but their words were lost to the grave, their stories distorted and forgotten by successive generations.

That is why I set about to write this book, to seize the unique opportunity to document from primary sources the stories of these migrants' lives in that mountain land and culture, the reasons for their coming, the connections that facilitated the move; and their struggles and successes in this new home. As a son of parents who migrated from West Virginia to Ashtabula County in 1956, I saw firsthand their intense love for the mountains and shared the pain they experienced every time the car headed north after a visit "back home." They were doing it to give me the opportunities they never had, to provide security for a future that seemed so bleak in those mountain hamlets. They faced the scrutiny and mistrust all migrants experience as they proved themselves worthy of the new land to which they were called and dispelled the negative stereotypes of their native culture and home.

It is that negative stereotype that I particularly hope to dispel with this book, to erase any conception of mountain people as lazy, dull, unmotivated, uncouth, fanatically religious individuals. Yes, every culture has its members who do not positively represent it. Yes, some migrants blew their wages on liquor, raising hell and creating headaches for Ashtabula County bar owners, policemen, and employers.[14] But the majority of those migrants didn't stay long. They worked enough hours to pay for their work boots, first month's rent, and transportation, then packed their belongings in a brown paper poke and bought a bus ticket back to the hollows and hamlets of home.

After interviewing scores of mountaineer migrants, I am convinced Appalachia gave the North its very best, hardest-working, most resourceful and ambitious individuals, who took on many of the jobs the locals did not want. They have set examples of honesty, industry, and loyalty wherever they have worked. They have established homes that are the pride of their neighborhoods. They have proven themselves to be friendly, caring, conscientious, responsible citizens.

Their numbers are dwindling. Almost every day an obituary appears in a northeast Ohio newspaper that reads "he/she was born in —, W.Va." The first generation of migrants who established a beachhead in the area from 1905 to 1940 is all but gone. Ruby Gillespie (chapter 4) and Larry Brown (chapter 8) died during the production of this book. The second generation is slipping away all too quickly and with it the stories of a way of life baby boomers and Generation "X" cannot comprehend.

My first effort to document their stories came in the form of a series of feature articles published by the *Ashtabula Star Beacon* during the week of March 28, 1994. The series was well received and many readers asked that it be published in book form. But I knew there were many more stories that needed to be told, and for the next three years I pursued leads and conducted interviews, basing chapters, whenever possible, upon the communities from which the migrants came. It has been a rewarding effort, but also a frustrating one, for time is always at a premium, especially when it is spent on an avocation. There are people whose stories I wish could have been part of this document, but who for one reason or another did not want to be included. And there are so many who have already gone home to the mountains of the Lord, their stories left to the cold Ashtabula County soil.

To make the project manageable, I have focused on one county, Ashtabula, which was a destination for West Virginia migrants primarily. However, the migrants could have been from Virginia, Kentucky, Tennessee, or western Pennsylvania and Maryland; their destination Cleveland, Dayton, Columbus, Lorain, or Cincinnati. An estimated 100,000 to 130,000 Appalachians lived in Cuyahoga County in 1973; one study sample showed 73 percent of the Cleveland Appalachian population to be from West Virginia and 15 percent from Tennessee.[15]

The Ford and Fisher Body automobile factories and steel mills were major migrant employers and recruited workers through newspaper advertising in West Virginia. In June 1951 an unidentified Cleveland steel mill ran Help Wanted ads on several Sundays in the *Charleston Daily Mail.* The ads sought "Male Help" with "no experience necessary." Transportation was furnished, rooms were arranged, and a representative was on hand at the West Virginia State Employment Service in Charleston. The mill went to considerable effort to make the employment process convenient.[16] Two years later, another unidentified mill ran similar ads in the *Charleston Daily Mail.* This time, the employer was seeking high school graduates in one ad and those with a minimum of an eighth-grade education in another. The applicants had to weigh at least 145 pounds and be between eighteen and forty. As before, transportation and paid housing would be arranged.[17]

The Lorain/Elyria area, west of Cleveland, was also a landing zone for Appalachian migrants, particularly those from the Huntington, West Virginia, area. National Tube Company in Lorain frequently recruited in West Virginia for workers through newspaper advertising and recruiters stationed at state employment agency offices.

A 1980 study done for the Appalachian Regional Commission ranked Cleveland as the sixth most popular migration destination for Appalachian migrants during the years 1955 to 1960; Cincinnati ranked eighth, Columbus twelfth, and Dayton fifteenth. In all, more than 68,000 Appalachian migrants had arrived in those four cities during the period from 1955 to 1960.[18] Regardless of which Ohio city the migrant came to, the reasons for coming remained the same: the push out of Appalachia by a lack of jobs and the pull of opportunity created by Ohio's rapidly expanding economy.

This book is intended to be a popular, oral history of the Appalachian migration to northeast Ohio, not a genealogical research tool, social or economic history, or textbook of the migration.[19] This is a book about common people in search of a better life. In the process, *they* created history, families, and fodder for research. Accordingly, my work is foremost meant to be enjoyed, not suffered through. Its purpose is to honor, not dissect, a wonderful, overlooked group of people who made significant contributions to every community they called "home."

Notes

1. The region known as the Western Reserve came into being in 1786, when Connecticut ceded to Congress all of its western lands except for a 120-mile-long strip of territory south of Lake Erie. This land, "reserved" for Connecticut, remained a colony of the state until 1800. The western section (the Firelands), containing half a million acres, was given to citizens whose property was burned during the Revolutionary War. The balance, amounting to three million acres, was sold to the thirty-five investors of the Connecticut Land Company in 1795. On Independence Day the following year, Moses Cleaveland and his surveying party arrived at the mouth of Conneaut Creek (Fort Independence and present-day Conneaut) to begin their work for the land company. James Kingsbury, with his wife and three children, had followed the company from Buffalo and settled at Fort Independence, but the surveying party continued west and founded the city of Cleveland along the Cuyahoga River.

Kingsbury's wife bore a child the following winter, the first white child born in the Western Reserve. Beginning in March 1798 with Alexander Harper, settlers began to arrive in Ashtabula County from New England. Communities took the names of their founding families (Austinburg, Harpersfield), the New England towns from which they hailed (Andover, New Lyme), or Indian names for the "river of many fish" (Ashtabula, Conneaut). For most of the nineteenth century, the Reserve remained a western double of its eastern parents in both appearance and nature. But the railroads and shipping industry that developed in the latter half of that century and heavy industry that came in the twentieth changed the region's flavor. Thousands of Italian, Finnish, and Swedish immigrants came to work on the docks at Ashtabula and Conneaut and to lay the rails that stretched from Lake Erie to the steel mills of Warren and Youngstown.

For more background on the Western Reserve, see Harlan Hatcher, *The Western Reserve: The Story of New Connecticut in Ohio* (Indianapolis: Bobbs Merrill Company, Inc., 1949; or Kent, Ohio: Kent State University Press in cooperation with the Western Reserve Historical Society, 1991; reprint of 1966 revised ed.).

2. The swath cut through the Ashtabula Township landscape by the Ashtabula River (known as "The Gulf" to locals) is as close to a valley as one gets in Ashtabula

County. Not surprisingly, this valley attracted the migrants as a fishing and recreation spot. As for mountains, the southern section of Ashtabula County has some hills, but to a true mountaineer these are just road bumps.

3. The Scotch-Irish trace their heritage to Englishmen who received grants of land in Ireland from the twelfth to fifteenth centuries and to Lowland Scots who moved to northern Ireland in the sixteenth century. From about 1700 to 1776 more than a half million Scotch-Irish immigrated to the United States. As country dwellers, they gravitated toward the outback country of New England, western Pennsylvania, the Shenandoah Valley and what later became known as Appalachia. Germans accounted for the other major nationality group to settle the Appalachians, although there were English, Dutch, and Welsh, as well. For more background on the Scotch-Irish and Celtic background of the Appalachian people, see B. B. Maurer, ed., *Mountain Heritage* (Parsons, W.Va.: McClain Printing, 1980), 32–37.

4. Harry K. Schwarzweller, James S. Brown, and J. J. Mangalam, *Mountain Families in Transition: A Case Study of Appalachian Migration* (University Park: The Pennsylvania State University Press, 1971), 58–67. The authors studied migration patterns from the Beech Creek communities of eastern Kentucky to the Ohio Valley over two decades, producing the most detailed sociological case study of the migration. Readers interested in the sociological implications of the migration will find this work of great interest.

5. John D. Photiadis, *Selected Social and Sociopsychological Characteristics of West Virginians in Their Own State and in Cleveland* (Morgantown: West Virginia University and U.S. Department of Labor, Office of Manpower Research, 1975). The author interviewed migrants from Mineral, Grant, and Raleigh Counties, West Virginia, who had moved to the Cleveland "West Virginia Ghetto" on the city's nearwest side and to Cleveland suburbs, either directly or by moving up from the ghetto. Cleveland's West Virginia Ghetto was defined as Lorain Avenue between West Thirtieth and West Sixty-fifth and the Tremont and Clark-Fulton areas. On the east side, North Broadway, Goodrich, and Collingwood neighborhoods also had large numbers of Appalachian families. Photiadis's study notes that Lakewood, Brook Park, Berea, Parma, Middleburgh Heights, and Brunswick were suburban communities to which the Appalachians migrated.

6. Jesus Antonio Rico-Velasco, "Immigrants from the Appalachian Region to the City of Columbus, Ohio: A Case Study" (master's thesis, Ohio State University, 1969), 121.

7. Schwarzwaller et al., 159. Of thirty migrant men interviewed in the authors' follow-up, sixteen were union members, "but only four were active in the sense of having attended a number of union meetings the previous year." The authors conclude that membership in a union for most Beech Creekers was "a nominal status."

8. Ibid., 154.

9. Dorothy Kunkin and Michael Byrne, in *Appalachians in Cleveland* (Cleveland:

Cleveland State University Institute of Urban Studies, 1973), quoted a 1970 statewide survey showing that one out of every three Ohio factory workers was an Appalachian migrant. "Statistically, Appalachian workers surveyed had held their jobs longer than non-Appalachians, had bought more houses per capita and had provided a stable labor force for Ohio manufacturing"; Kunkin and Byrne, 8. The study showed that after two years of living in the city, 60 percent of the Appalachian migrants had improved their occupational category. The study cited by the authors, *The Appalachian Migrants in Columbus, Ohio,* was done by the Junior League of Columbus in 1970.

10. John Photiadis noted that most of the problems reported by the Cleveland study group were related to social integration. The greater density of the population and the shift from rural to urban social interaction accounted for much of their dissatisfaction with Cleveland. Thirty-nine percent said city life bothered them "very much" or "quite a bit"; Photiadis, 18, 172–74.

11. An interesting observation among those "born-again" migrants interviewed is that while religion was an important presence in the mountains, many of them did not come into a "personal relationship with Jesus Christ" until they came north. For some, it was a matter of the gospel message being presented in a fresh way that challenged their approach to religion. For others, it was the security of the religion in a strange land or the realization of personal sinfulness after living on the wild side for a few years in a city filled with temptations. Finally, it may be observed that a number of the migrants went on to establish small congregations of Holiness and Southern Baptist in the region.

12. Schwarzweller, 214. The mountaineer viewed wealth as coming from the hand of God because he was living a good life. This thought obviously clashed with the more materialistic approach to wealth in the northern culture. To this day, many of the migrants see God's hand in the blessings they have received in the north. Lucian "Lou" Philo Tenney, a migrant from Buckhannon, West Virginia, said one of the differences he has noticed between the southern and northern cultures is that people in West Virginia always have something to laugh about and be thankful for. No matter how bad the times or problems, the migrant could gather with his friends and kin and find some elements of joy or humor. Among Ashtabula natives I have often observed the opposite to be true. Conversation is frequently negative and focused upon what is lacking and oppressive in one's situation.

13. This same mountaineer was also one to pull practical jokes on his neighbors and friends. He got into a disagreement with his neighbor and decided the best way to get even was public humiliation. So he called in to the local radio station's "Swap Shop" program and announced that he and his wife had to get out of town in a hurry and were giving all their belongings away. All you had to do was drive by and pick them up. Then he gave his neighbor's address. Within a few minutes the street was a traffic jam of bargain hunters being turned away by a very angry neighbor. After that incident the radio station changed its policy on taking addresses over the air.

14. The most infamous of these troublesome migrants was Arthur Lee Cole, who on October 21, 1957, shot and killed Ashtabula Police Department Patrolman Eino Toivola with a twelve-gauge shotgun as Toivola responded to a domestic dispute complaint. Cole, aged forty-seven, his wife, and three children came to Ashtabula County in the early 1950s from Floyd County, Kentucky. A June 3, 1959, *Star-Beacon* newspaper article noted that his court-appointed attorney, Robert H. Fuller of Ashtabula, described Cole as "the product of a marriage of first cousins in Kentucky's squalid coal fields." Cole had only a first-grade education and an I.Q. of 59. He had worked at the New York Central Reclamation Plant but was unemployed at the time of the murder. His police record included intoxication, disorderly conduct, and operating a vehicle without a license. In May 1958 he was found guilty of first-degree murder and sentenced to die in the electric chair the following June. But a series of appeals based upon insanity kept him on death row for six years, despite his admission of guilt and desire to pay the price with his life. He died at Lima State Hospital for the Criminal Insane in November 1965. One of his daughters told me that the family suffered great shame and felt ostracized from the community as a result of their father's deed; the taunting was so great, the children had to drop out of school.

15. Kunkin and Byrne, 5. The population of Brunswick, for instance, one of the Cleveland suburbs to which Appalachians tended to migrate in large numbers, was estimated to be 50 percent Appalachian.

16. *Charleston Daily Mail,* 1 June 1951, 21. Workers sought included boilermakers, blacksmiths, bricklayers, machinists, riggers, millwright and electrician helpers, as well as inexperienced laborers.

17. Ibid., 1 June 1953, 15. Birth certificates were required to apply for these jobs. One ad requested "Birth certificate if under 21."

18. Gary Fowler, *Appalachian Migration: A Review and Assessment of the Research* (Washington, D.C.: Appalachian Regional Commission, 1980), 26–27. A similar ranking for the period 1965 to 1970 placed Cleveland eighth, with 13,154 Appalachian migrants moving to the city during that time (Atlanta, Georgia, was first). Columbus ranked fourteenth, Cincinnati sixteenth, and Dayton twenty-second. The author quoted statistics given by Clyde B. McCoy in his presentation "Appalachian Migration Streams to Selected Metropolitan Areas" at the Conference on Appalachia in Urban Areas, Academy for Contemporary Problems, held at Columbus, Ohio, in March 1974.

19. For a scholarly treatment of the subject, see the aforementioned *Mountain Families in Transition;* Jack Temple Kirby's *Rural Worlds Lost;* and *Down Home, Downtown: Urban Appalachians Today,* edited by Phillip J. Obermiller. *Mountain Heritage,* edited by B. B. Mauer, is an excellent overview of Appalachian culture for the general reader.

1 the best location in the nation

ashtabula county and appalachian migration, 1900-1965

Lands of Contrast

IT WAS THE GATEWAY to "The Best Location in the Nation," an industrialist's description of northeast Ohio in the 1950s. The catchy slogan, first used by the Cleveland Electric Illuminating Company, was more than clever marketing. The region had land, water, railroads, shipping, highways, industry, and commerce. Fifty-eight percent of the nation's population lived within a five-hundred-mile radius. Sixty-seven percent of the country's manufactured products were produced there. Only one essential commodity was in short supply: labor.

For Ashtabula County, the state's northeasternmost county, the labor shortage resulted from overselling the region's advantages to heavy and chemical industry. During the war years Ashtabula County community leaders attracted several defense industry plants to the area, most notably Union Carbide and Carbon's Electro Metallurgical (Electromet) plant and National Carbide's carbide facility. These additions were followed by numerous postwar industrial and chemical plants that strained the local labor market beyond its limits. Within a decade, the county changed from a primarily agricultural economy to a significant manufacturing center with concentrations in heavy machinery parts, alloys, and chemicals. Employment within the county rose from 9,000 in 1943 to 15,000 just seven years later. The county's population rose from 68,674 in 1940 to 78,695 in 1950.

Northeast Ohio needed workers, and the Appalachian highlands, particularly West Virginia and Kentucky, provided a ready source. Although only three hundred miles to the south of this booming industrial region, the Appalachian Mountains sheltered a way of life that was significantly different from that of the North and less favorable to economic growth. Job opportunities in most Appalachian communities were limited to coal mining, lumbering, and farming. Most mountain children grew up on family farms where a self-sufficient lifestyle was practiced and instilled as their inevitable lot in life. As Jack E. Weller notes in *Yesterday's People,* pioneers who settled other regions of the country could look forward to mounting financial rewards, security, and comfort with each successive generation. But nature did not cooperate with the mountaineer; indeed it overcame him and molded him into a fatalist. With opportunities limited to the amount of farmable land owned by the family, the length of a coal vein, or the expanse of timber on the hillside, the mountaineer's future was one dictated by natural resources. The best he could hope for was the status quo; to maintain it was to be successful. The mountaineer's children could not expect to fare any better than their parents as long as they farmed their allocation of acres carved from a stony mountainside.

The farm often included a small coal mine, which, along with firewood from the forest, heated the modest farmhouse and cooked the breakfast and dinner of cornbread, beans, pork, and vegetables. There was no electricity, gas, water, sewer, or cable television. With the exception of footwear, dress clothes, and some work clothing, garments were made at home from yard goods purchased or bartered for at the general store. Chickens and eggs were commonly used as barter. Cash often came from the sale of moonshine the farmer made in the secret recesses of the woods or ginseng he and his family harvested there.

Expenses were minimal and every family had an account at the general store for acquiring staples. When the account reached ten or fifteen dollars, it might be settled through the sale of a calf, a few gallons of moonshine, or other farm products. Apart from store purchases, only the tax obligations on the land, a house call from the regional doctor, or a collection plate passed at revival made demands on the mountaineer's purse. It seldom held a surplus, but its owner rarely needed one.[1]

This economic system served the mountaineer for more than a century but began to collapse under the pressures of farm mechanization and the advance of an increasingly urban and materialistic society. In *Rural Worlds Lost:*

The American South, 1920–1960, Jack Temple Kirby describes the highland South as the most "backward" part of rural America in "the infrastructures and amenities of farm business and life. Few country people had gasoline-powered machinery of any kind, electricity, indoor water, or telephones. Most notably they lacked automobiles."[2] Kirby attributes the latter situation to the lack of paved roads in the highlands until the 1940s and 1950s. The remoteness intensified by the lack of a transportation infrastructure helped to preserve both culture and tradition, but also shut out mechanization and progress.

By the early 1940s many of the small, family-owned Appalachian farms could no longer meet the needs of a generation that wanted automobiles, refrigerators, electric stoves, telephones, and television sets. The farm families were just too big for the amount and quality of land allotted them. Most of the large farms laid out by the Appalachian settlers had been divided and subdivided as successive generations of children inherited equally their share of the land.[3] Many of these farms were too small to sustain a family or produce enough income to purchase labor-saving machinery. While farmers in the rest of the country were operating tractors and mechanized planting and harvesting equipment in the 1930s and 1940s, many West Virginia farms were still dependent on draft horses and the strong backs of a large family. Mountain farmers were trapped by the unprofitability of their farms' small size and the absence of labor-saving machinery. The Appalachian farm was simply uneconomical—in many cases, among the worst in the nation.[4]

The First Wave: Farmers

Migration for Land's Sake

But not all early-twentieth-century mountaineers had fallen into the trap laid by the fatalism of their culture and constraints of the land. Beginning around 1910 young men and women started to leave the Appalachian farms for the job-rich cities of the North. Thirty years would pass before Ashtabula County offered an industrial base sufficient to attract migrants, but at the turn of the century it did offer good farmland and access to mechanization. Savvy mountaineer farmers with the means and connections took notice. The rich, flat farmland of Ashtabula County seemed like a godsend to West Virginia farmers tired of struggling along rocky mountainsides with a team of horses and a barefooted family equipped only with hoes and tired backs. Beginning around 1900, peaking in 1908, and continuing into the early 1920s, a farmland-driven migration from West Virginia to Ashtabula County took place. Evidence of this can be gathered from the 1910 and 1920 U.S. Census Records, oral family histories, and the 1924 *History of Ashtabula County* by Moina Large. The last-named work recognizes at least ten of these migrant families as having established fine farms and businesses, earning the respect of their Buckeye neighbors in a relatively short time.

It is likely that many of these West Virginia farming migrants came as a result of the recruitment efforts of Anderson J. Cutlip, a Braxton County, West Virginia, native who came to Ashtabula County in 1906. His daughter, Opal Cork of Pierpont, said Anderson had been a grocery store owner and lumberman in West Virginia but turned farmland realtor when he saw the opportunity to lure mountaineer farmers to the North. Ross Boggs Sr. of Dorset Township said A. J. Cutlip sold a farm to his uncle, Clarence P. Baker, who came from Webster County in 1918. A descendant of Gideon Draper Stump also attributes that family's migration to Anderson Cutlip's marketing.

Other mountaineer farmers followed these pioneering families, as brothers and uncles wrote home extolling the ease of farming on flat topography. Arlene F. Daniels said her parents, George Hank William and Mary Bell Fink, had connections to a farmer in Denmark Township who convinced them to load their possessions and kids on a train and come north in 1917. They left a hundred-acre farm in the Grassy Meadows region of Greenbrier County—steep, rugged mountain country of West Virginia. "We had a good-sized farm," Arlene said. "We had an apple orchard and mother kept a fenced-in raspberry patch. We had some cattle, pigs. Mother had turkeys, chickens, and sold eggs." There were eleven children in the Fink family, but by the time George Fink decided to move north, only four of them remained at home. Arlene said their West Virginia neighbors sealed their decision to migrate. "I think really what made him move was problems with the neighbors," she said. "They were fighting all the time. Shooting in the air, sneaking around. Dad couldn't stand that." The farm was sold and the life in West Virginia pretty much forgotten. "He never went back, just to visit now and then," Arlene said. "Dad may have gone back to the farm two or three times —he just forgot about the place. It was a dickens of a big change up here. You had the country schools down there and animals running around the place."

Gertrude Richardson was only five years old when her father and mother, George and Stella Teter, migrated to Ashtabula County in the summer of 1919. The family came from Bridgeport, West Virginia, where George Teter was a butcher and meat cutter. Gertrude's mother had three brothers and a sister in Ashtabula County, and they provided the link that George followed north. George Teter purchased a hundred-acre farm, arranged the sale of the family home in Bridgeport, and brought his family north by train. Gertrude is unsure why her parents left West Virginia. The only reason she was ever given was that "they couldn't handle me living in town because I kept running away," she said. "So they brought me out here to the hundred-acre farm." The farm was located on Morgan Road in Plymouth Township. The sixteen-room house was more than adequate for the family: George, Stella, Gertrude, and her three siblings, Virginia, Kenneth, and Agnes. Cousins were left behind in West Virginia and an annual trip back home was made every summer. Gertrude recalls making the trip in a touring car that was ill-suited for travel in inclement weather or on mountain roads. The trip took two days and preparations involved cooking enough chicken and other provisions to feed the family on the road.

Travel conditions between Ashtabula County and West Virginia had improved by 1945 when Albert Franklin Viers sold his Greenbrier County farm and moved his son Robert and wife Katie Elizabeth to a 150-acre farm in Wayne Township. But the trip was still long and memorable for Robert, who was sixteen when the family moved north. "All we brought was our car and some canned goods in the back," Robert said. "It took us nineteen hours that time to get up here. We left Lewisburg around nine in the morning and didn't get here until after four in the morning the next day." Mountain roads, storms, a failed generator in the old Chevy, and fog accounted for the delay. "The fog was so bad that he couldn't find the driveway for the farm he had bought once he got here," Robert recalled.

Robert Viers said his father originally came to Ashtabula in 1943 to work on construction of the Electromet plant. He stayed with school chums, Roy and Eva Richardson, who had a farm in the southern part of Ashtabula County. "I think he had made up his mind to come to Ohio to live and went back down and got his ducks in order," Robert said. For Robert, who tended the farm back in West Virginia while his father worked in Ohio, the move demonstrated just how antiquated farming methods were in his home state. In West Virginia, he harvested wheat with a cradle scythe—a scythe with a frame of wooden fingers attached above the blade. The fingers caught the stalks of wheat as they were cut off, allowing the harvester to deposit them in a neat pile, where they could be bound together into bundles and eventually stacked in a shock. The stalks had to be released after each swipe of the scythe; the process was time-consuming and laborious.

Shocks were gathered into a barn or other building until a threshing machine could come to the farm. Robert said the machine that threshed at their West Virginia farm was powered by a steam engine, had wooden parts, and required three men to operate: one to throw the shock on the table, one to cut the bands on the shock, and a third to feed the wheat into the machine that separated the grain from the straw. Establishing a rhythm among the workers was critical for efficiency. If the second and third man became unsynchronized, injury to the third worker's hand was likely. "The guy feeding the machine would reach back and get a wicked slice across his hand if the other guy wasn't paying attention," Robert said. "Many a guy has been hurt that way."

Corn was hand-picked in West Virginia. Harvesting involved cutting the stalks and stacking them into shocks, which were left in the field until fodder was needed for the cattle. The corn was husked in the field. A hand-cranked shelling machine could be used to remove the corn from the cob, but Robert said he witnessed his grandfather shelling corn by hand many an afternoon. "My grandfather had a hundred sheep and, after he got old, he'd sit there in the afternoon and shell corn into pails," Robert said. "Then he'd dump the corn into wooden troughs where the sheep ate."

Robert estimates that mechanization on their Wayne Township farm was two decades ahead of the West Virginia one. On his father's Ohio farm, a combine cut a forty-inch swath through the wheat and threshed it in the field. Other township farms that used a binder only, which reaped and tied the grain into bundles, depended upon a threshing machine that came to the farm, as in West Virginia. But Robert said the threshing machines in Ohio had metal parts and used a blower rather than a conveyor system to separate the straw and grain. Corn was harvested and shelled mechanically.

Mountainous terrain prevented the use of some machinery on West Virginia farms—binders, for example, could not negotiate the steeper hillsides. Bottomland farms were generally more progressive because mechanization was better suited to flat terrain. This gave the lowland farmers an edge over their hillside cousins and created a window of opportunity to move beyond

the status-quo standard of the prevailing fatalism. But such land was not easily acquired, and for Albert Viers, moving north was a more viable alternative.
Robert said that his father liquidated the relics of this antiquated farming
system—including the cradle scythe, team of horses, and Farm-All F-12 steel-
wheeled tractor—when he sold the farm. "But father got a hankering for his
tractor back and went back to West Virginia, bought it back, and brought it
up here," Robert said.

From Farm to Factory
In addition to making farming less laborious, the move from West Virginia
gave Robert access to a boom job market after his graduation from Williams-
field High School in 1950. Robert traded his farming work for a factory job
with True Temper Corporation, a Saybrook Township company that manufactured hoes, forks, and rakes of all kinds from raw steel. Robert worked
there for thirty-three years and three months, many of them as general foreman of the Hot and Cold Metal Division, a section that encompassed about
half the plant. His father, who was fifty-three when he came to Ohio, kept
the farm for only a short time after his son found factory work. After selling
the first property, Albert purchased a ten-acre farm in Wayne and went to
work for Sanborn Wire in Rock Creek. He died at the age of sixty-two and
was buried in West Virginia. His wife remarried and died in Ashtabula
County in 1978, where she is buried. "I never heard Mom say she wanted to
go back, even after Dad died," Robert said.

    Perhaps, then, the greatest significance of this early farmland-based mi-
gration lay in the experience of Robert and many other young men who followed fathers and uncles to the county's farmlands—it helped connect a
segment of West Virginia's population to the northeast Ohio industrial jobs
that were to come. When Granvil and Abigail Bennett moved by rail from
Upshur County, West Virginia, in 1899, seven of their eight children made
the trip in the passenger coach with them, while Ralph, a teenager, traveled
in the boxcar with the livestock; some forty-five years later, Ralph's nephew,
Harold Hornbeck, traveled from the hollows of Kedron, West Virginia, to
the industry-rich flatlands of Ashtabula County in a 1940 Chevrolet. Harold
was taking advantage of the beachhead established by these farming migrants, an advantage that many other migrants would depend on during the
industrially driven migration.

Seedlings of Industrial Migration: Common Economies
By the 1930s, hard times had settled over much of Appalachia, hard times
that would not lift with the end of the Great Depression. The decline began
after World War I, when the blast furnaces no longer needed coal in the
quantities required by the war effort, and continued as alternative fuels began
to replace King Coal. In 1950 the mining industry employed 136,014 West
Virginians, about 21 percent of the labor force. A decade later, mining employment had fallen to 60,941. Another 12,000 mining jobs were lost in the
state between 1960 and 1970 as mechanization and decreased demand sent
miners to the unemployment line. Compounding the employment difficul-
ties was a decrease in West Virginia agriculture and forestry jobs, as well as
foreign competition in the glass and ceramic industries. Jobs in agriculture
and forestry in the state fell from 62,332 in 1950 to 11,637 just twenty years
later.[5] Appalachia simply had a surplus of people for the number of jobs
available. Lowell Long, a Tucker County, West Virginia, native who left the
state for Baltimore in the late 1950s, summed it up this way: "West Virginia
didn't want us."

That Appalachia could not support its own was documented in a mid-
1930s study of coal-producing counties of Appalachia. The study concluded
that 350,000 people should leave the area's agricultural industry and 60,000
leave mining. In all, it was determined that 27 percent of the area's population should leave to bring the living standards up to the level of the United
States at large.[6] But regional overpopulation did not deter the highlanders'
reproduction rate, the highest in the nation. Kirby notes that in 1940, when
1,000 statistical American women of child-bearing age bore 73.7 children,
their peers in Wolfe County, Kentucky, bore 174.3.[7]

During the 1930s many men did begin to leave the farms of the southern
highlands and head north. At the beginning of that decade, 54,043 Ten-
nesseans, 206,353 Kentuckians, and 130,363 West Virginians were living in
Ohio.[8] Kentuckians had found work in the Champion Paper Company of
Hamilton and the rubber industry drew many early migrants to the Akron
region during the World War I years. By the early 1920s, tens of thousands
of West Virginians working in Akron had turned the "Rubber City" into
"The Capital of West Virginia."[9] Mountain families also worked as seasonal
farm workers, following the vegetable harvest across midwest states. Many of
these farmers eventually grew tired of being on the move and returned to the

hills to sell their farms and start over again in one of the regions they had visited as migrant workers.

The Timber Connection

Appalachia and Ashtabula County had two economies in common during
the 1930s—agriculture and timber. A young mountaineer with the right
connections and a bus ticket could easily transfer his logging skills to the
North and make more money in the process. Virgil Eugene "Bud" Cole
came to Ashtabula County from Greenbrier County, West Virginia, in 1939
or 1940 to work in the lumber industry. His daughter, Polly Geyer, of Kins-
man, Ohio, said her father and several other bootleggers from the White
Sulphur Springs area were more or less forced out of the hills as a condition
of probation. "He got caught making whiskey and he come up here because
he said he'd go back to making whiskey if he didn't get away," she said. "He
was on ten-years probation." Polly said the revenue agents found her father's
still, pulled it out of the woods, and destroyed it. They put his wife in jail to
force Virgil out of hiding. He surrendered to the authorities and redeemed
his wife, unaware of the windfall he might have won had he recognized that
his wife's civil rights had been violated.

Virgil Cole worked for the G. L. Van Devender Lumber Company in New
Lyme, Ohio, as head sawyer at several camps. His wife Eula G. (née Eckard),
daughter Polly, and sons William and Virgil followed him to Ohio in 1941.
Polly recalls leaving West Virginia as being difficult for her because of the
pets she had to leave behind: a barrel of turtles, a woodchuck, and a black
snake that crawled onto the rabbit cage every morning to get its piece of
bread. "I really did miss all my animals," she said. Polly more than compensated for the loss in her adult life, harboring five indoor and two outdoor
dogs, seven outdoor cats, twenty-eight ducks, a dozen or so chickens, a goat,
and several dozen breeding rabbits at her home. Her love of animals comes
from her father, who, while living in West Virginia, kept a rattlesnake collection. "Father and these other guys always played with snakes," Polly said.
"I think it was against the law, but they used to get these rattlesnakes and
they'd pull the fangs." Wagering was one use of the snakes—a cruel one, as
each man laid a rattlesnake in the sun and bet that it would be the last to
succumb to the heat. The snakes also provided props for practical jokes. "My
Dad always put one in the glove compartment of his car," Polly recalled.
"He'd stop and pick up somebody, a hitchhiker, and he'd say to him, 'Reach

in that glove compartment and get me a cigarette.' This one poor guy just about went out the window." Bud Cole's love for the rattlesnake was so great that he even slept with one tucked under his shirt, much to Eula's consternation.

Polly's first year in Ashtabula County was spent with Harry and Ruby Gillespie in Ashtabula, who established a beachhead for White Sulphur Springs residents. But the next year she moved to the lumber camp at Kelloggsville with her parents and brothers. They lived in a two-room shanty consisting of a kitchen and communal bedroom. "That was the best life a kid could have had, it kept you off the streets," she said. "I liked it. That's a good life. Mom made it that way." Eula was the camp cook for the ten lumbermen, and she brought a measure of civilization to the camp. Polly said prior to her mother's arrival, the men "washed" their plates by running a piece of bread around the surface to sop up any food particles, turned the plate over on the table, and returned to work. Eula introduced the practice of washing dishes. The meals were mostly beans and potatoes—there was no refrigeration for meat. "It was ordinary, country food," Polly said. "We bought meat on Saturday when we went to Jefferson and Mom would cook it all up for the next three days."

Polly and her brothers were the only youngsters in the camp, but the isolation was not a problem for Polly, who liked the country. A school bus picked her up at the camp and took her to school. Her weekly treat was to go to Jefferson, where her father bought her a quart of ice cream and a movie ticket. "Mom and him would go to the bar," she said. "He drank a lot, but Dad was a good guy. He was never mean to his family." Polly lived in the camp two years before her father rented the upstairs of a house on East Jefferson Street. Characters who lived at the camp, many of them migrants from West Virginia and Virginia, continued to stay with the family on weekends. They included Raven "Muscles" Dean, Burt Morgan, Culver Burns, and Chester Scott—as well as her father's brother, Clile Cole, and Charles Wagner, one of her father's friends. She still has a teddy bear Burt Morgan and Culver Burns bought her for sixteenth birthday, a bear she named "Burtsy-Burnsy." Polly said the men enjoyed teasing her, and she enjoyed the occasional opportunity to get even. "When they would come over on the weekends to our house, I'd sneak in their bedroom and get their underwear and sew it up on the machine so they couldn't put them on," she said. "They were always a-teasin' me about something, so I got them."

Summer Job

"A. W. Hinchliffe Lumber Company, that's how my uncles got up here," said Lawrence Glenn Gatrell, who came to northeast Ohio from West Virginia in the early 1940s to work in the woods with three of his uncles—Thomas Tennant and Clarence and Lawrence Headley. Hinchliffe, a Chardon firm, cut timber throughout northern Ohio. During his teenage years, Glenn worked summers in the northeast Ohio woods, returning to his home in Tyler County to help his mother, Lettie Tennant, who had a forty-six-acre farm. Among Glenn's jobs at home was cutting enough wood to keep the house warm for him and his four siblings. The experience on a cross-cut saw led to his first paying jobs.

Employment options in Tyler County were limited to farming and mining by the time Glenn was old enough to leave the farm. "I'd work for farmers for fifty cents a day," he said. "Anybody who could hoe corn, they'd hire them for fifty cents a day. When I left there in '47, they were paying three dollars a day." He was drafted into the army in 1944 and served in the Philippine Islands. When he got out in 1947, he considered his options in West Virginia—coal mining or working in a Weirton steel mill—and headed back to northeast Ohio. "It was bright lights up here back then," he said. "This town was bright; it's dark today compared what it was like back then." He went back to working in the woods, this time around the Lorain area, where timber was being cut for blocking used at steel mills. Glenn said the pay was relatively good—workers were paid seven dollars per thousand board feet. "We could knock out seven thousand feet a day," Glenn said.

A crew consisted of two sawyers—one for each end of the cross-cut saw— a skidder, and two mill workers. The saw in the mill was powered by a diesel or gasoline engine, but the saws used to cut the trees were all cross-cuts, powered by men. The crews worked six days a week and stayed in three mobile shanties, measuring about eight by fourteen feet each. Married men were allowed to have their families stay in the camp. Glenn and his cousin Everett Headley were bachelors at the time and stayed in one shanty. The money was much better than working on a farm or lumber camp in West Virginia. But it wasn't much of a life, and after one of his cousins got blood poisoning from an ax wound to his foot, Glenn and Everett decided it was time to find a different line of work.

Glenn bounced between jobs—the New York Central Car Reclamation Plant, National Carbide, greenhouses, and Electromet—before his uncle,

Thomas Tennant, helped him get a job with the American Water Works in 1951. "My uncle worked there, my brother worked there. Then one day they asked me if I wanted a job, and I said 'Yeah.'" He retired from there in 1988. Many others followed Glenn from his Tyler County home to work in the woods, at the reclamation plant, or one of the carbide plants: four half brothers, Everett Kester, Ralph Thompson, and Howard and Robert Spencer; a half sister, Frances Leasure; and Jim and Earl Seese, who lived over the mountain from his West Virginia home.

Building the Best Location

Migration in Earnest, 1945–1960
Just as Glenn Gatrell weighed his options between home and the industrial north after World War II, many other young men of Appalachia found it difficult to return to the hills after seeing the lights and opportunities of the city and more prosperous regions. Many who had left for foreign lands became desperately homesick for mountains and kin. But even more realized after traveling beyond the hollows that there were easier, albeit more hectic, ways to make a living. After their discharge they returned home only long enough to pack a few things and say good-bye, then followed an uncle's or brother's lead to the North or East.

A combination of four major factors—overcrowding on the farms, lack of job opportunities, an expanded view of the world, and the North's wartime and postwar industrial boom—set the stage for this great migration of young men and women fleeing Appalachia's poverty and hopelessness for the prosperity and opportunity of the North. In general, the migration consisted of male household leaders under forty—strong, intelligent, determined men eager to improve life for themselves and their families. Their fathers and uncles seldom followed their paths—perhaps their roots were too entwined in the traditional ways of the mountains, an unskilled job, the homestead, or the fatalism that pervades this culture. Taproots nurtured by five generations are not easily torn from their mountain soil. Nevertheless, between 1940 and 1970, an estimated 3.5 million mountaineers yanked up their roots and headed to the northern cities of opportunity. Jack Temple Kirby notes that Ohio was the most important destination of "genuine hillbilly migrants." Kirby calculates that by 1960 there were 839,581 people living in Ohio who had been born in the nearby South.[10] The authors of *Appalachians in Cleveland* estimated that more than 2.2 million migrants left the region from 1950 to 1960 and another 1.1 million left from 1960 to 1970.[11] Leonard M. Sizer, a professor of sociology at West Virginia University, estimated in 1968 that one-third of native-born West Virginians, more than 650,000 persons, were living outside their home state.[12] U.S. Census figures for 1960 showed that 311,134 persons who were born in West Virginia were living in Ohio. From 1950 to 1960, more than 446,000 people migrated from that state to other states; more than 67,000 of them landed in Ohio in the years 1955 to 1960.[13] Additionally, the oral testimony of the migrants and studies such as John Photiadis's reveal that migrants often came north for a short period, became discouraged or disillusioned, and went back home. Others used Ohio's industries as a safety net in times of strike or unemployment but retained their mountain home as a primary residence.

The migration to Ashtabula County was not uniquely the experience of the Caucasian Appalachian family whose ethnic background was Scotch-Irish or German. The Deep South contributed many a black worker to the county, as well. Sol Ray, identified as a spokesman of the Ashtabula black community in the early 1950s, was quoted in an Ashtabula *Star-Beacon* article as saying that in 1948 there were only ten black families in the city. By the fall of 1953 the number had increased to 1,300 individuals, virtually all of them migrants from the Deep South.[14]

It must be acknowledged that, statistically speaking, Ashtabula County was not a leading migration destination compared to cities like Cleveland, Hamilton, Cincinnati, Akron, and Columbus. However, Ashtabula County provided hundreds of southern highlanders with the same opportunities available in these large cities without the stresses inherent in an urban atmosphere. In a sense, the area offered the mountaineer advantages of both worlds—jobs and a relatively rural environment. Furthermore, the area was accustomed to the migrant experience, having received many Finnish and Italian immigrants in the prior half-century. Finally, the earlier migration of farmers from West Virginia had provided beachheads for young migrants seeking work in factories.

Organizing for Growth
The industrialization that made the dreams of both local and migrant workers come true happened partly by the accident of war, partly by design. Prior

to 1940 Ashtabula County industry concentrated on shipbuilding, railroads, greenhouses, and tanneries. The *Ashtabula Star Beacon,* in a November 13, 1951, article on industrial growth, stated that "the Ashtabula of 20 years ago was not a highly-industrialized, aggressive community. It ignored its raw materials and thought of its lake only for shipping, not for a vast source of water. . . . The whole community lacked the spark, the drive, the flame that makes cities great. It had enormous potential; it possessed little." As a result, the Depression years saw an exodus of young people as the community became known as "a good town to be from." As the economic effects of World War II began to pull the nation from the Depression, "Ashtabula was ready to sit on the sidelines and watch the rest of the nation move forward."

Robert S. Morrison, Ashtabula industrialist, said in a 1995 interview that only one in eighteen Ashtabula area jobs was industrial in the 1930s. In contrast, Lorain, Ohio, which was similar in size to Ashtabula, had one in four and a half; Sandusky, Ohio, had one in six. "The five largest industries in town were the Ashtabula Bow Socket Company, American Fork and Hoe, Iten Fiber, Ashtabula Corrugated Box Company, and Aetna Rubber Company," Morrison recalled. "Not any one of them employed more than 240, and some were under 100." Other employers included two tanneries and several greenhouses, which provided low-paying jobs, mainly for women seeking a second income.

Progressive-minded citizens like Morrison recognized the opportunity at hand and on April 7, 1941, formed the Ashtabula Industrial Corporation with support from the Ashtabula Area Chamber of Commerce and Cleveland Electric Illuminating Company. "This group of Chamber members rolled up its sleeves, tossed in its dollars and traveled to industrial capitals all over the nation to preach the gospel: 'Come to Ashtabula,'" stated a *Star Beacon* article. Formed to provide the money and a site for one industrial plant, the corporation quickly posted a series of successes. The first move was to sell enough stock to purchase the Aetna Rubber building on State Road. Morrison helped raise $27,000 to acquire the structure, which was then leased to several manufacturing firms. Morrison also convinced American Fork and Hoe to locate a new defense factory in Ashtabula Township. The Industrial Corporation purchased the land and put up the building that would be converted into a bayonet factory during World War II. The factory produced more than 1.5 million weapons and gave many women their first taste of employment in the manufacturing sector.

Union Carbide and Carbon's Electro Metallurgical Company (Electromet) plant on Lake Road in Ashtabula Township was a sprawling, busy facility in the late 1950s, when this photo was taken. *Photo source:* Ashtabula Star Beacon *archives*

Postwar successes of the Ashtabula Industrial Corporation included attracting the giant Reliance Electric Company, Timken-Detroit Axle Company (Rockwell Brake), and Morrison's own firm, Molded Fiber Glass (MFG) Company. In all, seventeen new industries landed in Ashtabula and surrounding townships between 1943 and 1951. Six thousand new workers were added in just seven years and the total of county payrolls went from $19 million in 1943 to $46 million in 1950. Many of the new workers had come from southern states, with the highest concentration of Appalachian workers in one plant, the Union Carbide and Carbon's Ashtabula Township Electro Metallurgical (Electromet) plant.

Winding Down
The northward migration began to wind down in the late 1950s, when the nation's boom economy started to lag and employment in Ashtabula County leveled off. Ashtabula County, often referred to as the caboose on the economic progress train, would still attract migrants into the mid-1960s as chemical manufacturers and plants like True Temper continued expansion.

However, migrants arriving in the later years of the county's boom decades often had their prosperity pulled out from underneath them a decade or two later.

Robert Turner was working in the coal mines around Masontown, West Virginia, in 1965 when his nephew came back from Ashtabula and told him about job openings at Rockwell Brake. At the age of thirty-seven, Robert, who had already suffered injuries from coal mining, was ready for safer, less rigorous work. He asked his nephew to bring him an application the next weekend. Robert completed the application, sent it back to Ashtabula with his nephew, and awaited a phone call. It came the next day. He interviewed and was hired October 4, 1965. Bob moved his family—wife Mary Ann, sons Brad and Robert, and daughter Mary Jane—to Ashtabula. He worked at Rockwell for the next twenty-two years, until the plant closed in 1987. The nephew who got him the job returned to West Virginia and got a job mining coal. Bob stayed in Ohio and found work as a substitute school custodian and driver for an Ashtabula County transportation firm. Although the job that drew him to Ashtabula died out, Bob still feels Ashtabula County offered him better job opportunities than West Virginia.

Electromet and the Migration North

The Alloy Connection

Electromet was the outcome of the industrial corporation's preaching of the Ashtabula gospel to the federal government, which needed sites for its war production plants. On May 15, 1942, the Defense Plant Corporation announced it would authorize the Electro Metallurgical Company, a unit of Union Carbide and Carbon Corporation, to build a calcium carbide (Carbide Division) and ferrosilicon (Alloy Division) plant on Lake Road in Ashtabula Township. The Carbide Division produced calcium carbide, which when combined with water releases acetylene, a gas used in welding and the production of plastics, synthetic rubber, and chemicals needed for the war effort. The alloy steels would be used in armor plate and armor-piercing projectiles, gun barrels, aircraft assemblies, gears, axles, and cylinders. The announcement stated that the plant would employ several hundred men and promised a payroll in excess of $1 million annually. Ashtabula was chosen for the plant because it could provide the manpower as well as the water, electricity, and rail and water transportation for the raw materials and finished product.

On January 16, 1943, Morrison, president of the Ashtabula Industrial Corporation, told a group of Ashtabula Rotary Club members gathered for lunch, "There will be plenty of jobs for men who are willing to work with their muscles and minds together, jobs that will pay well."[15] Just four months later, 750 men had been selected to receive training for the new plant. Specialists from other Union Carbide and Carbon plants, including the Alloy (originally named Boncar), West Virginia, plant (one of the largest ferroalloy plants in the world at that time), would provide the training.

This Alloy/Ashtabula connection provided a pipeline for many Appalachian families in the years to come. Alloy's plant had begun smelting ferroalloys March 13, 1934, and transformed a small community along the Kanawha River into a thriving area. The Alloy plant provided a beacon of employment amid the dark future of the coal mining and lumber industries. Its impact on the small coal mining town of Boncar was so great that the community's name was changed to Alloy in honor of its benefactor's product.[16]

An Alloy Family
Entire families found work at the Alloy plant, which was located about thirty-five miles from Charleston. Among them was the Frank and Gertrude Myers family. Frank had been a coal miner in the early years of his working life, but silicosis set in and he had to find less strenuous work. A guard position at the new Union Carbide and Carbon plant provided it. All five of his sons would find work there, as well as five of his sons-in-law.

"We were a Union Carbide family," said Flavia V. (Myers) Cole of Jefferson, Ohio, one of Frank and Gertrude Myers' twelve children. "That plant was where everybody worked. It saved families, really." Flavia was twelve when her father went to work at the plant in 1934. The move brought a significant change in her way of life. "That was right on the edge of the Depression," Flavia said. "Dad worked the mines before the UC plant got in. I can remember he'd just get one day a week. We had a big garden plot and we managed, somehow. We were poor, but we didn't know we were poor." They lived in a house rented from the mine company, but Flavia said her father did not "owe his soul to the company store." And the mine company provided benefits not seen in industry today. When her paternal grandfather died, a funeral fund from the mine company paid his burial expenses.

The Alloy plant was across the road from the Myers home, which they rented from Union Carbide and Carbon. Flavia remembers the air pollution from the plant as a problem in the valley. "Some days you couldn't hardly see your hand in front of you," she said. "They eventually made them start to clean it up." Flavia graduated from high school in May 1940 and got married June 10. Her husband, Martin Russell Cole, grew up in Sugar Creek, West Virginia, "back over the mountains from Anstead." He came to Alloy as a teenager in search of work at Union Carbide and found both a furnace job and a wife there. Wartime service in the marines took Martin away from his job and wife for two years. When he returned, both were waiting for him, but things had changed. Martin had seen the world beyond the mountains. "He was restless," Flavia said. "He just wanted a change. So they sent him back up here in 1949. He knew the company was sending people up here and he knew the kind of work they had here. They told him if he would come up here he'd get to keep his seniority. They were a good company to work for."

Flavia and Martin set out for Ashtabula over Memorial Day weekend 1949. It was not her first time out of the mountains. During World War II, Flavia had moved to Detroit, Michigan, where Martin's sister lived, to work in the office of a food products company. But she didn't like it there and returned home after six months. This time, Flavia did not have to make the trip alone. Accompanying them in another car were Martin's brother, Bill, and his wife Reva. Bill also worked for Union Carbide and had a job waiting for him in Ohio. "We just took our time coming up," Flavia said. "I remember we stopped at a park and cooked our breakfast. I thought it was one of the most beautiful places. We came up through Mentor and all the azaleas were in bloom. I don't think I'd ever seen so many flowers in my life. We both liked it here."

Housing was hard to find. Bill located a place on Route 20 and Martin and Flavia stayed there until they could buy a farm on Thiel Road in Jefferson, using the proceeds from the sale of their West Virginia home. They purchased their farm in 1950 and lived there twenty-nine years, until lung cancer claimed Martin.

War Shortages

By September 1944, six hundred production workers were employed at Ashtabula's Union Carbide and Carbon plant.[17] World War II draft quotas were cutting into the northeast Ohio male labor force, creating a shortage of manpower for the new industry. Harold Gladding, an Ashtabula car dealer and builder, was selected as the first personnel manager of Electromet. He hired the plant's original two thousand workers, many of them from Appalachia. "Harold Gladding would rent a couple railroad passenger cars and run them down to West Virginia," Morrison said. "He'd take sixty people, put them in that car, lock the door and come back up here with them." The men were housed in West Fifth Street apartments owned by Joe Moore and provided transportation to the nearby Electromet plant. Some of the workers stayed only long enough to work off their transportation and first week's room and board. Then they got on the next train or bus departing for West Virginia. Some stayed to enjoy the nightlife and create a ruckus in town. "On Saturday night there would always be a fight or two," Morrison said. "I had my reservations about them, they were the bottom of the barrel. Yet some of these people have made good lives for themselves in Ashtabula." Morrison later hired some of these mountain people to work in his factory. "There were some good, some mediocre, and some bad," he said.

The Boom Years

The end of the war brought temporary closure of the plant, but in June 1946 the War Assets Administration sold the plant and its equipment to Electro Metallurgical for $5 million. The war plant had cost the government almost $8.5 million to build. Electro Metallurgical announced that it would spend another $9 million on a power plant and dust/fumes control system. The hastily constructed war plant had been designed with little regard for air pollution control, and the area was cursed with the stench and dust from its furnaces. (Such was the haste of construction that the contractor used U.S. Treasury silver as electrical conduits for a short period because copper was unavailable.)

During the 1950s the sprawling Ashtabula Union Carbide complex grew to include steam, carbide, alloy, acetylene black, air products, and welding rod plants. In the peak years, the mid- to late 1950s, combined employment reached three thousand men and women who earned relatively high wages for the mostly unskilled work they performed. Yet the local labor pool could not provide enough workers to meet the demand. Merlin Mead, an Ashtabula County native who served as treasurer and president of Local 3081 United Steelworkers of America, said many locals considered Electromet a "black man's" job—too dirty, hot, and hard for the Anglo-Saxons and Italians. Merlin said the labor shortages became particularly bothersome after the war, when the plant could no longer serve as a refuge from the draft. Many of those who sought asylum in the dirty plant later rose to leadership roles in the community. "I was always a little disgusted with our city fathers," Merlin said. "This plant was a war baby and workers got a deferment. The day they were no longer eligible for the draft, they left in droves."

To meet the labor demands of the Ashtabula Township plant, Union Carbide encouraged workers to recruit relatives and friends from back home. Harold Hornbeck, who migrated to Ashtabula in the early 1950s, said Electromet's management paid employees ten dollars for referring a new employee who would work at least six weeks. But Ralph Ware, who came from White Sulphur Springs, West Virginia, in 1947, refused to lure his acquaintances to the place, despite the attractive bonus. "I felt too sorry for them to do that," he said.

Merlin Mead said black workers were recruited from Mississippi and Alabama. Union Carbide recruiters also scoured the southern highlands for workers, offering them the transportation, housing, boots, and gloves necessary to get established in the job and area. Foremen Arthur Hazen and Emil Tremblay traveled from the Ohio River to Georgia posting "Help Wanted" notices in community halls and talking with potential workers. Harold Hornbeck believes the company liked to hire mountaineers because they were the only ones who could handle the hard work and heat. "Mostly, they were used to hard work and they could do it," he said. "When I was at Union Carbide stoking the furnaces, we had a guy come in and worked a half-hour. Then he threw the shovel and all in the furnace and said 'I can't take this.' The West Virginia guys, not all of them, but most of them would stick it out."

Newspaper advertising throughout West Virginia and particularly the Buckhannon, White Sulphur Springs, and Charleston areas drew many a young mountaineer from his hollow to head north in search of steady employment and a liveable wage. Ivanhoe, Virginia, was another area targeted for recruitment, because a National Carbide plant was located there. Recruiters also worked in Portsmouth, Ohio, and netted the company at least two men, brothers Herb and John Fetters.

It was either 1948 or 1949, Herb Fetters recalled, when he saw the sign in the unemployment office advertising jobs at Electromet in Ashtabula. He'd been unemployed since coming home from World War II and was running out of money. "There were no jobs back then. The state gave us twenty dollars a week for fifty-two weeks . . . we just laid around and lived on the money from the service," he said. Herb applied for a job and Union Carbide gave him an advance on his pay so he could buy a bus ticket to Ashtabula. A plant official met him at the Ashtabula bus terminal and helped him find a room on West Fifty-second Street. "After thirty days, I paid the fare back," he said.

Herb Fetters was one of seventy-six men who started that day. Their first assignment was scrubbing carbide residue from insulators. Many of the men didn't come back for a second day. "They'd hire a hundred people at a time and maybe the first day seventy would quit," he said. But Herb found the job and location to his liking. Although his weekly pay was less than forty dollars, he always sent a few dollars back home to help support his five siblings and parents. After he got some money under his belt, he went back to Portsmouth and got married. The first of thirteen children was born while he was still living in the West Fifty-second Street apartment. Health problems caused by silica dust inside Electromet forced Herb to quit after ten years, but he has no hard feelings toward the company. "They treated me good," he said. "That was the best company, even though at that time you were making only ninety-five cents an hour."

John Fetters was twenty-six and recently married when he followed his brother north in January 1950. He'd spent his youth and early adult years working on his father's 160-acre farm. With a wife and two daughters to support, he needed a job that paid cash for his hours of labor. He caught a bus to Ashtabula and hired on at Electromet January 24, 1950. His first nine months in Ashtabula were spent in a twelve-by-eight-foot shanty that he rented from Ziggy's Big Fish Resort, a cabin/restaurant/boat rental development on Lake Road across from Electromet. The Big Fish was a first stop for many migrant families who faced a severe shortage of affordable housing in Ashtabula City. John paid twenty-four dollars a month for the privilege of eating and sleeping in a room heated with a kerosene cookstove. Snow blew in under the door and the curtains waved in the draft. A daybed provided a place to sleep and sit. There was no indoor bathroom and he had to take his showers at the plant. "You couldn't find a place to live that was decent," he

Glenn Gatrell used to hoe farmers' fields for fifty cents a day
back in West Virginia. He found a better way to make money
in northeast Ohio lumber camps, although he still raises a fine
garden behind his Kingsville Township home.
Photo by Carl E. Feather

said. The singular advantage of the shanty was its proximity to the plant. John didn't have a car and had to walk to work and the store. Once a month, he'd catch the bus back home for a visit with his wife and family.

After seven months of living alone at the Big Fish, John found a cottage to rent and moved his family—wife Viola and her two daughters, Connie Sue and Ruth Ann—to Ashtabula. They rented a series of small houses before finally saving enough money to purchase a new home in 1962. Overtime helped pay for the house. Not only was the rate better, but men pulling a double also got free lunch from a nearby beer garden. But the men paid for it in tedium and fatigue. "Sixteen hours in that place seemed like it was a week," he said. "It was rough working, but I made a good living." John worked around furnaces the entire thirty-four years he was with Union Carbide. Work-related injuries and burns furloughed him for at least a year. The worst burn occurred when the men were required to wear leggings for protection. A piece of molten slag fell into John's legging and lodged against his ankle, burning its way through the flesh and into the tendon. "I was laid up for six months from that," he said.

Strikes, both frequent and lengthy, also took their toll on the men. John Fetters said he was on strike in 1956 when his landlord, Bob Hill, put him to work roofing sheds and completing a garage. Bob owned a car dealership in Kingsville and asked John if he was any good at washing and waxing cars. "I told him to look over there at my Ford," John said. "I went over there the next day and cleaned up a green Plymouth. I went back the next day and saw the car was gone from the lot. I asked him where it went and he said a man came up on the lot, looked at the car, and bought it. I had a job there from then on." John worked part-time at Bob Hill's garage for the next thirty years, until the dealership was sold. He also took double shifts at Electromet whenever they were offered him. John recalls being snowed in at the plant for up to three days at a time and working sixteen-hour shifts with only a nap between them. One December he worked three days straight, sixteen hours on, eight off, until he was able to come home Christmas night for dinner. "I needed to work," he said. "It was hard work. But after I learned the ropes, I took care of myself."

Merlin Mead observed that the mountaineers and black workers were often eager to take the overtime while locals would pass it up, especially if it meant extra hours in the hot, dirty areas of the plant. But there was always a feeling of resentment toward the migrants when payday came and the local workers' checks reflected their unwillingness to turn an extra shift or two. "A lot of those people would not do the dirty jobs," he said of local workers. "If it was a dirty, stinking job, they'd turn it down. And who would work it? The boys from West Virginia."

The occupational hazards of Electromet went far beyond the stench and heat. It was a terribly noisy plant, and as Viola Fetters points out, former furnace tappers share a physical handicap: they are hard of hearing. John Fetters attributes his hearing loss to the combination of poor ear protection and the job of firing an eight-gauge shotgun into the furnace. The shot from the gun opened the tap hole, and John said it would sometimes take forty to fifty rounds, fired inside a metal container, to open the hole. The plant's monthly budget for shotgun shells was $4,000.

Merlin Mead counts at least ten work-related deaths during the thirty-four years he worked at the plant. Among them was a foreman who was burned to death when Furnace Thirteen exploded, spewing hot gases onto the metal catwalk where he was standing. Another foreman in the carbide packing department died when an extension cord was dropped into a storage bin, shorted out against the metal lining, and ignited the explosive gases. A six-ton electromagnet fell from the ceiling onto a worker, killing him instantly, and in Building Fifty-seven, a worker was burned to death when molten metal poured on him from a tipped ladle. In Building One, a worker was incinerated when he fell into Five Furnace.

"It was not a safe place to work. It was one of the dirtiest places I ever saw in my life," Merlin Mead said. He believes the company was also remiss in prematurely releasing injured workers to return to their jobs. Merlin said a black migrant, Bob Jackson, was "absolutely cooked" when Zero Furnace blew. Surviving despite serious burns, he was soon released for return to the job. Seeing him working around the furnaces with bandages still on his oozing burns, Merlin raised heck with the company nurse, Gertrude Kotila, until she agreed to keep Jackson out of the plant for another couple of months.

The air inside and around the plant was heavily laden with particles of lime, carbide, coke, and other materials used in the manufacturing processes. "You can't pour all that stuff into those furnaces and burn it without dust coming out," Merlin said. For many recruits, the noise, dirt, dust, and heat were overwhelming. Dixon Greenwood, a New England native, was hired at Electromet in February 1947. He was one of fifty men hired that day, but only he and another man stayed with the job. Greenwood said the pay was good, five cents an hour more than what other factories were paying, but Electromet workers viewed their job as just a place to pass the time until something better came along. "It was hard. I don't imagine that other than those who had been miners, they had any idea what that kind of work was." He tells of one worker who asked him how long he'd have to work to pay off the shoes the company provided. Dixon told him four hours. When lunchtime came, the worker bid him farewell. Merlin Mead tells of another occasion when the safety department head was giving a new employee the facility tour and stopped in the furnace room where an alloy furnace had just blown. "The guy told him, 'I got to go back and get my sweater from the locker,'" Merlin said. "He's still looking for his sweater. He never did come back. They'd take one look at that and disappear."

The Great '50s

By 1955 combined employment at Union Carbide's Ashtabula Alloy and Carbide divisions was around two thousand, making it the city's largest employer. Don Booth, who came from Elkins, West Virginia, in 1952 to work at the plant, said many of those workers were from Appalachia. Don's uncle, James Bennett, worked for Union Carbide and was responsible for helping Don get his first job at the plant. Don worked a year in the Carbide Division, then headed back to West Virginia. Don said his wife, Opal (née Newlon), didn't like living in Ohio. And he wasn't fond of working in the carbide stench and being burned by the chemicals. "That carbide would get on you and you'd start perspiring and it would turn to acetylene gas," he said. "It would stink—you'd get in the shower at the end of the day and the water would hit that carbide and turn it into gas. You couldn't smell nothing but that acetylene gas. And that lime would get on you and burn you, cause blisters."

Don and Opal Booth went back to Elkins, where he and a partner got into the sand and gravel business without much success. His next venture was with his brother Charles. They purchased and operated Rock's Snack bar, a novelty eatery built from rocks. Located across from a drive-in theater, the eatery had a hopping business that could have provided the men with a good living had Route 33 not been relocated. The new route bypassed their business and spelled doom for an eatery that depended heavily upon the highway traffic. They sold the snack bar and parted company, Charles going to Baltimore to work for General Motors, Don back to Ohio and Union

Carbide. Don figured the company wouldn't give him a second chance, but they gladly rehired him in the Alloy Division.

Don Booth's job at Union Carbide was in the packing section of the plant, where five-thousand-pound slabs of alloy were broken with sledge-hammers and the slag and other dirt knocked off with chip hammers. "It was hard, hard work. Hot, heavy, dusty work," he said. "I was staying with my uncle and I'd come home from work and say, 'That's it. I quit, this was my last day.' But he drove me, mentally drove me to get out of the house and go to work until I got used to it." The work was so demanding that Union Carbide wouldn't hire anyone who weighed less than 140 pounds. "I just hardly made it," he said. "If I hadn't had rocks in my pockets, I probably wouldn't have been hired." After pounding metal for six months, he was made shift supervisor. When he retired in 1985 from Elkem Metals, which purchased the plant from Union Carbide in July 1981, Don Booth was supervisor of operations, testimony to his perseverence.

Many of the other southern workers who started in the 1950s also stayed on until retirement. "Some of the best people we had were from the South and some of the worst people we had were from the South," Don Booth said. "And the same was true for the local people." Merlin Mead is more emphatic about the mountaineers' role at Electromet. "If every West Virginia worker had suddenly not reported to work, they would have had to close the plant down," he said. "Most of them were good, solid working people."

Growth of the Chemical Shore

A Brotherhood of Industries
Just two months after reporting its construction plans for the Union Carbide and Carbon war plant, the government announced a second Ashtabula County carbide plant. The $3.5 million plant was built and operated by National Carbide Company and financed by the Defense Plant Corporation. Located on fifty-one acres along State Road a mile south of the Electromet plant, the National Carbide facility had an annual capacity of seventy thousand tons of calcium carbide. Wartime use for the product was the manufacture of synthetic rubber and cleaning solutions for airplane engines. The July 18, 1942, announcement carried with it the promise of three hundred

new houses for Ashtabula. The full employment estimate for the National Carbide plant was set at 170 to 200. Ashtabula was on a roll for victory, jobs, and migration. The plant went on line with little fanfare in early September 1943. Sam A. Pope was transferred from the firm's Ivanhoe, Virginia, plant as manager. His connection to the Ivanhoe community provided a link to migrant workers from that state.

Like its Electromet cousin, the plant was hot, dirty, and dangerous. At least one worker was killed by a National Carbide furnace blast. Everett Lee Bishop, a twenty-four-year-old tapper from Indiana, died when one of the furnaces exploded August 20, 1951. Equipment failure was blamed for the explosion. National Carbide's Ashtabula plant did not fare as well as the Union Carbide and Carbon plant in the postwar years. The government put it on the auction block after the war, but rejected a series of bids, forcing National Carbide to close it in 1950. Union Carbide leased the plant, but discontinued operations there in May 1952 because the carbide market had gone soft.

Lake City Malleable

Another factory to come out of the war effort, also known for its less-than-desirable working conditions, was Lake City Malleable. Construction of the plant was announced December 4, 1943, and the first metal was poured at the plant on June 5, 1944. The product was gray iron castings for bombs as well as castings for military trucks and pipe couplings. After the war, the War Assets Administration sold the plant for $1.6 million to Lake City Malleable, which produced castings for automotive, agricultural, and electrical uses.

Like Electromet, the plant provided job opportunities for many unskilled but eager workers from Appalachia. Loye Wilfong, who migrated to Ashtabula from Ten Mile, West Virginia, considers it one of the best jobs he ever had because it was piece work. A hard-working man could make a good wage at Lake City Malleable, although the conditions were hot, dirty, and physically demanding.

Peacetime employment at the foundry peaked around 375 in the early 1950s. But the numbers began to tumble after Machinery Terminals, Inc., of Akron purchased a controlling interest in the firm. The work week was reduced and twenty-five employees were furloughed. Employment levels continued to fall over the next three years until it was closed and purchased by National Distillers for its new zirconium production plant in June 1956.

Queen Chlorine

Many of the industries built one upon another and created synergistic relationships. This was particularly true of the chemical plants that rose upon what was once farmland and orchards east of Ashtabula. The first such plant, built by National Distillers in 1950, produced metallic sodium used in making gasoline anti-knock compounds. Chlorine, a byproduct of the process, was initially released into the atmosphere. The stench from the combined carbide, alloy, and chlorine production in the Lake Road area of Ashtabula Township was often unbearable. Clothes hung outside to dry would be bleached out by the high chlorine content of the air on humid, still days. But by the end of the year a plant that could use the chlorine, Hooker-Detrex Corporation, was in operation south of the National Distillers plant. The Hooker-Detrex plant manufactured trichloroethylene, an industrial solvent. Hydrogen chloride was a byproduct of the Hooker-Detrex operation. In turn, General Tire and Rubber built a polyvinyl chloride plant to make use of the hydrogen chloride. And not coincidentally, processes used by both General Tire and Hooker-Detrex required acetylene supplied by Electromet.

The Lake Erie shoreline between Cleveland and Ashtabula quickly developed a reputation as "The Great Chemical Shore."[18] But the Chemical Shore's heyday was relatively short lived. The economy began sputtering in the 1970s and suffered greatly during the '80s, when thousands of high-paying jobs were lost to foreign competition and southern locales. Estimates of industrial job losses during that period range from three to five thousand; unemployment rates in the county went above 15 percent in 1982. Some industrialists, like Morrison, blamed it on unreasonable wage and benefit demands from a workforce that was largely unskilled. Others saw it as part of the much larger shift in the economy that could not support high wages for unskilled workers. Whatever the reason, the opportunities available in the 1940s and 1950s no longer existed for the migrants' offspring as they graduated from the county's high schools two decades later. Like their fathers, they were forced to migrate to other states in search of the very thing that had drawn their parents from their mountain lairs two decades earlier. Indeed, many of the migrants who had been lured to Ashtabula as young men found themselves without jobs as they entered the fourth and fifth decades of their lives. Loye Wilfong summed it up this way: "Every place I worked closed up."

The community's appearance, social structure, and quality of life suffered as the sour economy took its toll on individual lives. Alice Herpy, a migrant from White Sulphur Springs, West Virginia, believes Ashtabula was a much better place to live when she first came to the city in the spring of 1942. "This place was just booming when we came here," she said. "Smokestacks everywhere." The Ashtabula Bow Socket was near her home and the sound of the hammers beating out their products was heard around the clock. The hammers of that industry, which began as a manufacturer of buggy parts in 1880, were the heartbeat of Ashtabula industry for decades. They were silenced for good in 1982. "When that hammer stopped, it seemed like Ashtabula stopped," she said.

But in the Chemical Shore's golden years of 1940 to 1965, there were jobs to be had for any ambitious young man able to handle the heat, air pollution, and grime of the factories clustered in this gateway to prosperity. Many of those who blazed that trail from Appalachia to Ashtabula County have passed on from this life. A few have returned to their homeland. And many stay, their roots still drawing nourishment from mountain hollows and streams, while they enjoy the more prosaic benefits of the service industries and retirement funds of the north coast.

These are their stories.

Notes

1. Jack Temple Kirby, *Rural Worlds Lost: The American South, 1920–1960* (Baton Rouge: Louisiana State University Press, 1987), chap. 4. Kirby quotes the observations of Rev. Raymond Adkins, a schoolteacher-preacher in West Virginia circa 1933. Adkins observed that a large family required only about $3.75 a week in cash, "because all they had to buy was flour, chewing tobacco, smoking tobacco, coffee, baking powder, saltlick, and the rest was raised right there on their little farm." A barrel of corn mash reduced to three gallons of moonshine could supply the family's cash needs for nearly two weeks of store purchases (121).

2. Kirby, 119–20. Kirby notes that even the cotton sharecroppers of that era fared better than those in the highland south, for the sharecroppers had cars.

3. O. Norman Simpkins, "Culture," in *Mountain Heritage* (Parsons, W.Va.: McClain Printing, 1980), notes that the Celtic culture, upon which the Appalachian system of land inheritance was based, used an equal inheritance system for land. Both girls and boys were assured their share of the land. As the farm moved through generations, it got split up into smaller and smaller plots, until the farms were too small to sustain a family.

4. Rupert B. Vance, "The Region: A New Survey," in *The Southern Appalachian Region: A Survey,* ed. Thomas R. Ford (Lexington: University of Kentucky Press, 1962), 5; quoted in Jack E. Weller, *Yesterday's People* (Lexington: University of Kentucky Press, 1965), 18. Weller notes that some mountain farms returned less than $600 per year value in gross products, while the density of farm population was some 50 percent higher than that in the best farm areas of the Middle West. Cumberland Plateau farmers were found to be the lowest income group in United States agriculture.

5. Dale Colyer, *West Virginia Employment by Industry Category* (Morgantown: Division of Resource Management, Agricultural Experiment Station, College of Agriculture and Forestry, West Virginia University, June 1973), 10.

6. Vance, 5; quoted in Weller, 18–19.

7. John L. Thompson, "Industrialization in the Miami Valley: A Case Study of Interregional Labor Migration" (Ph.D. dissertation, University of Wisconsin, 1956), quoted in Kirby, 327.

8. Thompson, in Kirby, 327.

9. Phillip J. Obermiller, *Down Home, Downtown: Urban Appalachians Today* (Dubuque: Kendall/Hunt Publishing Company, 1996), 8.

10. Kirby, 236–37.

11. Dorothy Kunkin and Michael Bryne, *Appalachians in Cleveland* (Cleveland: Cleveland State University Institute of Urban Studies, 1973), 4.

12. Leonard M. Sizer, "Population Change in West Virginia," *West Virginia University Agricultural Experiment Station Bulletin* 563 (May 1968), quoted in John D. Photiadis, *Selected Social and Sociopsychological Characteristics of West Virginians in Their Own State and in Cleveland* (Morgantown: West Virginia University and Office of Manpower Research, U.S. Department of Labor, 1975), 4–5.

13. William F. Schweiker, *Some Facts and a Theory of Migration* (Morgantown: Office of Research and Development, Appalachian Center, West Virginia University, 1968), 9.

14. *Ashtabula Star Beacon*, 15 September 1953. A serious housing shortage was created by this influx, resulting in "Box Car Villages" that lacked modern plumbing. The reporters did not note the states of origin for the black migrants, stating only that they came from the "South."

15. Ibid, 16 January 1943.

16. Various authors, *Explorer: The West Virginia History Database Timeline Module* (CD ROM) (Charleston: The West Virginia Division of Culture and History, Archives and History section, 1995). The Alloy story has a very dark side. In the process of digging the Hawks Nest Tunnel at Alloy for the New-Kanawha Power Company (a Union Carbide subsidiary), many of the workers were exposed to silica rock particles that resulted in silicosis and death. At least 476 workers, mostly migrant African-Americans, died from silicosis. Fifty years later, some studies have

placed the death toll as high as 764, making it the worst industrial disaster in United States history.

17. *Ashtabula Star Beacon,* 1 September 1944. Labor problems had already started to occur at the plant by this time. A work stoppage had shut down the entire production side of the plant after a head furnace man was ordered by his foreman to do maintenance work. The furnace man refused and was sent home. A spontaneous walkout of the employees followed.

18. The 1951 Industrial Review published by the *Ashtabula Star Beacon* (November 13) called Ashtabula the "Chemical Capital" of the Chemical Shore. The November 12 article of the same series called Ashtabula a "lusty, new industrial giant." For an excellent account of how the Chemical Shore developed, see William Adams Littell, "The Great Chemical Shore," *Inside Ohio* (April 1954): 15-17.

2 coal miner's daughter

west virginia—a synonym for hard times

Late Arrival

BERDELL SEIBERT hasn't lived in West Virginia since 1924, but the few hard years she spent there as a child were enough to keep her from wanting to go back.

That's not to say that her early childhood in Randolph and Tucker Counties, West Virginia, did not give her many pleasant memories. Berdell will pick a basketful of fine tales and recollections from those days and relishes sharing them in hours of storytelling. But she has no regrets about leaving her mountains and being part of the first migration wave from West Virginia to northeast Ohio.

The Bessemer Railroad, a line that ran between Conneaut and Pittsburgh, delivered Berdell and her family to Conneaut at 7 P.M. on a June evening in 1924. Berdell remembers the time because they were late arriving, having boarded the wrong train in Pittsburgh and traveled to Conneaut Lake Park, *Pennsylvania.* They had to wait at the amusement park town until the Conneaut-bound Bessemer train came through.

With seventeen-year-old Berdell were her mother, Lela (Davis) Brown, and her stepfather, John Brown. Younger siblings Rosalie, June, and Edgar also were in tow. Personal possessions and furniture came later, after John Brown found a job at the Nickel Plate, one of Conneaut's largest employers. In 1920, the Nickel Plate completed a twenty-eight-stall roundhouse and 110-foot turntable in the city's engine terminal and shop complex. Many jobs were created in this large complex, which included flue, boiler, and car shops. The prosperity of Conneaut contrasted with the grimy pall of unemployment settling over Tucker County as coal mines and lumber camps gave out. John Brown was a miner—he had worked at mines in both Pierce and Davis before answering the call to come north. It was the Butcher family who gave that call. Berdell recalls that the Butchers and Browns had been friends when she lived back in Coalton, West Virginia, near Elkins. Berdell believes the Butchers were the first to come to Conneaut, perhaps followed by the Markijohns—Modesto and Josephine (Tucci) and their sons Tony, Sam, Mike, and Reuben—another Coalton mining family. Both the Butchers and Markijohns made the transition to the North easier for Berdell and her parents.

"They called and said they were hiring at the Nickel Plate," Berdell said. "So we packed up and came out here. I was glad to leave. It was getting so terrible there. My dad went over [to the Nickel Plate] right away and got a job. I wasn't here too long before I got a job, too." Berdell's jobs included working at a clothing store on Main Street, the Conneaut Creamery, and her parents' business, Brown's Cash Grocery Store, on Sixteenth Street, where she served as bookkeeper and ran the store with her mother. Berdell's teenage employment at Coffman's Store in Davis, West Virginia, where she worked weekends to help supplement the family's income, had given her the experience to handle these jobs.

Training Grounds

The rugged mountains and her mining-town childhood imparted a tough spirit to Berdell. She was born November 13, 1906, in Bemis, West Virginia, a small logging community in Randolph County. Her mother divorced her father, an itinerant preacher recalled only as "Mr. Funkhouser," when she was a toddler. "I remember very little about my father," she said. "But my father didn't do anything for us." Her early years were spent in Coalton. After her mother married John Brown, the family moved to Tucker County, West Virginia, where her three siblings were born: Edgar in the town of Henry, Rosalie in William, and June in Pierce. The family lived in a mine-company house in Pierce. The 1920 census placed the population of Pierce at 1,500 souls, many of them of Italian descent. The Brown family lived on the hill,

Berdell Seibert, Conneaut, Ohio (originally from Randolph and Tucker Counties, West Virginia). *Photo by Carl E. Feather*

away from "Hunky Town," as the Italian area was dismissively known. Berdell said it was a rowdy community where drinking and fighting were common. She recalls a mass murder in the Italian section that left seven people dead. "Boy, it was a rough town," she said.

The relative prosperity of the community ensured the Brown family food on the table, although variety was sometimes lacking. "We always had something to eat, it wasn't much, but we had it," she said. "But I never ate so much bacon in my life as I did back then. Seems as though we always had bacon, and I still like it. I can't figure that out."

John Brown and Lela's brothers, who stayed with them, worked at Mine 40 at Pierce. Lela had promised her father that she would take care of his boys after he died. She stayed true to her promise, even after remarrying. She made extra money by taking in boarders and baking pies and bread. The three-bedroom house, already stretched beyond capacity with the six members of the Brown family, was remodeled to provide some privacy and comfort for the boarders. "They built a room off the back for the boarders," she said. "We had a tub out there and a big stove. We kept it heated and sealed it up so we could have a place to bathe. But we had to carry the water in from way out in the yard; there was a pump out there."

The house had three bedrooms upstairs and a living room, dining room, and kitchen on the first floor. It was illuminated with gas lamps and heated with coal. A small garden out back provided vegetables; a white fence enclosed the front yard. The nearest town was Thomas, about two miles away, and accessible by the railroad that ran between Pierce, Thomas, and Davis. Berdell rode for free when she could convince the conductor that she was a relative of a railroad worker. Otherwise, she walked the tracks to deliver her mother's grocery list to DePollo's store in Thomas. Home delivery of the order was a service provided by the store owner's son, John. But the customer returned to Pierce on foot.

One trip to Thomas is forever etched in Berdell's mountain memories. Her uncle had just returned from the army and brought a new pair of shoes for her. Berdell wore them to Thomas and was fortunate enough to get a ride home on the train. But the sole passenger coach jumped the tracks and went over a ravine. With help from other passengers, Berdell climbed out of the tilted car to safety. "The coach went off at the Thirty-nine Mine and killed a man," she said. "I got a few bruises, but the only thing that happened to me was I got water on my new shoes. There must have been a water fountain on the train. My uncle was sitting on the porch, and when they got news of the wreck, he asked my mother, 'Wasn't Berdell supposed to be on that train?' Mother said, 'My God, she's in a wreck.' They ran down to the mine and when they got there I was all upset about my shoes. My uncle said, 'The hell with the shoes, I can buy you a new pair of them.'"

The woodlands surrounding Pierce offered their share of hazards as well. Berdell earned extra money selling blackberries harvested from the woods between Pierce and William. "This one time I went up there and had one pail full and was getting pert near full with the other one," she said. "I sat down to eat lunch, and the thing I was sitting on started to move. It was a big snake. It took off and they couldn't get me back up there after that. My uncle went back up there to get the berries and said the snake was gone, but he could tell where it had been. I sat down on that thing and thought it was a branch." An uncle built a table near a spring in the woods so the family could enjoy picnics there. Berdell said the children were warned to watch out for bobcats and bears. "We forgot something and had to go back to the house," she said. "We left our stuff at the table and when we got back, it was gone. The bears had got it. But we weren't afraid of bears. If you saw one, you'd just stop and they'd go away, unless you bothered their cubs."

Although relative wilderness surrounded their community, both culture and learning were available to the townspeople. Square dances were held in the school and homes. "People would take their furniture out of a room and have a square dance," she said. "My Uncle Bud used to call for them. And they had a picture show in Pierce until the damned thing burned down. Then, when we wanted to go to the movies, we had to go clear to Thomas."

The six-room schoolhouse doubled as a community center. Church was held there, as were dances, holiday celebrations, concerts, and school lessons. Berdell completed eight grades in the school, and even served as a substitute teacher while still a student. "You couldn't get teachers down there," she said. "So they put me in to do the teaching. I didn't have trouble with any of the youngsters except Rosalie. I earned enough from that to buy my clothes for graduation." Commencement was held in the Sutton Theater in Thomas. Berdell continued her education at Davis High School, where her family moved after Mine Forty closed at Pierce. John Brown worked the mines sporadically, and Berdell eventually quit school so she could work and help with family finances. Her uncle and aunt, Bob and Bertha Davis, had a farm north of Thomas and supplied them with land for a garden and laying chickens. But when the call to go north finally came, there was no hesitation. Berdell said the outlook was simply too bleak to stay.

Better Days in Conneaut

The family had little difficulty making friends and fitting into the new community. Berdell worked and her siblings continued their education. She credits her involvement in the United Brethren Church in north Conneaut for assimilating her into the community. "I got along beautifully," she said. "I started church over there right away and got to know a lot of people. I know some families that came here had trouble, but I never had any. My family didn't either."

One of the persons Berdell met at church was David Seibert of east Conneaut. They were married in 1928. David, who died in 1986, ran a gas station until the stock market crash of 1929. After that, he worked for Dick Tyler's service station for many years. The couple did not have any children.

Berdell made numerous trips back to West Virginia to visit her uncle and aunt on their farm as well as friends she grew up with. But the aunt and uncle eventually sold the farm and moved to Maryland. And like Berdell, many of her friends were scattered north, east, and west in search of better jobs and futures for themselves and children. Two of her childhood friends remained behind. Berdell recalls visiting them many years after she had migrated north and having one of them tell her, "I wish to Christ that I could get out of here. I hate it." The second told her that she was satisfied, then whispered in her ear, "I want to be sure my two boys get out of here." David liked West Virginia and especially enjoyed visiting the farm. But any ideas of moving there were quickly squashed by Berdell, who had seen the down side of the area. "He liked it all right," she said. "If he had moved back there, though, I'd broke his neck. If there had been anything worthwhile there, it would have been different."

The company store at Pierce was eventually closed and torn down, as was the company house with the white fence around it. The town that had been home to some 1,500 souls at one time is today but a small community of several houses. Berdell traveled back to West Virginia one last time in 1987. Although she could still pick out the ghosts of streets and buildings from the abandoned land, the Pierce, Thomas, and Davis Berdell saw were vastly different from the ones she knew as a child. Sixty years of hardship had redrawn the portrait of communities that had been painted almost overnight.

"God, Davis was so different," she says. "The only thing I could spot was the post office."

Planting the Seed

Twenty-five years after Berdell's family came to Conneaut, another generation of Tucker County young people looked northward for jobs in the postwar boom of northeast Ohio. John Brown would provide the link for his nephew and his wife, Harry and Norma Brown, to come to Ashtabula County in 1948 (chapter 10). In the interim the increased demands for coal during

World War II gave Tucker County's coal miners and railroaders a reprieve. But in those parts of West Virginia where family farms were the mainstay of existence, the 1930s soil brought forth a crop of hard times. The flat farmland and timber of Ashtabula County began to draw northward a trickle of young farming migrants, many of them nephews of farmers who had come north twenty years before. Weary of working the rocky fields with a side plow, they left family, hills and—in the case of Ross Boggs Sr.—a tradition of legendary kin, to create new legends of their own—in Ohio.

3 strong stock for legends

the ross boggs family in ashtabula county

It Started with Big Andy

THE GRANDFATHERS AND great-grandfathers of mountain people have given many a mountaineer a generous spool of yarn from which to weave tales of strength, bravery, and ingenuity. Like an afghan knitted beside the hearth night after night until it is so large no bed can hold it, these tales sometimes grow beyond the boundaries of reason. It is at that point they become legend more cherished even than the reality of having a public figure in the family.

History eventually revisits those in the public eye and revises their accomplishments and honors. Bones are dragged out of the dusty closet and displayed in bookstore windows as long as the revisionist's revelations occupy the best-seller list. Legends, however, are seldom debunked, especially when their subject's stage is a deep, remote valley along the Little Kanawha River in Webster County, West Virginia. Who is there to disprove the heroic deeds, the Herculean build, or incredible output of "Big Andy" Boggs, who lived in this valley from 1815 to 1880? "Big Andy" is long gone, but stories of his strength and achievements continue to provide fascinating conversation whenever Boggs family members gather. And given the impressive accomplishments of his great-great-grandsons, one can wonder if Big Andy's story is not more fact than legend.

Andy's legendary status is a favorite topic of Webster County oral and print historians, who record that Andy could pick up a 150-pound anvil by its snout end and pitch it thirty feet into the air. He stood five feet eleven inches, weighed more than two hundred pounds and had very broad shoulders, according to oral sources. His shoulders were said to be so broad that when he lay on his side with his arm beneath him, his head would hang clear of the surface on which he was lying.

He was a good blacksmith and gunsmith, enjoying a reputation for making the most accurate guns of his day. Like many a mountain man, Andy also had a reputation for being a prankster, bear hunter, wrestler, and fiddler. But Andy's most celebrated feat was constructing the dam for "Boggs Mill" on the back fork of the Little Kanawha River. The mill timbers have long since disappeared, but remaining in the stream is a stone twenty feet long, five feet high, and six feet wide. Legend has it that Andy singlehandedly moved the stone from the opposite bank of the river to dam up the water for his gristmill. Depending on who is telling the story, Andy either carried the stone or skidded it on saplings to its place in the river. Either way, Andy did it by himself.

Another favorite tale places Andy in his blacksmith shop shoeing a mule for a Mrs. Perrine. Andy wanted his customer to stay for dinner, but she refused. He insisted and found a practical way of ensuring compliance. Andy picked up the mule, heaved it onto the roof of his shop, and told Mrs. Perrine to go home on foot or go back to his house and wait for dinner. She accepted the invitation. There are bear-hunting stories as well. One version puts Andy near Kanawha Head in Upshur County shortly after the Civil War. Andy and Bob McCray were flushing a bear from a laurel thicket with their dogs when the bear broke out. Disgusted with the dogs, Andy chased the bear quite a distance until it finally stopped and reared up against a fallen tree. Andy caught it from behind the ears and held it there until Bob caught up with him and slit the bear's throat. The story also is told of Andy's loyalty to the Confederacy and how he hid from the Yankees on a high and desolate mountain between Cleveland and Williams Camp. He later said of his mountaintop, "It is so high and rugged that if one could escape the Yankees, surely it would provide a good place to hide from the devil." Accordingly, Andy was buried there in 1880, the first mortal laid to rest in what became Boggs Cemetery.

These are tales that are told, re-told, embellished, and debated when the embers glow orange in a Boggs family hearth, the last piece of apple pie is up for grabs at the family reunion, or a visitor stops by a Boggs farmhouse for an evening of conversation. It is a rich treasure to have a legend in the family and an equal honor to have a section of the Mountain State bear your family's name. To this day there is a Boggs Mill (a town also known as Bois) and Andy's Run (a stream) in Webster County, although many modern maps fail to note their existence.

But legends do not fill the belly with food nor buy the necessities and amenities of a modern world. Unless one is fortunate enough to have inherited the broad shoulders, gunsmithing skills, legendary strength, and ingenuity of Andy Boggs, the valley and mountains of the Little Kanawha can be as much a breeding ground for poverty and despair as legends and stories. And so it was that in the spring of 1933, Andy Boggs's great-grandson, Ross Boggs Sr., left this valley for Ashtabula County.

Planting New Legends

Ross was seventeen years old when he headed north, but his childhood and youth in the mountains had prepared him well for the work that he would find in Ohio. His mother, Hesther, died in the great influenza epidemic of 1918, when Ross was still an infant. His father Robert Elliott could not care for all three children, so Ross and his older brother, Walter, went to live with their paternal grandparents, William and Margaret Boggs, who owned a mill along the Little Kanawha.

"It was just out in the country," he said, describing his childhood home near Replete. "I'd say it was a mile from any place, anybody, a half-mile up from this Andy Boggs's Mill. Andy's three boys owned that whole valley down there. My granddad was down the river from Andy's place and he had a gristmill." Ross spent six years with his grandparents before his father remarried and moved to Salem, in Dodridge County. His memories of life around Boggs Mill are carefree and happy ones. "School was two to three miles away," he said. "I'd go till the weather got bad, because that was too far for a six-year-old to walk in bad weather." The area was sparsely settled and wilderness was not far from the back door of their grandfather's home. Ross recalls meeting up with a treed bear while walking with his father to the circus in Cleveland, about five miles from Boggs Mill.

His grandfather's home was a log structure covered with wood siding. The boys' bedroom was upstairs, and their grandfather woke them by pounding

The West Virginia farm about a half mile from Boggs Mill along the Little
Kanawha River, where Ross Boggs Sr. went to live with his paternal grandparents
after his mother died in the influenza epidemic of 1918, when he was an infant.
Photo courtesy of Ross Boggs Sr.

on the ceiling with a broom handle. "I was back there after I was married
and you could still see the marks on the ceiling where he'd wake us up," he
said. The boys had chores, but they also had time to play and enjoy their sur-

roundings. The river provided a constant source of recreation, from swimming after chores to catching suckers in the spring. For entertainment, they watched pedestrians cross the swinging bridge fifteen feet above the river. Ross said there were no hand rails or cables on the bridge to keep the pedestrian from falling off. "There was an old fella that would come up the river. . . . He'd go up the path around the hill to this swinging bridge, and he'd come across to the gristmill," Ross said. "My brother and I would see him coming and we'd run out there and watch him, because when he got to the swinging bridge he'd get down on his hands and knees. He'd put that sack of corn on his shoulders and then he'd crawl across the bridge. I found out afterwards that that old fella was in his eighties, and he'd go across that swinging bridge like that. They got cables for you to hold on to now when you cross it. And now I know why he got down and crawled, but when we were kids, that was fun to watch him. That was big treat for us to go out there and watch him crawl across the bridge."

His grandfather was of Irish stock. Ross recalls him as the "easiest going, nicest man" he ever knew. "I never saw him lose his temper," he added. His grandfather didn't have much in the way of material goods, but the family ate well, despite the addition of two more mouths to feed. The hundred-acre farm and orchard supplied most of their food.

Ross moved to Salem with his father and stepmother when he was seven. His father continued to work in the lumber business until the Depression, when the bottom dropped out of the market. Ross completed seventh grade, a bit of the eighth, and headed off to work for his mother's brother near Clarksburg, West Virginia. He worked there less than a year. "I plowed on the old side plow when I was sixteen," he said. "You'd have to stand up so close to hold the handles, you'd hit a rock or something and get your ribs cracked up good."

Follow the Brother

With no desire to torture his body on the steep slopes of West Virginia until his dying day, Ross followed Walter north. Drawn to northeast Ohio by his uncle, Clarence P. Baker, who had migrated to Dorset Township in 1918, Walter had found work at Diamond Alkali in Painesville. He wrote back to

Ross and told him "there's work in Ohio." It was the spring of 1933 when Ross Boggs made the trip to Ashtabula County in an old Plymouth. He would never live in West Virginia again.

"When I got here, I had an uncle that lived up the road from here, [the husband of] my dad's sister, and I went up and visited him," Ross said. "They were saying they needed a hired man [at the Guy Divine dairy farm]. Now you want to know the wages? Ten dollars a month, room and board. I worked almost two years. . . . They was good people, and they treated me good. A lot of people were working for their room and board at that time. I left there and went to another fella from West Virginia, [Austin B. and Ellen] Musgrave, from Buckhannon. They had a big dairy farm. I went to work for him and he said 'I'll give you fifteen dollars a month and more if you are worth it.' We were filling silos, worked thirty days straight and at the end of the month he gave me thirty dollars. That made me feel pretty good."

While visiting his uncle in Dorset, Ross met his future wife, Ruth Spencer, at her high school graduation ceremony in 1935. They were married two years later and had four children: Ross Jr., Barbara, Robert, and Ron. They moved from farm to farm in the early years of their marriage, starting with the Welser farm on East Union Road, where Ross worked as a farmhand. In the spring of 1939, the couple moved to Pat Kennedy's farm on Kyle Road, stayed a year, then moved on to the Leiby farm on the same road. Two years later they moved to the Neely place on Mells Road, and, in the fall of 1942, bought their present farm and home on Route 307. Also, beginning in 1939, Ross worked during the winter months at Ashtabula Hide and Leather, an Ashtabula tannery that made leather for bookbinding and automobile upholstery. He made forty-two cents an hour and worked on an as-needed basis.

Ross said there were several other West Virginia natives working in the tannery, including Joe Gillespie, whom he recalls as a slacker. Joe and another worker, Joe DeAngelo, spent most of their time talking, and a few of the workers decided to teach them a lesson. Catwalks made from planks ran across the vat in which the hides were tanned. These planks were easily moved, and the men decided to adjust to within a whisker of the vat's edge the one that Gillespie and DeAngelo would be walking on. The men were, as usual, talking and paying no attention to their work when they started across the plank, and it gave way with both of them on it. "From that time on, the vat was known as 'Two Joes Inn,'" Ross said with a mischievous laugh.

Ross Boggs Sr. and his wife Ruth (née Spencer) at their Dorset Township, Ohio, farm. *Photo by Carl E. Feather*

The two Joes were in good company, he added, for the tannery's owner, a Mr. Hill, also took a dunking in one of the vats—with his dress clothes on. Ross said the men tried hard not to laugh as they pulled him out, but sensing the difficulty they were having, Hill gave them permission to let loose. "He said, 'Go ahead, God damn it, laugh!'" recalled Ross.

Quitting the tannery in the spring of 1947, Ross started a new career with the Morris Lumber Company. He skidded logs by day and farmed by night and on weekends. Ross's hard work won him the respect of his employer, who by the early 1950s had made Ross a field man in charge of ten sawmills. Ross eventually decided to go into the lumber business for himself, and started by cutting a 170-acre tract on Kyle Road that yielded more than three million board feet. Ross cut wood for himself for seven years, until a heart attack in 1962 forced him out of the strenuous business. After his recovery, he drove truck (a hill-country expression) for the county for ten years and started a convenience store at Pymatuning State Park. He and Ruth operated their "Boggs Service" for twenty years before selling it in 1987.

Fighting Words

Like many a pioneer moving into land rich with opportunity, Ross's northward migration paved the way for other relatives. His father followed the trend set by his two sons and came to Ashtabula in the early 1940s. He found work in the factories and died in Ashtabula County in 1953. Ross's sister, Mildred Robinson, came to Ohio in 1939. "She was living in Shinnston, they were working on a farm there," he said. "So I bought this farm and I had another farm rented then and I was working in the shop. They moved here and lived here. He got a job offer in Painesville, where my brother was, making a lot more money. So they moved up there and we moved in here, and been here ever since 1941."

Thus, Ohio was most accommodating to those willing to work, despite an occasional barb about a mountaineer's accent. But no one messed with Ross Boggs, for he came from the hills well-trained in the art of holding his ground. "When I was fourteen or fifteen, we'd go down to Salem to the old feed mill on a Saturday afternoon and start boxing," he said. "But off would come the gloves and we'd have a fistfight." Ross put those skills to use when he arrived in Ashtabula County. Amateur boxing was a popular pastime all along the lakeshore and Ross's experience at the feed mill made him a good bet in the ring. He boxed middleweight for several years until he got "worked over pretty good" one night in Buffalo and decided to become a trainer in the Golden Gloves league. He went back in the ring one last time to raise some quick cash after he was married. "I had a chance to make some money and signed up for a match," he said. "But I was out of shape. I just didn't move as fast as I did before." After that, Ross's boxing career was limited to training young amateur boxers and organizing boxing matches in the Dorset fire hall. Among his students was Eugene Turner, a black youth from Denmark Township who went on to become a boxing pro.

New Land, New Legends

Ross Boggs's greatest victories were not in the boxing ring but in the voting booth. Ross was first elected Dorset Township trustee in 1957 and served for the next twenty years. He also served one term on the Dorset School Board.

The example of public service set by Ross encouraged two of his sons to enter politics and go much further than their father ever dreamed. Robert, a teacher by training, was elected Ohio representative for District Ninety-seven (northern Ashtabula/eastern Lake counties under the old districting plan) in 1972, at the age of twenty-four. He was one of the youngest representatives in Ohio history. His work in the Ohio House focused on the formation of joint ambulance districts to serve rural communities, protection of Lake Erie waters, and creation of the Ohio 828 tax credit for businesses.

Robert Boggs was appointed to the Eighteenth District Ohio Senate seat in 1983 and elected in 1984, 1988, and 1992. He served as Democratic head of the Ohio Senate from 1990 to 1996. Bob chaired numerous committees and commissions during his senate terms, including the Ohio Rail Transportation Commission, Midwest Inner City Rail Commission, and Great Lakes Commission. Much of his senate work focused on public education funding and bringing equality to districts where costs of educating students were higher. He also worked on environmental legislation to keep Lake Erie waters from being diverted to other regions. He left state government in 1996 and was elected Ashtabula County commissioner that same year.

Ross Jr. began a career in baseball with the Brooklyn Dodgers as a catcher. But a pulled hamstring on the last day of spring training abruptly ended a promising career. He returned to Ashtabula County, entered the workforce, married, and started a family. He enrolled at the Ashtabula Campus of Kent State University to obtain his teaching certificate and work on a degree. But a surplus of teachers kept him from making a career in the classroom. He got a job at Rockwell Brake and entered politics with a seat on the Pymatuning Valley School Board and as an Andover Township Trustee. He was appointed to fill his younger brother's position in the statehouse January 11, 1983, and was elected as District Two representative the following year.

As representative, Ross Jr. served on committees that dealt with agriculture, natural resources, public utilities, children and youth, commerce and labor, finance and appropriations, and townships and elections. He worked to create the Ohio Issue Two bond program, which gave local governments access to funds for infrastructure repair. He also helped mobilize many different groups to bring pressure upon the Ohio Department of Natural Resources to build causeway parking at Pymatuning State Park. The speaker of the house appointed Ross Jr. to chair a select committee on child abuse and juveniles in the state. The one-and-a-half-year, statewide project ended with the publication of what became known as "The Boggs Report."

Both Bob and Ross Jr. say their father's work ethic inspired them to accomplish and serve. "At a very early age we learned to work and work hard," Ross Jr. said. "Dad's saying was 'A hard day's work for a fair day's pay.'" "I think we both will tell you that in our own minds—despite all the public notoriety we've received—we've never been able to accomplish what our father did in his life," Bob said. "They eked out a tough living with nothing. And he is symbolic of the hundreds and thousands of others who came up here and did the same thing. Our country, state and county have been moved along by the toil and sweat of these people. But as baby boomers, we don't often recognize their accomplishments."

The other two children of Ross and Ruth Boggs are Barbara Lizert of Medina, a nurse, and Ron of Ashtabula, a dock worker. Unlike their brothers, Ron and Barbara wanted no part of politics.

Ross is proud of his family and their accomplishments in Ohio. "I've got a nice family. I'm the luckiest guy in the world," Ross says as we sit around the dining-room table of his farmhouse on Route 307. Ruth has just served up slices of her legendary apple pie and filled our cups with hot coffee. The top of the table is covered with clippings documenting his family's accomplishments, from Andy's encounter with the bear to Ross Jr.'s latest battle at the polls.

It could be tempting for Ross to consider himself and his sons twentieth-century legends, just as their ancestor Andy was a legend in his own century. But that kind of recognition comes only with time and often only after the subject has passed on to his eternal reward. "I don't really see myself as a legend," he says. "I worked hard and tried to raise a good family. I had a good wife and I raised the kids to do the right thing only. . . . I come up the hard way and I made up my mind that my children would have more than I had. I've never made big money, but we've always had enough to eat. It was never anything extravagant, but we've had warm clothes. It makes me feel pretty good to think that a hillbilly can come up here and have two sons go to the statehouse. I've rubbed elbows with the governor and some pretty important people."

With more than eighty years of living behind him, Ross Sr. admits that his days at the farmhouse could be drawing to an end. Florida calls every winter and could entice him to become a year-round resident. Would he consider West Virginia, instead? Not if his wife has anything to say about it. "She says it's a good place to visit, but . . . ," Ross says. "I got pretty deep roots in West Virginia, but I've been here so long."

Ross Boggs has no regrets about his life or leaving the mountains, even though it was the backdrop for some amazing feats by his legendary ancestor. Indeed, the Boggs family has shown that the stuff of legend is in the genes and upbringing, not the environment. But one would like to believe that the ruggedness of their ancestors' world might have played a role in conditioning them for the challenges of the flatlands.

"I'm a tough hillbilly," says Ross, with a determined, satisfied look on his ruddy, weathered face—the face of a legend, despite what he says.

Turning to Industry

Ross Boggs came to Ashtabula County in the region's final decade as a primarily agricultural community. In the 1940s, World War II transformed the lakeshore orchards and meadows into a Chemical Shore of furnaces and smokestacks. Young men drawn from Appalachia to build and work in these wartime industries established beachheads—migrant welcome centers for kin in need of a week's spending money, food, and lodging before moving out on their own. In Ashtabula, Harry and Ruby Gillespie's house became a classic beachhead for this purpose, a conduit of Appalachian workers during the peak years of migration. The front door of their West Thirty-seventh Street house was never closed to West Virginia kin in search of a better life in Ashtabula, and dozens took advantage of their hospitality.

4 the gillespie beachhead

harry and ruby's migrant welcome center

Ticket to a Better Life

HARRY GILLESPIE took a week's wages and purchased a one-way bus ticket to Ashtabula in July 1941. He promised his wife Ruby that he'd send for her when he'd made enough money up north, and two months later Harry made good on that promise. But Harry didn't stop there. Before the migration years had ended, more than four dozen White Sulphur Springs workers and their families had come to Ashtabula on Harry's ticket.

During the 1940s and '50s, the Gillespies' West Thirty-seventh Street home served as welcome center, boardinghouse and reunion hall for parents, brothers, sisters, cousins, and shirt-tail relations seeking better lives in Ohio. It is safe to say that no two individuals did more to stock Ashtabula County with West Virginia workers than Harry and Ruby Gillespie. Time and illness have stolen many of the names from the couple's combined memories, but Harry estimates that fifty West Virginia migrants got their start at the Gillespie residence.

Harry was born in White Sulphur District of Greenbrier County June 22, 1910, to John Brown and Mary Lou (Remley) Gillespie. The seventh of eight children, Harry grew up on farms around the White Sulphur District area. "I just worked the farm, that's all," he said. "I had a hoe on my back from the time I was seven years old." Harry's father taught him to plant by the moon. Plants that produced their fruit above ground were planted in the light phase of the moon. Vegetables that grow underground—potatoes, turnips,

Harry Gillespie still keeps a garden of tomatoes, beans, and peppers in his West
Thirty-seventh Street backyard. *Photo by Carl E. Feather*

and carrots—were planted in a dark phase. Harry said the rule was even followed when setting fence posts. He's seen fence posts set in the dark phase
settle into the ground after a couple years; those set in the light phase stay
put. But there were other farming superstitions practiced by John Brown
Gillespie that Harry can't vouch for. "If he didn't get his potatoes in by Good
Friday, he'd just as soon not plant them at all," Harry said. And Harry's father didn't believe in using the kernels from either end of the ear for seed
corn. Harry's father believed that those kernels, which were not uniform in
shape or size, would produce entire ears of deformed corn. When seed corn
was shelled off, the odd-shaped kernels went to the hogs. "I don't know if
there was anything to it or not, but we always had nice corn," he said.

There were rattlesnakes and copperheads on the farm, and Harry's brother
Joe discovered the hard way why their mother insisted they wear shoes when
working the fields. One day, his mother told him to take the cattle into the
pasture—and be sure to wear his shoes. Joe did, until he was beyond his
mother's sight. He took them off at the rail fence and hopped into the pasture
—and onto a copperhead. The snake bit Joe on the foot and it appeared

likely he would die from the bite. A woman down the road from their farm was summoned to administer her homemade snakebite remedy. She had the older boys gather poke root from the woods and boiled it in a pot with water. They forced Joe to put his foot in the concoction, as hot as he could stand it. "That took all the poison out of there," Harry said. Regardless, Joe had to use crutches for four or five months before his foot fully recovered from the bite. Harry said the dangers inherent to going barefoot around mountain farms make the stereotype of "bare-footed hillbillies" an inaccurate generalization. As Joe's experience demonstrates, mountain youngsters enjoyed going barefoot as much as any other youngster, hill country or flatland, but the consequences of going barefoot were more serious in the mountains.

Another stereotype that doesn't hold up for Harry is the mountaineer's supposed taste for wild game. "I didn't like bear meat," he said. "I don't like deer meat. I'm not much of a deer eater. And I never ate 'possum. 'Possum, I don't like their grimy face."

Harry's family included some excellent musicians, among them his uncle Glenn Gillespie, a state champion fiddle player. One day Harry's uncle came in from working the fields, took his fiddle down, and told his wife he was going to teach her to play. He played sweet mountain music for her that afternoon, then went to his bedroom and prepared to die. Harry said a stick from a peach tree had pierced his uncle's ear, but he's always suspected that Glenn died from killing a rabid lamb a few days prior to taking ill. Whatever the cause of death, his funeral created some controversy in the family. Glenn's family had convinced him to get a pair of dentures as he got older, but Glenn despised them. "Made him sicker than horse," Harry said. Glenn dumped the dentures in a hollow stump in the field while he was plowing and told his wife he wasn't going to wear them anymore. But after his death, Glenn's wife insisted he be buried with dentures in his mouth. Harry's father came to his rescue. "He told them he didn't want to wear them when he was a-livin', so he sure wouldn't want them when he was dead." Glenn Gillespie departed this world just like he entered it—toothless.

Following Buzzie North

Harry recalls the Depression as being a particularly brutal time in Greenbrier County, and things had not improved much by the early 1940s. He was working at the Buskirk cattle ranch, earning $1.25 a day—small wages for a man who had his heart set on marrying the Buskirk family cook, Ruby May. Ruby was born February 28, 1914, in Alvon, West Virginia, the daughter of Pinkney and Mary (Cole) May. She and Harry were married March 18, 1941, in Lewisburg. "I don't know how we met," Harry said. "But we met and we got married. I certainly was proud I did meet her."

Harry's wages were still not of the magnitude to support a family, so he decided to follow Ruby's first cousin, Buzzie Lewis, to Ashtabula. Buzzie was a golf caddy at The Greenbrier in White Sulphur Springs, a resort for the rich and famous. One of The Greenbrier's guests was Hosea Hill, who owned the Ashtabula Hide and Leather Company. Hosea offered Buzzie a job at his tannery and Buzzie, eighteen at the time, took him up on the offer.

Buzzie came to Ashtabula in the summer of 1938. Three years later, he extended the same invitation to Harry. "I quit my job down there and I came back up here with him," Harry said. He recalls very little of his bus trip or first impressions of the land. "I wasn't looking too much at the land," he said. "All I wanted was work." He found it at Ashtabula Hide and Leather, making thirty-five cents an hour. "That was a lot better than what I was getting," he said. The tannery, located along the Ashtabula River off Main Street, was the city's oldest industry. It had operated in Ashtabula since 1879, when it was moved to the city by its founders, McKay and McDonald, bookbinders from Massachusetts. Sometime after 1883, the tannery was purchased by Hosea Hill and operated by him and his son, Lawrence; the tannery was sold in 1948.

Harry said the tannery was busy place in the 1940s, with twenty-five people employed on the "wet" side, where he worked, and at least as many on the dry side. Four hundred steer and 450 cow hides were processed every two days. The hides arrived in railroad cars from Swift and Armour meat-packing plants. The stench of the hides, dyes, and chemicals was terrible, but Harry said he got used to it after a couple of weeks. He also easily adjusted to the new community. "I never got homesick," he said. "When you're a grown man, you don't get homesick." Harry boarded on Ashtabula's east side, paying a dollar a day for his meals and lodging. After two months, he returned to White Sulphur District and brought Ruby to Ashtabula County. They lived in Jefferson until the end of 1941, then moved to West Thirty-seventh Street in Ashtabula. The following year, they purchased a house down the street and have lived there ever since.

Ruby also got a job at the tannery and worked there for several years before the couple adopted their daughter, Vicki (Partridge), in 1954. Ruby's daughters, Leota (Suplinski) and Hester (Stickney), were also raised by the couple.

Although getting a steady, good-paying job was a blessing to Ruby and Harry, he says the greatest thing that happened to him in Ashtabula was the day he found the Lord at First Baptist Church. "When you've found the Lord, you've found it all," he said. The couple's commitment to the Lord and their family was not a shallow one. They shared the wealth they had been blessed with, be it a Sunday chicken dinner, a brown bag lunch, or their own bed. "[Guests] were all over the place," he said. "We'd just give up our beds to the rest of them."

Kin Stop

The first family members to follow Harry and Ruby to Ohio were Eugene and Alice "Doodle" (Ware) May and their five-month-old daughter, Mary Jane. Eugene was Ruby's brother and grew up in the White Sulphur Springs area. Alice grew up on a twenty-four-acre farm on Big Draft Road, about three miles from The Greenbrier. Her parents, Omel "Homer" and Lena Bell (Loving) Ware, had twelve children; Alice was the oldest girl and had the responsibility of caring for her younger siblings like a second mother.

The four-room house was built from slab wood scraps. "It was terrible," said Ralph Ware, Alice's brother. "At night the snow would blow right in on us." Alice said the house was heated with wood and it was the older children's job to cut and chop the fuel. "We'd get a beating if we didn't help saw wood," she said. The farm provided the staples for the family's diet: "Beans and 'taters, 'taters and beans," Alice said. "We'd walk five or six miles to get a bag of apples," Ralph added. "Just so you could have fried apples for breakfast." Meat was unknown unless Ralph or one of his brothers caught a rabbit in a trap.

Christmastime and spring brought seasonal culinary treats to the children. "We'd get an orange for Christmas," Alice said. "You knew we were getting them because you could smell them in the house for a week before Christmas." And Ralph added, "If we got an orange, bananas, and nuts, you felt like you had a million dollars." Spring brought watercress, which was gathered by the bucketful from a nearby pond. The green was eaten into early summer, when it became too bitter.

Omel worked at The Greenbrier as a maintenance man for more than forty years, but Ralph said Greenbrier jobs paid more in prestige than cash. The family lived in poverty the first half of the century, and it wasn't until after the children had left and the couple got a small place in town that they enjoyed indoor plumbing, electricity, and gas. "Mom insisted on taking her wood stove with her," Alice said. "When she finally got an electric stove, she couldn't believe how much easier it was to cook. It took her half the time."

Ralph said it was a given that the children would move out and become self-supporting as soon as possible. If nothing else, having to share a bedroom with four or five siblings was incentive enough to find less crowded quarters. Homesickness was something he never felt because he grew up knowing that leaving home was a part of life. But there was homesickness in Alice's heart when she left West Virginia for Ashtabula in the spring of 1942. She said the weather was cold and the trip long and miserable in a car she can describe only as a "jalopy." "It took forever and a day to get here," she said. "I had just about had it. We got to Jefferson and I saw the sign 'Ashtabula—10 miles,' and I wanted him to turn around and go back to West Virginia. I didn't care if we did have to drive all that ways back again." The need for work kept Eugene going, and Alice followed out of love. "When you love somebody . . . when you got a husband, a baby, you wanted to be where he was," she said.

Love/Hate Relationship

That didn't change the way Alice felt about her new home. "I hated Ashtabula the minute I saw it," she said. "It was just different. I didn't know what I was getting into." The first difference Alice noticed was that you could see the sunrise just by looking out the window. "It was kind of strange to get up and look out and see the sun instead of looking up for it," she said. The second big change took longer to accept. "The people were different. No hospitality about them. Down home, you'd walk down the street and people would say 'Hi' even if they didn't know you. Here, they were so cold," she said. "I had a terrible time. So finally I said if you think you are better than me, then I'll just let you know that I think I'm just as good as you are!"

Brother and sister Ralph Ware and Alice Ware Herpy relied on the Gillespie beachhead as they migrated to Ashtabula from the White Sulphur Springs area. *Photo by Carl E. Feather*

Alice and Eugene stayed with Harry and Ruby for about a week until they could find their own apartment. They eventually moved to Madison Avenue, where Alice still lives. Another child, Shirley, would be born to them before they divorced. Eugene found work at Ashtabula Hide and Leather and Alice did housecleaning for other families. After the divorce, she supported herself and daughters with odd jobs. "It wasn't easy, but we got by," she said.

Returning to West Virginia was not an option after the divorce. Ralph Ware was living in Ashtabula by that time and provided familial support for his sister. He and their brother Carl Edward first came to Ashtabula in 1943, fresh out of high school and tired of working at The Greenbrier as golf caddies. "We'd caddy for eighteen holes of golf and make a dollar," Ralph said. "Sometimes, they'd give you a quarter tip." The boys stayed with Eugene and Alice and worked at the New York Central Reclamation Plant for a couple of weeks, then got drafted into the navy. At the war's end Ralph headed off to West Virginia University on the GI Bill. But after two years of trying to get by on $110 a month for books and meals, Ralph decided he could do better in Ashtabula. He came back and started all over again, this time at Electromet, where Carl also worked.

Land of Temptations

Ralph said war and its many horrors had changed his brother Carl from a meek, gentle man to a hard-drinking womanizer quick to start a fight. "He was just wild," Ralph said. And it was true not only of his brother. Ralph's observation is that some of the mountaineers who came north could not handle the abundance and accessibility of alcohol. In West Virginia bars were few and far between; most alcohol was home brewed or purchased at State Stores or private clubs. But in Ashtabula, rows of bars and taverns beckoned the workers flush with their pay to stop, socialize, and meet a pretty girl or two. Alice blames this free-flowing atmosphere for the demise of her marriage to Eugene. "Alcohol ruined our marriage, ruined him," she said. Ralph saw what the alcohol was doing to his brother, brother-in-law, and other migrant workers at Electromet. "I came to the conclusion that if I was going to work forty hours a week, I wasn't going to spend my money on that." Taking the advice of his grandfather, who told him to wait for a woman who had the qualities of his grandmother, he married Jennie Meola, an Ashtabula girl, in 1952. They had two daughters.

Transplanting the Family Tree

Both Alice and Ralph praise Ruby and Harry for their contributions to the family. Alice said Ruby worked constantly to feed the flow of mountaineers newly arrived in Ashtabula and established ones coming back for a visit. Family members still recall the holiday dinners Ruby prepared: one Thanksgiving, she made twenty-two pies for about two dozen family members. There were twelve varieties, including three different kinds of apple, candied sweet potato, and her forte, grape pie. Despite all the work Ruby put into each meal, it was her policy never to sit down and eat until all the family was finished.

The Gillespies' home was always open, and it made no difference to Harry or Ruby whose side of the family the new arrivals came from. Kin is kin to a mountaineer, and shirt-tail cousins received the same welcome as parents and siblings. The largest family group to benefit from the Gillespie beachhead came from Ruby's side, the Allen and Velma (Cole) Lewis family. There were ten surviving children in the Lewis family, nine boys and one girl, and all of them came to Ashtabula as a result of the Gillespies. There was little reason for the Lewis offspring to stay behind in West Virginia as they came of age to support themselves. Their father, a woodsman, had gone blind in 1932 and the Depression was brutal on the large family. "You made your living off the land," said Ken Lewis, one of the sons. "Everybody tried to chip in. Other brothers caddied at the [Greenbrier] golf course. I worked at the Justice Lumber Company since I was fifteen or sixteen years old. I ran the buzz saw, cutting slabs for firewood. I cut timber there, then, during the war, I worked on the truck hauling logs to other places."

At eighteen Ken followed his brothers Melvin and Buzzie to Ashtabula after World War II. His first eight months here were spent working in the timber business. But Ken grew tired of living in shanties in the middle of swamps. "You were in water up to your knees all the time," he said. He found a job with the New York Central Reclamation Plant, then got hired on the railroad in the summer of 1947. He worked there until 1963.

Ken returned to West Virginia in early 1947 and brought his parents and siblings Jasper, Fraley, Manuel, James, David and Charles to Ashtabula. Allen Lewis told his son he'd come north on one condition: that when he died, his body would be returned to West Virginia for burial on the homeplace. Ken promised, and later made good on that commitment. The family moved into a house on West Thirty-eighth Street, near the Gillespies' house. Ken's sister, Cassie, also lived in Ashtabula for a short time during World War II, before marrying a Cleveland man and moving to that city. After retiring, Ken sold out and moved to Birch River, West Virginia, in 1995. The pull of homeplace was just too strong for him to stay north, even after fifty years of living in Ohio.

Ruby's parents also came to Ashtabula and stayed with Harry and Ruby. Her mother died in their home. Virgil Eugene "Bud" Cole, Ruby's uncle, his wife, Eula, and Virgil's brother Clile and his wife Goldie migrated to Ohio and stayed with Harry and Ruby on occasion. Harry's brother, Joe Gillespie, and his wife Una, and their three children got their start at Ashtabula Hide and Leather with Harry's help. Their daughter, Alice, was about twelve at the time and fondly recalls the short stay at the beachhead before her parents found a house. "He was my favorite uncle on my dad's side," Alice Lewis said (Alice later married Melvin Lewis).

Others might come, stay a short while, and then go back to West Virginia. That was the case of John, Joe's brother who came here with his son, Dan, in the late 1940s, but stayed only six weeks (chapter 16). Eula Cole's stepfather, Clarence Kale, came to Ashtabula from Virginia in the 1940s and worked in the lumber camps for several years. Harry said Clarence's wife, Ollie Grace, stayed with them while he was in camp.

Ruby's hospitality extended to her adopted family in Ashtabula. She taught and worked with the children of First Baptist Church for forty years and conducted Bible classes for neighborhood children on her front porch and in the garage. Whenever there was illness at the home of a friend, Ruby prepared and delivered a bowl of soup to the back porch. Her children sum it up this way: "She is the 'Golden Rule' personified."

Ruby and Harry seldom see the many folks who got a start in their home. Most are dead, Harry says; the others just don't come around any more. The large dining-room table, around which so many West Virginia families shared their first meals in the new state, is seldom used. Ruby and Harry eat their meals in front of their kitchen window at a small dinette set. The window looks out on their garden, where Harry still raises his peppers, beans, and tomatoes. Upstairs, in one of the bedrooms where many a weary West Virginia migrant slept, Harry works on a latch-hook rug. The pattern is haphazard, a snowstorm of bright yarn threads worked into the mesh with strong, mature fingers. On a twin bed in the other bedroom, Ruby has loosely assembled the blocks for her latest quilt. Like Harry's rug, the pattern has no name. Each block contains a flower made of fabric scraps; a gridwork of green cloth holds the blocks together.

The quilt and rug are symbolic of the lives that have come to this home from distant sources to be sewn and fitted into the quilt of Ashtabula. The crafter has briefly touched each scrap of material or length of yarn, worked it into place, and then moved to the next piece. When the work at last is finished, it appears to the viewer, standing back to get a good look, not as migrants, immigrants, or natives—but as home.

5 nothin' but hard times

novel forinash: thumbing to ohio

Hitchhiking Miner

THE EARLY 1940S were tough times in Webster and Lewis Counties, West Virginia. Mines were closing and sons leaving for war. The farms, weary from decades of use, yielded a crop of rocks. Despite the inherent beauty of its mountains and streams, rural West Virginia was more likely a place to starve than to live in 1942.

Like many a miner, Novel Mortimer Forinash was out of work again. This time, it was a mine at Shinnston that had closed and put him back on the road in search of work. He thought of heading home to Little Skin Creek, where his wife Della, three sons, and a couple of brothers-in-law depended upon him for support. But Novel was tired of mine closings and the menial farm work that had kept the family from starvation during the Depression. His thoughts turned to northeast Ohio, where he had worked in the Ashtabula shipyards some eighteen years earlier. With his last paycheck in his pocket for traveling money, Novel began hitchhiking toward Albion, Pennsylvania, where his sister Anna L. and her husband Hampton G. Heaton lived. He'd write his family when he got there—and had a job.

"I didn't know where he was going," Della Forinash said. "Me and the kids were there alone. Then we got this letter from him in Albion. He said he was working in Conneautville at a pickle factory and as soon as he got enough money saved, he'd send for me and the kids. I think it was two months before he had enough because he had to pay his room and board, too."

It was August 1942 when one of Novel's cousins made the trip to West Virginia to bring Novel's family—Della and sons Allen, Dana, and Willoughby "Bill"—to their new home. The family's possessions, consisting mainly of the clothes on their backs and her brother Gid's guitar and radio (Gid was in the wartime service), fit in the car with room to spare. Della left without regret and felt no sorrow as the mountains of her home state faded in the rearview mirror. "I wanted to leave because all I could think of was hard times," she said. "All I could think of up here was there would be better times. It was kind of rough here, but not as bad as back there."

Growing up in Cleveland, West Virginia

"Back there" was Cleveland, a Webster County fork in the road. Flanked by towns with colorful names like Ireland, Wildcat, Duffy, Hacker Valley, and Canaan, Cleveland proper was a store building, the storekeeper's house, and the post office, which was housed in the store. Eight or nine farms, including the one where Della spent most of her childhood, rounded out the community. Her parents, Jacob Hanson and Daisy Faye (Summers) Casto, moved to the 169-acre farm in 1912, coming from Jacob's family farm in Braxton County, West Virginia. Della, who was born September 21, 1908, in Hermoia, recalls making the move with horses and wagons. She felt the home they left behind was much better than the one into which they moved—an old one-and-a-half-story farmhouse. There were only three rooms downstairs— kitchen, living room, and bedroom. The upstairs was never finished.

Her father invested his carpentry energies in building a larger barn rather than expanding the house to meet the growing family's needs. There were eight children: Della, Cliff, Gid, Homer, Nan, Elbert, and Willard. A sister, Lora, had died before the family moved to Webster County. Della and her sister slept in the kitchen, the boys in the bedroom, and their parents in the living room. Wood heated the house and cooked their meals, oil lamps provided their light, and telephone service was jerry-built. "Neighbors went together and used common wire," she said. "You'd go so many miles and then put a switchboard. I still remember our ring—it was four longs." Party lines were essentially neighborhood conference calls. Telephone service subscribers shared a common or "party" line under this arrangement, which meant that every time a call was placed to another subscriber on the line, all the phones on that line would ring. The number and pattern of rings distinguished whether the call was for you or the neighbor. Eavesdropping was simply a matter of picking up the receiver and listening to—or joining—the conversation.

The farm was the family's means of support, although Jacob Casto was a versatile man who could have earned his living at carpentry, stone masonry, or mining had the opportunities been present. But farming was his lot in life, and he did it with the help of two horses, seven children, and an ailing wife. "He raised corn, wheat, oats (for the livestock), and we raised practically everything we ate," Della said. "He had meadows and raised his own feed, and he always had a surplus he could sell." Della said the soil was tired and rocky, the mountains steep and demanding. The family didn't own a tractor, and it would have been of little value on that terrain. "You had to stand on one side of the hill and shoot corn in with a shot gun," Cliff said, joking about the challenge of planting crops on the hillsides. The bull work was done with two horses, Frank and Dan. Frank weighed around 1,800 pounds and was a mean cuss when he wasn't bridled. "Put a bridle on him and he was tame as a dog," Cliff said. "But when he ran loose, he was dangerous."

Della began working long before she was even fully able. The mountains and their hardships stole her childhood. "I can't remember when I didn't work. I can remember standing on a chair to make bread and wash clothes," she said. "You had to be old while you were still young. That's the only way I could figure it out." Schooling was sporadic and a two-and-a-half-mile walk from the farm. Because the area was heavily agricultural, youngsters went to school only four months a year—they were needed on the farms the other eight months and to hold class then would have been futile. Teachers were also in short supply. Della recalls one winter when no teacher was available and the entire community had to forgo school. Teacher qualifications were minimal—anyone with an eighth-grade education who could pass the teacher's test could take the post. Della said her later grades were taught by students she had gone to school with in her childhood days.

Even when there was a teacher, Della often had to give up school to stay home and help her mother, who was frequently ill. And morning and night chores often left her too tired for learning. "I had to milk eight cows before I went to school," she said. "When I came home I had to milk eight cows and cook supper." She completed grades three through eight, then left school for good at the age of fifteen. Della said her foundation of learning came from her father, who taught her the alphabet and how to read before she set foot in a classroom. "I followed Dad around in the wintertime with a slate and he taught me the letters and figures," she said. "Dad thought you didn't need to know anything except reading, writing, and spelling."

Della developed a great love for reading and read every one of the three dozen books in the school library. *Black Beauty* was her favorite. But at home there were only a few old schoolbooks and readers that had belonged to her grandmother. This shortage of material only served to increase her hunger for the printed word, and throughout life she has read everything she could get her hands on, except science fiction.

Her dream was to become a nurse—a cousin and heroines in storybooks provided her role models. "But my folks, they had it in their heads that nurses were bad people," she said. "Them old people had funny ideas." Della's other dream was to own a red dress. "But my folks wouldn't let me buy me a red dress," she said. Novel did, however. Cliff grew up without dreams. "Nothing. That's one thing you want to keep out of your mind, is dreams about doing something," he said. "I wanted to be rich, but I never got there. The thing I wanted the most was I wanted to get out of them hills. I got tired of beating my brains on rocks. That's all."

Family, landscape, and imagination provided the children's recreation, what little there was of it on the Cleveland farm. Summer games included horseshoes and baseball. Dominoes and sledding were winter pastimes. "I played dominoes with my father," she said. "I soon learned to let him win. He was a poor loser. He liked to play jokes on you, but he didn't like you pulling them on him." When it came to recreation, ingenuity took over where poverty left off. Della said her brother, Elbert, decided his sled didn't go fast enough on its wooden runners, so he invented a hybrid, replacing the runners with wooden wheels. "He was smart enough to tell me not to ride on it," Della said. The contraption gave him the speed he was seeking—it barreled down the mountainside, crashed through the bars on a pasture gate, and stunned its daredevil pilot.

It was also Elbert who owned a 22-gauge rifle, purchased with money earned by working for other farmers. Della said Elbert decided to give his siblings a demonstration of his marksmanship one afternoon by shooting at a telephone pole that was riddled with nails. The youngsters were sitting on the front porch, except Della, who was on the steps. "He shot that gun and

Cliff Casto and Della Forinash. Growing up in West Virginia, they knew nothing but hard times. They are shown at their Saybrook Township home, where they moved in 1947. *Photo by Carl E. Feather*

the bullet came back and hit me in the leg," she said. "I got up and started shouting, 'I'm dead, I'm dead.' Then they started following me around the house, running after me." Della said the wound was only superficial and the bullet fell out of her leg. While it scared her and the other youngsters, Elbert didn't learn his lesson. "We were forbidden to use the gun after that," she said. "But he got it out one day and he wanted me to put up an oak board for target practice. I did it and ran behind the milk house. When he shot that thing, it came back at him and buried in his forehead. He never used that gun again, he traded it off for something else."

Della said her parents kept strict discipline with the use of a paddle. "We knew what we were allowed to do and wasn't," she said. "But we'd do a lot of things behind their backs and cover up for each other . . . they never could figure out who did what." A rule laid down for each youngster as he or she headed off to school was that if you got a licking in school, you'd get another one at home. One day Elbert said "damn" in the schoolhouse and the teacher administered punishment with his six-foot hickory whip. Della, who was only seven or eight at the time, witnessed the whipping. "I was literally scared to death," she said. "The other boys were at home helping put up crops. Elbert made me promise not to tell it. And I never told on him. So he didn't get a whipping at home." Della also witnessed the whipping of another student who was first punished by being made to stand in the corner for hours with a dunce cap on. "[The teacher] held that whip by both hands and whipped him until he fell on the floor, but he kept whipping him," Della said.

The schoolhouse did provide Della with one pleasant childhood memory, for it was there she received the only Christmas present she had as a child: a small doll that she was not allowed to play with. Della learned about Santa Claus at school, where the tree was decorated with ornaments and symbols of the season. "But Santa Claus never came to our house," she said. Nor was there a Christmas tree in the Casto farmhouse. "There was never a place to put one," she said. "By the time you got eight people in three rooms, there was no place for a Christmas tree." Only a special meal of chicken or duck marked the holiday.

Marrying into Poverty

Della and Novel were married September 2, 1928, at Hampton and Anna Heaton's home in Cleveland, West Virginia. Novel had grown up in Cleveland and was eight years older than Della. But his seniority was not a guarantee of greater wealth—Novel couldn't even buy his new bride a ring after paying for the license and minister. The couple moved to Fairmont, then Worthington, as Novel followed coal mining jobs throughout West Virginia. But the Depression had taken its toll on the mines, and in 1929 the couple moved to her brother-in-law's farm in Cleveland. Their first son, Elbert Alan "Al," was born there in 1929. A second son, Dana Hanson, came in 1932. A midwife presided at both births. Willoughby "Billy" Steele was born in 1938, after they had moved to Weston, and was the only one of Della's children delivered by a doctor.

Della's mother died in 1930 and her father remarried. Three of her brothers —Gid, Homer, and Cliff—left home and moved in with Novel and Della. Novel supported the family digging coal from small family mines that were a part of virtually every farm in the area. The coal veins were usually only one or two feet deep. It was slow, miserable, hard work. "You did well if you got a dollar a day," she said. "You'd make fifty cents a day to start." Even at that, many of the farmers could not pay in cash. One of the farms Novel worked at was owned by the widow of a man who had committed suicide by tying a large rock to his chest and jumping in the river. The widow and her five daughters were left with the task of surviving and Novel was occasionally called upon to help with the bull work. "My husband worked three days there for one chicken," Della recalled.

A small flock of sheep provided Della and Novel with fifteen dollars every spring, when the sheep were sheared. Otherwise, cash was hard to come by. Novel worked for the WPA for a while, making three dollars a week. But when the government discovered he also had sheep, they dismissed him. "We almost starved to death," Della said. She recalls the years of 1940 to 1942 as the worst. Novel found work delivering coal in Lewis County and the family moved off the farm. But no one had money to pay for the coal, and the job dried up. Food was hard to come by, and World War II rationing made eating even more of a challenge. The family lived on cereal, bread, and milk. The landlord paid them a quart of milk a day for milking his cows. Novel boarded at his job—when he had one—and had to take his rationing coupons with him. Della earned $1.50 a week doing housework for better-off families. "Washing, cooking, cleaning," she said. "I didn't have to milk no cows, but I did have to chop wood." Della made clothing for her family from nickel-a-yard dry goods. Their neighbors had cows, and the white feed sacks were passed on to Della, who made shirts for the boys from the material. Nothing was wasted. "You just didn't know where your next meal was coming from," she said.

Thumbing to a Better Life

It was against this bleak background that Novel thumbed his way to Hampton and Anna Heaton's house, near Albion, Pennsylvania. The Pickens and Heaton families of Webster County had come north to Kingsville Township earlier in the century. Hampton brought his family out of Wildcat on a log train into Weston, West Virginia, where they caught the main line to Ohio.

They lived on a farm in Kingsville for a while, then Hampton traded his Kingsville Township farm for one near Albion in the mid-1930s.

Della said her husband's cousin, who lived in Meadville, Pennsylvania, drove to Webster County to take her and the three children to Albion. "It was rough," she said. "I didn't know what to expect. I'd never been out of West Virginia. But I was too tired to be excited." Her other memory of that day was Billy's battle to bring his cat. The cousin didn't want it in his car, but Billy threw a fit and the cousin agreed. The cat barely survived the trip, however, and once they got to the Heaton home, Anna wouldn't allow it in the house. The cat went to the barn and was killed when a cow lay on it. Billy's thoughts of the cat were soon diverted by a pet snake. "Every evening after supper he'd go out in this orchard and sit on a log out there until dark," Della said. "I asked him what he did out there, and he said, 'I eat apples and my snake eats with me.'" Della challenged his story, but Billy insisted. "'Oh yes there is a snake,' he said. 'I take a bite, and the snake takes a bite,'" she said. A couple of the boys decided to watch Billy from the barn loft and check his story. To their surprise, there was indeed a snake that crawled on the log next to Billy. Whether or not the reptile took a bite of apple from Billy is unknown. When Novel learned his son was keeping company with a snake, he went to the orchard and killed it. "Billy cried and cried," Della said.

The family lived with the Heatons from August to April, awkward, long months in a crowded home. Then the Albro Pickle factory closed, and Novel and Della were on the move again looking for work. This time their search took them to Ashtabula, where Novel found work at the shipyard. Della recalls that it was very difficult to find a place to live—they bounced from a room on Park Avenue to a small flat above the old post office to a rented house on Route 45, near Route 531.

It was tough going for the family. A hearing problem prevented Novel from getting a driver's license and he depended upon friends and co-workers to get to work. He often had to pay for his ride to work. "He spent a lot of money paying for it," she said. "He always kept a truck and somebody drove it for him." Della eventually learned how to drive, but not until she was in her fifties.

Shipyard work was dangerous and painful. Paint scraped from the hull fell into Novel's eyes and caused inflammation. Della said the company didn't provide safety goggles, just eye drops to help reduce the swelling and pain. The Ashtabula shipyard closed and Novel headed west to Lorain and another shipyard. Della and the boys stayed behind. Then the Lorain shipyard closed, and Novel headed west again, this time to Pearl Harbor, Hawaii, where he worked for eighteen months as a civilian rigger raising and refurbishing ships sunk in the Japanese attack. Della and the boys stayed in Ashtabula rather than return to West Virginia and their family. "All I could think about were the really, really hard times I had down there," she said. "You'd plant a garden and all you'd hit were rocks."

She took in washing and ironing for people to make extra money, and Dana and Al had *Star-Beacon* newspaper routes to supplement the family income. Della later got a job at Bugler's Inn on Route 20 in Saybrook Township. She worked the night shift there for seven and a half years before growing weary of the late nights. Her next job was The Sundry Shop on State Road, Ashtabula Township. Della said adjusting to the social differences was often the most difficult part of the jobs. "I was shy," she said. "Well, I guess you couldn't tell it now because I can talk the leg off a donkey." Some people made fun of her West Virginia accent, but Della was careful not to volunteer information unless she was asked. "I talked when they talked to me and I made an awful lot of friends," she said. "I didn't say too much, but I thought a lot." There were phrases and words that were unfamiliar to Della, but none bothered her more than the method of giving directions. "My neighbors were always talking about my south window," she said. "I was going nuts. I didn't know where my south window was and I didn't know how to answer them. Down in West Virginia, they don't say north or south, east or west. It's right or left." Della said she finally got straightened out on north and south by her landlord, who explained to her that north is always toward Lake Erie. After that, Della understood where her south window was, and how to navigate her way around Ashtabula using Yankee directions.

After the war Novel found work at the New York Central Car Reclamation Plant and in the furnace room of Electromet, a job he hated. Della said the company was so desperate for workers that sheriff's deputies would come and take Novel to work each day. A stint at Lake City Malleable followed. "He didn't like factory work," Della said. "So he got construction work and stayed with construction the rest of the time. I didn't like construction, it was feast or famine."

The Beachhead Established

The couple faced another crisis in 1947 when they were forced to move from the home they had been renting. "We could not find a home anywhere," she said. "We'd find them for rent, but when they found out we had three kids, they'd say nothing doing." Gid returned home from the army about this time and purchased a fifteen-acre farm on Route 45, Saybrook Township. Novel, Della, and their children moved in with him. In the years that followed, the Forinash/Casto home became a haven for brothers returning from the armed forces and cousins, nephews, and nieces coming north in search of a job. Della recalls a time when she packed five lunches every morning for the working men in the family: Novel, Dana, Gid, Homer, and Delbert Boyer.

Delbert was married to Nan Casto, Della's sister, and alternated between Ohio, where there was work, and West Virginia, where his father stayed. Their daughter, Audrey Ann Boyer, came north, only to be killed in an automobile crash in Ashtabula. Two of Delbert's sons—Chester and Leroy—found lodging at the Forinash home while they worked in construction and other local industry. Chester eventually bought a home in North Kingsville; Leroy went back to West Virginia. A third son, Ronnie, came up and made his home in Ashtabula.

Gid found work at the Bow Socket. Cliff hopscotched across jobs—a mushroom farm, Lake City Malleable, Ward Products, and the New York Central—before settling into a job with the Dunbar Hopkins Greenhouse for twenty years. He married Ann Parish of Akron in 1947 and made his home in Ashtabula. After a divorce, Cliff ended up back at the Forinash farm.

The many relatives and friends of the family made for lively gatherings and a well-used house. "It wasn't nothing for me to cook dinner for forty people on a Sunday," Della said. Len Forinash, Al's son, recalls those gatherings as boisterous and unrefined, with language to match. "It was a pretty rough place, but it was all family, and I could take comfort in that," he said. Len said his grandparents' home provided a familiar, friendly place where family members could test the local job market before deciding if they wanted to relocate. Della's strong work ethic and dedication to her family, both immediate and extended, helped the migrants accomplish their goal of a better life in Ohio. She assumed the roles of mother, job counselor, and sister as she helped them adjust to their new lives in Ohio. "I said if they'd all repay me for what I did for them, I wouldn't have a want in the world," Della said.

All three of the Forinash boys studied electronics and Dana started a radio and television repair business. Al bought into the business and Forinash Radio and Television became an established retail business in Ashtabula. Billy also worked for his brothers, and after selling the business, all three men went to work for General Electric.

Novel died December 29, 1983. Della insisted upon staying in the house that was home to not only her, but Cliff, Gid, Homer, and many others over the years. She admits she is too worn out from hard work to maintain it the way she once did. But it's home, and there is no place to go back to in West Virginia. The land is overgrown; the old farmhouse and barn but a memory. The property was sold to pay for her mother's funeral. She still tries to get back for the Forinash reunion every year, but Della says the mountains are just too steep and the paths too rutted for her weary frame to walk them. "I love the scenery, but I wouldn't want to live there," she says, looking out her kitchen window at the tired farm and collapsed, gray buildings beyond the back doorstep. "All I can associate with that is hard times, and I mean hard times. I haven't had it easy up here, but it wasn't like it was down there."

But hard times in West Virginia weren't limited to the coal mines and farms. By the late 1930s, the timber industry was also giving out. Young men like Elbert Snyder, who had planned on making a living from the state's forests, began to think about careers beyond the mountains of Upshur County. Two of his cousins had found work on Great Lakes ships, and their reports convinced Elbert he should trade his saws for a lifejacket, his home hamlet of Kedron for Ashtabula. All he needed was an opportunity. Ironically, it came at the expense of his own cousin's job.

6 kin from kedron

the snyder home

Sailing Man

HEAD EAST FROM Buckhannon on Route 33, go about ten miles to Sand Run, turn on the dirt road, and follow it down the hill about two miles to the right-hand prong of the Middle Fork River.

Those are the directions Elbert W. Snyder gives for getting to his hometown of Kedron, West Virginia, a place so small and forgotten that map makers no longer put either it or the turn-off point on the map. Although ignored by the official state highway map, Kedron is very real to Elbert and his wife Kathleen. It was real to Howard Riffle, Kathleen's late brother, as it is to Cecil Hornbeck and his brother Harold. It is more than a memory to brothers Wayne and Claude Montgomery, and Ernest "Shorty" Osburn and his son, Maurice. They all grew up in Kedron, and they all migrated to Ashtabula County in search of the jobs that Kedron could not provide. For many of the kin who came, Elbert and Kathleen provided a few nights' lodging and hot meals until the migrants got established on their own. Then again, Elbert and Kathleen were simply doing what had been done for them when they migrated to Ohio in the spring of 1941. His aunt and uncle, George and Belle (Hornbeck) Dawson, had lived in Ashtabula County for several decades before the great migration. Elbert recalls visiting them in 1923 with his mother, grandmother, and sister. George and Belle had a farm in Kelloggsville, "ninety-nine acres, and he wasn't satisfied with just ninety-nine and bought one acre to make it an even hundred," Kathleen said. The Dawsons sold that farm and moved to Kingsville, then to Ashtabula, where Kathleen and their son Willard stayed for several months in the spring and summer of 1941.

The Dawsons' son, Earl "Pete," worked for Cleveland Cliffs, the Great Lakes carrier, as did Marple Hornbeck, Earl's cousin, who went back to West Virginia every winter when the boats were laid up. The cousins kept each other informed of sailing opportunities. Elbert said Marple got his spring call to catch his boat in Cleveland the same time he got his draft notice. "He knew I was looking for work, and I asked him if they might hire me," Elbert said. "So I took him up to the county seat, Buckhannon, to make the phone call to Cleveland Cliffs. They told me to come on up here and apply. I went on April 1, 1941, and signed on the *Yosemite.*" Elbert had never been in a canoe before, let alone a Great Lakes vessel. That didn't stop him from trying something new. He needed a job and in 1941 Cleveland Cliffs and other Great Lakes shipping firms needed men with strong backs and constitutions. Elbert had both, courtesy of a Kedron childhood.

A Kedron Childhood

Kedron was part of the Union District, which included another small farming town, Gale, about a mile and a half beyond Kedron on the Middle Fork River. Farming and coal mining were the sources of income. The district encompassed enough territory and farms to support a Kedron post office and general store, owned by Clint Simmons, the grandfather of Wayne and Claude Montgomery. The Hornbeck family owned the town's other business, a gristmill.

Elbert was born October 15, 1910, to Jesse and Edna (Hornbeck) Snyder atop a hill that overlooks Kedron. The homeplace is gone, but the little community that was a stage for the mountaineers' joys and sorrows is recalled in the Mount Union Cemetery. There was a church there, and its bell tracked the cemetery's gains and community's losses. "If the person was twenty-five, they'd toll the bell that many times," Elbert said. "You'd just have to guess who was that age and who had been sick. I'd run out there to find out who'd died, it was only about a half-mile from home. Or we'd see the hearse a-coming, they'd stand there tollin' the thing. Uncle Ed Tenney was the bell ringer. They'd toll that old bell 'till [the hearse] got up to the church. It was a mournful old sound. I don't know if it did any good, but I guess it didn't do no harm, either."

Elbert Snyder's family was small by Kedron standards, just Elbert and his younger sister, Geneve. Their parents owned a small farm, three scattered pieces of land that totaled thirty-six acres, just enough to raise the corn, potatoes, vegetables, fruit, hogs, and other staples the family needed to survive. "Dad picked up work where he could get work," Elbert said. "He'd cut logs, timber, work in the stone quarry, and was cemetery caretaker. People would help keep the cemetery up and around Decoration Day [now called Memorial Day], the thirtieth of May, they'd take up a collection for the upkeep."

Ten families lived along the river in Kedron; Kathleen's was one of them. Kathleen was born January 18, 1919, to Roy and Goldie (Hornbeck) Riffle in Pickens, West Virginia. Her father worked in timber and the family moved often to keep up with the opening of new coal mines, which needed timbers for ceiling supports. Roy Riffle finally went to work in one and ended up living in Kedron. Kathleen has only good memories of her childhood, which was shared with six brothers and two sisters. "I had a wonderful childhood," she said. "I didn't have to work on the farm because I was one of the older girls. I took care of the house and the babies. Yes, I had a wonderful childhood, and I wouldn't trade it for any of the childhoods today." Among the good memories are the meals her mother prepared from the vegetables and pork raised on their plots. "My mother was very economical. She was a good cook. She could go in the kitchen and get a good meal out of little bit of nothing," Kathleen said. Bread was always baked at home, usually six loaves at a time.

Elbert said corn for meal was raised on the farms, and one year, his father raised their own wheat. Otherwise, the family's supply of flour, a half-barrel or about ninety-six pounds, was purchased in the fall. The bounty from the farm was stored in a fruit cellar. Elbert doesn't like to boast, but the Snyder cellar was one of the finest in that part of the country. It was built by his grandfather, made of cut stone, and had a rock bottom. A small amount of moisture trickled up through the rocks, creating an optimum level of humidity and temperature for long-term storage of everything from home-canned vegetables to rutabagas and potatoes.

There was no shortage of recreation in Kedron, despite its isolation. In the evening youngsters came down from the hills to hang out at the post office or organize a game of volleyball or baseball. Many of the recreational activities centered around the church, where Sunday school and revivals were eagerly anticipated. The woodlands provided plenty of recreation as well. Kathleen recalls "birch peeling" as a favorite activity. Birch bark was peeled from the tree using the metal lid from a snuff can, then the soft underside of the bark scraped off and chewed like gum. The flavor was aromatic and sweet, like teaberry. Autumn brought the cane harvest and making of sorghum molasses. The community's youngsters helped, whether by leading the mule or horse around the mill, which reduced the cane to sap and fodder, or by boiling down the sap into syrup. Winter fun included sledding and riding skippers. Elbert said a skipper is a single-runner sled, a homemade affair constructed from hardwood. The runner was usually made of cherry, about four to five feet long and six inches wide. The front end of the runner was curved upward so it wouldn't dig into the snow. Attached midway on the runner was an upright two-by-four-inch piece of lumber topped with a seat. The piece of wood was braced to the runner with two other pieces of timber. The timber supporting the seat was just long enough to allow the rider room to drag his feet in case the skipper got out of control. The only handles were the sides of the seat, the only controls the rider's feet and swaying motion. Using the single-runner sled required some skill in balancing it, but Elbert said a skipper with a good buildup of ice on its runner could go faster than any sled. Elbert has often wondered why some big manufacturing firm never picked up on the idea.

Elbert and Geneve went to the Mount Union School, a one-room schoolhouse with twenty-five to thirty-five students in grades one to eight. The school was almost within sight of Elbert's home, a mile up the hill from Kathleen's. Elbert went to all eight grades, then said good-bye to book learning and hello to the hard work of the woods and sawmills.

Sawmill Man

Elbert Snyder moved from job to job, at one time working eighteen months straight on one end of a cross-cut saw. But most of his jobs were in sawmills, where railroad ties were a common product. Elbert said many of the hardwood logs that went through the mill measured thirty to thirty-six inches in diameter. The hundreds of fine, ancient logs he sent through the buzz saw would be worth hundreds of thousands of dollars today, but most of them went into railroad ties and roof supports for the coal mines.

Elbert said his job at the sawmill was one of the easiest—he operated the carriage that held the logs as they went through the saw. It was still hard work, and the pay was low, thirty-five cents an hour. Elbert made extra money at the mill by working over an hour or two a night in the Dutch oven, where scrap from the mill was burned. He tended the fire in the oven and got the boilers pumped up for the next day's work.

He and Kathleen were married March 26, 1936, in the pastor's parsonage. There were no big church weddings or receptions in Mount Union, just a simple ceremony, after which life went on as it had before. Their first summer of marriage was spent with Elbert's family. Then Elbert heard of work in the lumber camp at Durbin and he, Kathleen, and baby Willard left to establish a new home of their own. Kathleen recalls ordering everything they needed to set up housekeeping from the mail-order catalog—a beige and green wood-burning stove; forest green breakfast set; bed, mattress, and springs; pots and pans—for $100. Rent at Durbin was six dollars a month. The cottage lacked electricity and indoor plumbing, but Kathleen said it was clean and comfortable.

Elbert sawed fifteen thousand board feet a day at Durbin, but the logs eventually gave out and he moved on to Coalton, then Clay County. He was there from 1939 to 1941, when he got fired over a pay dispute. "That was the best thing that ever happened to me in my entire life," he said. It was because of that unemployment that he headed north to work on the Lakes. Elbert, Kathleen, and Willard came to Ashtabula in their 1934 Ford. Elbert's son, Junior Ray "J. R.," stayed in West Virginia and was raised by Elbert's parents. But after he graduated from high school, he followed his dad to Ohio and found a job at the Ashtabula Bow Socket in 1951.

Kathleen and Willard lived in a three-room cottage the first summer they were in Ashtabula. "It was actually a playhouse that had been built for the owner's daughter," Kathleen said. "But it was a pretty nice playhouse." The playhouse had a large room that doubled as a sitting room and bedroom, a small kitchen, and a bedroom just big enough for a cot. There was no indoor plumbing; a hand pump near the house and an outdoor toilet met those needs. "It was nice enough for Willy and me until Elbert got home from the Lakes," she said. When the sailing season was over, Elbert moved his family into a duplex on North Bend Road in Saybrook Township.

Kathleen had no trouble adjusting to the change in culture and found the people of Ashtabula to be friendly and accepting. Likewise, Elbert found camaraderie aboard the ship, thanks to the war that brought young men from across the United States to work on the Great Lakes. Elbert's job got him a deferment from military service, but it did not provide him with much home life. He sailed from the first of April until January. One year, the boats ran into February as the Great Lakes shipping fleet hustled to keep up with wartime demands for iron ore and coal.

The vacation weeks of winter were spent in Kedron, where Elbert shared stories of job opportunities in northeast Ohio. More than one person followed him north and found temporary lodging at the Snyder home. Among them were Kathleen's brothers, Bruce and Howard, who also found work on the lakes; Dale, who went to work at the Ashtabula Bow Socket; and Frank, who drove a semi-truck as a self-employed contractor. Even their parents left their homes in the hills for a better life in Ohio. Kathleen's father worked at Copperweld for a while, then got a job at Electromet while it was still under construction. Neighbors also followed them north. Wayne Montgomery, fifteen years younger than Elbert, came up on a Sunday in 1951 and went to work second shift the next day at Lake City Malleable. He stayed with Elbert and Kathleen until he got established, then told his brother Claude about the opportunities in Ashtabula. Claude found work at Electromet. Wayne also worked at Electromet after being laid off from Lake City Malleable. "It was the easiest job I ever had. I don't know why I left there. Well, yes, I know. I got a job at Bow Socket," he said.

Farms, Beachheads, and the Hornbecks

Elbert's cousin, Harold Hornbeck, also followed him to northeast Ohio. But Harold had a link to Ashtabula County even before Elbert began his sailing career. Harold's uncle, Ralph Bennett, was a son of the farmland migration to Ashtabula County in the early 1900s. Ralph was the teenage son who rode in the boxcar with the Bennett family's livestock when they migrated to Monroe Township via rail. He married and established his own farm in Monroe Township.

Harold was born September 13, 1921, to Burton Cecil and Jessie (Bennett) Hornbeck. He grew up in Kedron in a family of four brothers and two sisters. His goal in life was to get out of school so he could go to work. Driving a truck was his ambition. "My teacher told me if you want to drive truck, you don't even have to think when you come to a curve, you just automatically turn the wheels. And I said, 'That's what I want to do,'" he said. Harold's wish came true, but only after a few years of working in the woods on a cross-cut saw, felling and cutting up 120 to 130 trees a day. He finally got his dream job, hauling coal for a contract trucking firm owned by his future wife's uncle. The pay was seventy-five cents an hour. "That was a lot of money then," he said. "And I could work as many hours as I wanted to."

Harold took seventy-five dollars of his earnings and purchased a Model A Ford. Things were going well when Uncle Sam drafted him into the army in August 1942. He ended up in a 40 mm anti-aircraft unit in the South Pacific. For Harold, there was no problem adjusting to the army, even though it marked his first time out of the state. "I just made up my mind that this was it and there wasn't much I could do about it," he said. He continued to drive trucks while in the army, and when he returned home in November 1945 he got a job with a trucking company owned by Basil Watts. The firm did road work for the state in the summer and hauled coal and timber in the winter months. There was a romantic element to Harold's employment, as well. Watt's niece, Garnet "Jean" Osburn, was Harold's sweetheart. The Osburns and Hornbecks had lived near and known each other for years. Marriage between the families was just a matter of time and Cupid's discretion. Jean and Harold fulfilled the destiny July 20, 1946.

Jean was the oldest child of Stella and Ernest "Shorty" Osburn. She was born in Ellamore, Randoph County, West Virginia, about four miles from Kedron. Ellamore was a coal and logging town, and the Moore and Kepple Company owned the Osburns' residence. The backyard of their Ellamore home was an Indian burial ground, and Shorty Osburn didn't allow his children to dig in the mound for fear of disturbing a Native American's rest. There was sufficient land beyond the mound to raise corn, potatoes, and a couple of hogs for butchering. "My mother canned everything she could get her hands on," Jean said.

Jean said Moore and Kepple's sawmills, lumber camps, and coal mines were the lifeblood of the Ellamore economy. Miners and sawmill workers, like Shorty Osburn, were required to shop at the company store, where prices were higher than stores that didn't trade in scrip. Shorty earned some cash and rebelled against the company's policy. His boss discovered that Shorty had purchased goods at another store and threatened his job if he shopped elsewhere again. Maurice, Jean's brother, said his father began planning for that day. Shorty fixed up the farm owned by his parents in Kedron and saved his money for a shopping trip. When all was in order at the farm, he went shopping, got fired, and moved his family from Ellamore to Kedron.

The year was 1944 and Jean, a teenager, was not happy about the transition. She had to switch high schools after her freshman year and make new friends. Further, there was less entertainment in Kedron than Ellamore, which had several community centers that hosted country and western stars from Wheeling's Grand Ole Opry. The stars arrived and stayed in a bus that they parked at the house of Jean's friend and neighbor, Nelda Goodwin, who was a musician herself. The connection allowed Jean to meet many up-and-coming country stars, but the ones she remembers best are Grandpa Jones and Sleepy Jeffers. Jean said the men walked her home, about two miles, after a show one evening. She recalls Grandpa Jones as looking, dressing, and talking old, even when he was a young man. But her real interest was in Sleepy Jeffers. "I was really flirting with Sleepy," she said. "He was really good looking."

A Better Life than Kedron

Two children had been born to Jean and Harold and a third was on the way by the fall of 1950 when Elbert Snyder told his cousin there was work up north. Harold was tired of trying to support his family on a three-day-a-week paycheck, but the death of his wife's uncle clinched his decision—Basil Watts was killed when a log rolled off a truck and fell on him. Harold took it as a warning that driving log-laden trucks and longevity do not go hand-in-hand. Harold's sister, Bessie, had already spent several years in Ashtabula County working on her Uncle George Dawson's farm. Harold decided it was time to head in the same direction and took Elbert's son, Willard, as navigator. Joining them in Harold's 1940 Chevrolet was Maurice Osburn. Maurice got a job at Electromet, stayed twenty years, then heeded the call back to the mountains. But for Harold, the separation from the mountains was permanent. "I didn't have a job," Harold said. "But the first place I went to, Lake City Malleable, I got a job. I didn't go anyplace else."

The job at Lake City Malleable was piece work and Harold earned up to fifty dollars a day on the grinding line. It was a lot better than Kedron, where everything had played out. Harold stayed with his sister and her husband, Bessie and Howard Riffle. Jean remained in Kedron with their children, Ron and Judy, until their second son, James, was born. She moved north in the spring of 1951, to a rented home on Route 45 in Saybrook Township. Jean said an early association with a church family, Saybrook United Methodist Church, helped ease them into the community and made them feel welcome. A third son, Doug, born in Ohio, also helped the transition. "I liked [Ohio]," Jean said. "I was really glad to get out of Kedron. I didn't like living on a farm." Jean got a job, too, working at the Tom Thumb Drive-In in Geneva. She was a car hop for six years there, then worked at the Kenny King's Restaurant in Saybrook Township for thirty years before retiring to full-time domestic life.

Harold worked at Lake City Malleable for seven years, went to Union Carbide, then Zherco Plastics, and finally, Rockwell Brake. They moved to their North Ridge West home in 1969. Other family members followed. Cecil, Harold's brother, found work at Electromet. Jean's parents and siblings moved to Ashtabula in 1951; Shorty found work at Lake City Malleable and in greenhouses. They stayed with the Snyders until they could find housing.

Elbert left the sailing life after the 1946 season. He went to work at Ashtabula Bow Socket February 12, 1946, and retired October 1973. He liked the lakes, and they had given him a start in a new part of the country. But he longed to be with his family and have more freedom. "I wanted to stay home a while," he said. "I was gone all summer and you couldn't go anywhere. You just couldn't jump off that thing if you wanted to go anywhere."

Trips back to West Virginia became fewer as more and more of the family and Kedron neighbors came north. In time, there was no need to return to West Virginia, for many of their family and neighbors were already here, including Kathleen's parents. "They liked it here, they really liked it," Kathleen said. "But they always thought they'd like to retire and go back to West Virginia. But they were too old, too sickly by that time." Elbert said he had seen enough of West Virginia while working in the woods, although he is still inspired by a fine autumn day in his home state. Kathleen's love for the Mountain State is much stronger, especially when she thinks of the scenery and her childhood. "There's poverty down there, but there's poverty everywhere," she said. "To me I can see beauty in a lot of things, even a big old rock."

There is no chance they will return to West Virginia to live, although

Elbert's sister is still there. Their home on Nathan Avenue in Ashtabula is comfortable and suited to retirement. The afternoon sun brightens the living room where they sit and chat with Wayne Montgomery, who has stopped by for a visit. They talk about sawmills, Kedron memories, and try to top each other's moonshining story. Wayne tells of an Upshur County moonshiner by the name of Frank Coon who boldly carried his jug down the streets of Buckhannon. Anyone who wanted a drink simply slipped into the alley with him for a couple of minutes. Elbert's story is about a bootlegger's wife who hauled the liquor into town under her flowing dress. "Her bloomers were full of it," he says. "She had these bottles in there and they caught her one time with it on her."

There is a round of gentle laughter as Kedron's migrants share their tales and relax in the comfort they have rightly earned. The yellowing sunset plays across Elbert's kind, round face and sets aglow the gentle waves of his gray hair. More than fifty years have passed since he has claimed Kedron as his home, yet the hills dialect remains in every word he speaks. It is a homey sound on this cold January afternoon, a familiar voice that gave welcome to many a nervous neighbor looking for work in the flatlands. "We just came first and others followed," Elbert says, succinctly summing up the migration of kin from Kedron.

Kedron Apple Butter Reunion

Every three or four years—depending upon the supply remaining in the pantry and the inclination of the parties—transplanted kin from Kedron, West Virginia, gather at Harold and Garnet "Jean" Hornbeck's home in the fall for a weekend of reunion, reminiscing, and good food around a kettle of apple butter.

The tradition dates back to the 1940s, when Elbert and Kathleen Snyder first established a beachhead on Ohio's north coast. As the Hornbecks, Osburns, Riffles, and Montgomerys arrived from Kedron and environs, the autumn reunion was held to preserve a tradition of their agrarian roots and fill pantry shelves with a flavorful reminder of simpler times in Appalachia.

For many years the centerpiece of the activity was a brass kettle Harold and Cecil Hornbeck's father purchased in 1914 for twelve dollars. It came north with Harold in the 1950s and served the family well for another four

Friday night before the Saturday apple butter stir, kin from Kedron and friends gather at the home of Harold and Garnet (Jean) Hornbeck. (From left): Elbert Snyder, Tony Klokoc, Jean (Mrs. Cecil) Hornbeck, Kathleen Snyder, and Cecil Hornbeck fill a washtub with apple slices late into the evening.

New copper pennies are tossed into the brass kettle by cousins Tyler Hornbeck and Erin White. The pennies help keep the apple butter from sticking to the bottom of the kettle.

Apple slices are slowly converted into apple butter by constant heat and stirring.

In addition to constantly stirring the apple butter with the paddle, the process calls for a second party to stand by with a wooden spoon, ready to skim off pips, tree leaves, and the occasional insect that may stray into the kettle. Doug Hornbeck does the job.

Kathleen Snyder shows Harold Hornbeck how apple butter is supposed to look and behave when it's done. Apple butter ready for canning will stay in a mound when it's piled up with a spoon.

Harold Hornbeck looks on as Elbert Snyder performs another test on the apple butter: if water separates from a spoonful placed on a plate, the apple butter needs to cook longer.

While apple butter cooks down outside, Jean Hornbeck prepares lunch for the workers—a big pot of vegetable soup on the stove; a buffet of salads, entrees, and desserts in the dining room; and loaves of homemade bread for sampling the apple butter.

During the apple butter stir, Cecil Hornbeck (left) and his cousin Elbert Snyder talk about a diversity of subjects, from friends they knew back in West Virginia to the Cleveland Indians' performance in the playoffs.

Ron Hornbeck (left) and Randy Osburn remove the kettle of apple butter from the fire.

An assembly line fills the jars and puts the lids on as the apple butter is finally cold-packed. Elbert Snyder wipes the rim of a jar while Jodi Osburn fills one.

Maurice Osburn gives a smile of approval as he tastes the apple butter on a slice of his sister's home-made bread.

decades before a crack forced its retirement from the flames. To preserve the tradition, Harold and Jean Hornbeck's youngest son, Doug, purchased a new fifteen-gallon brass kettle in 1997. With guidance from Elbert, Kathleen, Harold, and Cecil, Doug and his brother Ron and cousin Randy Osburn learned the fine art of apple butter making.

The work began on a Friday night in early October, when five bushels of McIntosh apples were peeled, cored, and sliced into a large washtub. Sitting around the kitchen in a circle, the migrants from Kedron recalled memories both bitter and sweet as they pared the tart apples. At a table in the kitchen nook, Harold whirled the red and green orbs on an apple peeler that shaved the skin from the fruit. Shorn apples were passed down the line for paring knives to finish the task. Within three hours, the washtub was overflowing; hands were sore and stiff, the floor sticky with apple juice.

Harold built a wood fire shortly after six the next morning and filled the brass kettle with its initial supply of apple slices. A soup kettle on the kitchen stove simultaneously heated raw slices to provide fodder for the outdoor cauldron. Kin and friends took turns continuously stirring the big kettle with the stirring paddle attached to a long pole; without constant stirring, the apple butter at the bottom of the kettle would burn. A 1928 silver dollar (the year Garnet was born) was tossed into the mixture for tradition's sake and to keep the apple butter from sticking to the kettle's bottom. Each grandchild also tossed a few new copper pennies into the pot for good luck.

There was no break from the stirring or fire tending. "Too much fire and it jumps right out of the kettle," said Elbert as a glob of hot apple puree hopped overboard into the flames. As the hours wore on, the kettle's brass exterior turned black; its lip became crusted with the overflow. The stirring paddle was passed from generation to generation and back again as each assessed the mixture's consistency and predicted the hour of completion.

The last pan of cooked apples was fed from the stove to the kettle about eight hours after fire was first put to brass. The smell of homemade bread baking emanated from the kitchen and revived the workers as they anticipated spreading hot apple butter on a slice of Garnet's light yellow bread. An hour or so later, Doug began to add the sugar—roughly two pounds for every gallon of apple butter. In the Hornbeck family, the tradition is to use white sugar. But Harold acknowledged that some families use brown sugar with equal success, just as Cortland apples can be substituted for McIntosh, with a corresponding increase in sugar to compensate for Cortland's tartness.

Eleven hours after fire first licked the kettle's bottom, the apple butter was ready to can—but only after some debate. Elbert insisted it needed more sugar, but was outvoted by the other tasters. "I got nothing to say about it," he said, conceding victory. "It's *their* apple butter." Minutes before removing the kettle from the fire, cinnamon oil was added to the cauldron; the smell spread quickly across the backyard and mingled wonderfully with the October evening's breeze. A bowl of the thick sauce was scooped from the kettle and set next to two warm loaves of bread. The fruits of their labor were sampled and approved by each worker with big smiles and second helpings.

All hands leaped into action as the kettle was then moved to the garage by husky volunteers. In assembly-line fashion, canning jars that had been sterilized by baking in an oven (cold pack process) were filled with the hot apple butter. One worker wiped clean the rim of the jar, then passed it to a tong-wielding family member who pulled a sterilized canning lid from a pot of boiling water and eased it onto the opening. A ring was whirled onto the jar and tightened. Within thirty minutes, the kettle was emptied and the table spread with half-pints and pints of the dark brown tradition. The sun set across the backyard tinged with wood smoke and cinnamon. Family members and friends packed up and headed home with their allocation of apple butter and memories. Harold and Garnet, weary from the two long days, announced that the next apple butter stir would be someone else's responsibility. "This is it," declared Harold. "If they want it, someone else will have to do it."

Jodi and Randy Osburn made plans to purchase a kettle so they can continue the tradition at their home in Pennsylvania. And with Doug already owning a kettle, there's little question as to who will preserve it among the northeast Ohio kin.

7 ten mile's contributions

a small west virginia crossroads

NOT ALL DISPLACED West Virginia families are as fortunate as the Horn-becks and Snyders from Kedron. For some, health or economic reasons prevent trips back home to family reunions. Others have no kin with whom to share traditions, no mountain home to revisit. The population of their hollows has been emptied and scattered to the urban areas of the East and North, leaving little trace of former habitation. Like Kedron, hundreds of West Virginia hamlets appeared overnight, bloomed in the reign of King Coal and Queen Lumber, and faded with their demise. One such community was Ten Mile, just over the mountain from Kedron.

The old settlers thought the little stream flowing through this plot and emptying into the Buckhannon River was ten miles long, and so named both the creek and town. John L. Tenney was the first settler here, coming from New England with his team of oxen in 1850. Lumbering became an important industry in the valley town, and the Buckhannon Lumber Company built a mill there. The Baltimore and Ohio Railroad arrived in 1890, and oil and gas wells sprang up thirty-four years later. But a century after John Tenney brought his oxen to Ten Mile, the migration direction was reversing. Perhaps Tenney might have saved his kin a lot of traveling had he, like many other New England settlers, settled in the Western Reserve rather than what was then western Virginia. But hindsight is always perfect, and if Tenney had never settled in Ten Mile, at least three generations of kin would have been cheated of a rich legacy of memorable characters.

Big Feet and Old Timers

Loye Wilfong still remembers the sound his father Asa made at the start of a new day in Ten Mile. "He stood on that porch and hooted like a hoot owl," Loye said. "His voice would travel through that valley and wake everybody up."

If Asa Wilfong were alive today in Ten Mile, only a few souls would hear his melodic summons. There are only a half dozen homes in this valley community located along the Buckhannon River, ten miles south (via the Baltimore and Ohio Railroad line) of Buckhannon. But if the call were given in Ashtabula County, many would recognize it. Ten Mile sent many of her sons and daughters north in the 1940s and '50s. Among them was Loye Allen Wilfong, born January 13, 1925, to Asa and Grace (Strader) Wilfong. Two younger brothers, Coye Ashur and Junior Oval, followed him north. Ten Mile native Lucian "Lou" Philo Tenney, born February 18, 1923, migrated to Ashtabula County in 1947. His younger brother, Virgil, came north the same year. His sister, Naomi, and her husband, Claude Montgomery, came in 1951. Carl DeBarr, another Ten Mile native, and his wife Sue, came to Ashtabula in the mid-1950s.

Ten Mile was like many of the small communities that sprang up in the hollows of West Virginia during the nineteenth century. Agricultural and self-sufficient in its economy, it was a post office address that encompassed smaller hamlets over the next hill, beyond the rail line's reach, or across the creek. In the environs of Ten Mile were the communities of Pickens, where the B&O line terminated at a turntable, and Laurel Run, where the Tenneys' maternal grandparents lived. Loye Wilfong recalls the Ten Mile of his childhood as a community of about thirty homes. Lou Tenney counts three general stores, three churches, and a railroad depot. There was a two-room schoolhouse that served the children of Ten Mile and, at times, those of outlying districts when they could not afford a teacher.

Lou Tenney spent the first five years of his childhood in his birth home, which was about two hundred feet from the Buckhannon River. One of Lou's favorite stories about the river concerns a despondent young man who decided to commit suicide by drowning himself in the stream. To gather sympathy and attention, he announced his plans ahead of time and a crowd turned out for the event. But a few of the spectators noticed that the man appeared to be holding his nose as he disappeared into the water. Their suspicions were confirmed the next day, when he appeared back from the dead —he swam underwater, emerged out of the spectators' view, and hid out for a day to allow the mourning and appreciation for his life to build. The river, which is strewn with large rocks, was more than a place to meet your maker or to swim and fish. It was also the bathtub. "You didn't use any suit," Lou said. "You just had a lot of trees to hide you. And the river is crooked, so you could find a bend or take your bath behind one of those big rocks."

The hardiness of the local young men and women was further proved by their practice of going barefoot. "We'd start going barefoot in March," Loye said. "We had shoes, but we were saving them for the next winter. Dad always said, 'If you can stand your feet on the ground, take your shoes off.'" Lou Tenney said the children and youth went barefoot around the house and yard, but shoes were necessary when they worked the fields. "If you had to work you had to have shoes on," he said. "I went barefooted until I was fifteen, as long as I wasn't working in the field. But you couldn't go in the field without some kind of shoes on. There were too many rocks and briars." Lou said adults almost always wore shoes, unless they were in the house.

Loye's grandfather, Philip Wilfong, had tough, huge feet that were legendary in Ten Mile. Loye said each foot was at least twelve inches wide and twenty-four inches long. "It looked like an elephant had walked out in the snow, the tracks he left behind," Loye said. "He never wore a pair of shoes in his life. When he'd go out to get firewood, he'd warm up this board by the stove and he'd take it and an axe to the shed with him. He'd stand on the board and cut the wood up." Philip Wilfong's shoulders were equally strong and massive. "He used to pick me up and set me on his shoulders, and he'd walk me up there for five miles," Loye said. "I was the toughest one of the family, and the littlest. He'd put his hand down on my head, grab hold of my hair, and go to swinging me around and around in the air." He had legendary finger strength, as well. Loye said his grandfather could grab hold of the rafters on the front porch and pull himself up using only his fingertips. It was strength born of hard work and times. Perhaps that is why Loye still gets upset when he thinks about his grandfather's death and the split it brought to the family. Some family members thought it fitting to buy their father his first pair of shoes for the burial. Others felt it would be best to bury him without shoes. After all, he'd never worn a pair in his life. But

Philip Wilfong returned to dust wearing shoes. "Dad didn't like it one bit," Loye said. "The way they were fighting, the family just kind of broke up after that."

Spending Money

Both Asa Wilfong and Dewey Tenney, Lou's father, were coal miners—when they could find work. The cash they earned paid their taxes and purchased sugar, coffee, fabric, shoes, coal oil, and train tickets. But when it came to food, families were essentially self-sufficient. Father, mother, and children labored in the fields to feed themselves and the livestock. Most Ten Mile families raised chickens for eggs that were traded for merchandise at the general store. Eggs and poultry purchased from the family farms in the hollow supplied the stores in Buckhannon. "I raised chickens one time to get my spending money," Loye said. "I'd carry three eggs in each hand and go down to that old country store and trade them for candy. . . . Then I had to walk about two miles back home."

Some Ten Mile adults extracted spending money from the abandoned coal mines and limestone caves that concealed stills. Loye's parents were among them. One of their best customers was a judge from Buckhannon. "There was a big old stump down there, and they'd hollowed out the inside of it and set a cover over it," Loye said. "I'd have to hide and watch that old judge. He was the only one around there who owned a car. He'd come right after dark and Dad made me stay out there by that stump and watch the judge get the moonshine out of it. Then the judge would back out of there and go back to Buckhannon."

The Wilfong family was constantly on the move, but always within the environs of Ten Mile. They had homes at Truby Run, Sago, Salt Block, and Ten Mile. There was always a little land for farming, and somehow, food on the table. Breakfast was the big meal at the Wilfong house, where ten children and two adults gathered around the table. The meal might include pork, oats or rice, eggs, pancakes, or biscuits and poor man's gravy, made from lard, flour, and milk. For lunch, there would be corn bread, meat, potatoes, and pinto beans. The evening meal was similar. "We ate well. But you didn't crawl across the table at Mom's house. She put it on your plate. She knew what you could eat," Loye said.

During the Depression meat from the farms became more difficult to come by, especially for the community's older residents who could no longer farm. Lou Tenney recalls one old woman, Mrs. Reeder, who was happy to get an opossum in her rabbit trap. "We'd eat a groundhog once and a while, but I never knew us to eat opossum. But she was thrilled to get that in her trap," Lou said. "When we got down to eating opossum, I quit then," Loye said. "The meat is full of grease on an opossum. . . . Meat wasn't too bad on a groundhog. My mom had a hundred recipes for groundhog."

The woman Loye would marry, Jean Perry, lived about two miles from the center of Ten Mile, across the Buckhannon River and up the mountainside. She was one of eleven children born to Dave Miller and Edna Virginia (DeBarr) Perry. Only one sister, Ruth, who married Zeward Copelan, and a brother, Bob, followed her northward. Bob worked in Painesville for twenty years, then returned to live out his days in West Virginia. Loye teases his wife by saying Jean's family was more affluent than his—they owned their farm, the entire side of a mountain. But like Asa Wilfong, Dave Perry also had to turn to the WPA and public relief in the 1930s before he finally found steady work in the mines.

Lou Tenney's parents were also land owners, fifteen acres of bottom land devoted to vegetable gardens and corn for the livestock. They did not own a horse and Lou's father traded work with someone who did when it came time for spring plowing. "We'd cut the corn by hand," he said. "I cut it with a German bayonet until that thing got lost. That was a beautiful knife, just as beautiful as could be."

Grandpa's House

The Tenney family lived in a small house—two bedrooms, kitchen, and parlor. It got crowded as more children came along, and when Lou was six, he moved two miles over the mountain to his grandfather's house at Laurel Run. That residence, an old country farmhouse, had four rooms up and four down, plus the pantries. His maternal grandparents, Ithiel and Maude Tenney (another family of Tenneys apparently no more than distantly related to the Tenneys on his father's side), had raised four children in that house, but when Lou arrived there was only one child left at home—Ross, the half-brother of Pearl Tenney, Lou's mother. Her mother had died after having three children, and Maude was Ithiel's second wife. (Lou's mother was a Tenney before marriage, most likely a very distant cousin to her husband.)

Ithiel's farm had 260 acres. He raised sheep, beef cattle for the family's use, five or six milking cows, and several hogs. "The hogs always got a lot of that milk," Lou said. "You always got good hogs that way." Three horses and strong male backs bore the brunt of the labor for plowing and other farm chores. Lou went to work on the farm shortly after arriving. "In the beginning my job was water boy, and that is one of the hardest jobs you can have," he said. "Those fellas can drink more water on a hot day." He also had responsibilities on his father's farm. Dewey Tenney often worked in Grant Town and had to leave his family alone for extended periods. Lou was put in charge of operating the family gristmill, which was powered by a small gasoline engine. "Everybody brought cornmeal to be ground," he said. "Cornbread was the big thing there and corn was used for dairy feed. Dad would take a toll from every load of corn he ground, so we always had plenty of corn and feed. They would come from all around that neighborhood . . . some of them would bring in a whole wagonload to get ground." His father's other sideline was a breeding bull. "He had the only one in the area. That kept you busy all the time," he said. "When he first left me to take care of them, he gave me a pipe as long as a baseball bat and told me, 'If you have any trouble with it, hit it across the nose.' I never had to hit him once."

There was little in the way of organized recreation in Ten Mile. Ross taught him how to hunt and fish, but in the Depression years, there was not much game to be found in those woods. "When we were growing up, I never saw a deer in that country," Lou said. "Now you can't go down there without seeing a deer. But during the Depression, everything that moved was killed if it was wild. We'd fish the Buckhannon River by dynamiting it. The fish would float to the top. Even in the '50s, it was hard to find enough squirrel to go around."

Lou's other pastime was playing baseball with the neighborhood boys, what few of them there were. "There were a lot of older people there who had been raised and lived in that area all their lives," he said. For Loye Wilfong, the town elders were entertainment in themselves. "Those old men would sit on the store porch of an evening and they'd start telling tales," he said. "It wasn't long before all those kids were at the store with them. They were eating it up and I was right there with them."

Lou's wife, Avalon, also spent most her childhood in Ten Mile. She said

Lou and Avalon Tenney have lived on Edgemere Drive in Ashtabula Township since 1963. The Ten Mile natives are firmly rooted in Ashtabula County.
Photo by Carl E. Feather

that although her father, Fred Hollen, was without work for seven years, the family did not suffer. Her memories of a Ten Mile childhood are sweet. "People were smart back then, they had no bills," she said. "They didn't have an electric bill to pay, and you canned everything you ate. We had an acre of ground and canned up everything that grew on it. And we were never sick and had to worry about doctor bills." Avalon's father got along with assistance from public relief, building roads for the WPA, doing odd jobs, and bartering for the family's necessities. Every man over twenty-one had to pay a poll tax, but Lou said most of the men worked it off ditching. "You'd spend a day ditching," he said. "Of course, you started with the ditch in front of your own property first, then if there was still time, you'd move down the road."

To Great Society sociologists, the people of Ten Mile were living in poverty. But Lou and Avalon said it didn't seem that way because everyone in the town shared the same economic status. Lou said his aunt, who lived in Washington, D.C., sent used clothing to the family. He got knickers or other "city clothes" that were so nice he didn't want to wear them for fear of being ridiculed by the less-fortunate children. But just about any style of dress was acceptable in Ten Mile, because everyone was in the same economic situation. Most younger children wore hand-me-downs from older siblings. Lous described the standard dress for Ten Mile as "overalls and just about any kind of old shirt you could find." He even wore bib overalls to high school. "Sometimes I'd wear Dad's clothes," he said. "I wore Dad's suit for my graduation picture."

Baseball and War

If there was one serious drawback to living in Ten Mile during the 1930s, it was the lack of local transportation. The train provided the only speedy way into and out of the hollow. But Loye Wilfong said the freight train didn't stop unless there was a big parcel to be deposited at the depot. Otherwise, the conductor hung the mail bag on the post as the train passed through town. Lou Tenney recalls two passenger trains and one freight train coming through town each day. His first year in high school, 1937, the passenger train was his transportation to Buckhannon High School in Tennerton, about twelve miles north of Ten Mile. The lack of transportation was a particular problem for students who participated in extracurricular activities. Lou Tenney loved baseball and played for Buckhannon High his senior year. By that time, a school bus ran to Ten Mile, but it did not make a return trip for students who participated in high school sports. To get home after practice or a game, Lou had to walk at least ten miles.

"We'd get home 10:30 at night from school and baseball practice," he said. "I only had two meals a day when I was in high school. I'd have breakfast before six in the morning. and there wouldn't be any more food until ten at night. I might have been a little bigger if I'd had three meals a day." His lack of food did not affect his performance on the field. Lou helped pitch and hit the team into the 1941 state finals. And although the high school had won a dozen state championships, it was the 1941 team that first enjoyed the benefit of new team uniforms. "I never had a pair of baseball shoes of my own," he said. "People would loan me their shoes. And I didn't own my own glove. We had ten or eleven gloves that belonged to the team and we'd all use them depending on what position we were playing." Lou's other love was table tennis. He spent his lunch hours drilling on the game and quickly advanced to school champion. Like Forrest Gump, he realized that the secret of the game was to keep your eye on the ball. But as high school graduation neared, Lou realized that making a living in the mountains was going to be a much greater challenge than keeping his eye on the ball. Three local employment options faced him: the mines, the lumber industry, or trying to survive on the farm. Lou already knew that farming was not going to pay much. He'd tended his uncle's livestock and cleaned the barns for a nickel a day. "You'd work all week and have only a quarter," he said. "I think he took advantage of me, really."

Mining was an unpleasant thought. Lou had worked in the family mine, which provided coal for the Tenney stoves. Hauling coal in a wheelbarrel had left him with a tired back and cold feet about a career underground. Then Lou got lucky. "I never had any hopes of going to college," he said. "I never prepared for college. I just figured I'd go to the mines or putt around on the farm. But my typing and bookkeeping teacher in high school got drafted. He asked me if I'd go to Marlington and help his dad keep the books that summer. I caught a ride to Marlington that Saturday after I graduated from high school and stayed there the summer working a half day in the office and a half day in the mill or on the trucks." Lou's career in the lumber business was cut short when the army rejected his former teacher. He had an offer to stay on and learn the lumber grading business, but Lou decided to follow his cousin Zane Neely to Baltimore.

Zane's father, Delbert, had married Dewey Tenney's sister and moved to Baltimore in the 1920s. "My cousin told me there was a lot of work in Baltimore, so I headed that way," Lou said. "I got off that train in Baltimore and I'd never seen a building like that in my life. I went outside and boy, I'm telling you, the cars and lights would make you dizzy. I had the impression I could just get out there and yell out Zane's name and he'd find me. But I didn't see him, and I got back on that train, the next train to Buckhannon, and took it home. I wanted out of there. When I got back home, I wrote a letter to my cousin and told him I was out there and I couldn't find him. Then he sent me instructions and I started out all over again."

That was in the fall of 1941, and six weeks after arriving in Baltimore Lou still had not found work. He kept applying at the Glen L. Martin aircraft plant, where the B-26 bomber was made. Lou's luck changed December 8, 1941. "Pearl Harbor had been bombed the day before, and I went down to the plant with my cousin and he dropped me off in front of the personnel office. I was standing there in the dark when somebody pulled me inside and asked if I could go to work that day," he said. Lou worked nights at the plant and played baseball by day. That was the sum of his year in Baltimore, which ended when he received a postcard from the draft board in Buckhannon. They advised him to volunteer so he'd have a better chance of getting his choice of assignments. Lou headed back to the mountains, determined to become a marine.

But the selection process at the intake center didn't work in his favor. The recruits were asked to raise their hand if they had been in jail. "The ones who held up their hands went to the marines," Lou said. "A friend of mine from Ten Mile had been in jail the night before and he didn't hold his hand up. I nudged him and told him to put his hand up. He said he didn't remember being in jail." Lou protested the selection process, but ended up in the navy. He was sent to the Great Lakes Naval Training Center, where his boot camp company was composed largely of men from West Virginia, Kentucky, and Tennessee. "When you're at boot camp, you're mixing with people from all over the country," Lou said. "Our company, we were all pretty much at home with each other and didn't have any problems as far as hillbilly stuff is concerned." And if there was harassment, the Appalachian boys could easily hold their own. "We were all pretty good fighters," Lou said of the 120 men in his company.

The navy gave Lou an opportunity to further sharpen his baseball, football, and table tennis skills. "I played tournaments and always won," he said. "I thought I could beat anybody, and I did." He spent two years teaching in anti-aircraft gunnery school in Washington before being shipped to the South Pacific. As he prepared for an invasion of Japan, the war came to an end. Lou returned to Ten Mile in May 1946 and settled down to taking a vacation. "I figured I owed myself one," he said. "But when I started to look for a job, that was the first difficulty I ran into."

Heading North

He could have gone back to Baltimore and picked up at his old job in the aircraft factory. "To this day, I can't answer why I didn't do that," he said. Instead, Lou set his sights on Ashtabula, where his Uncle Ross had moved in 1943. After the death of his parents, Ross had sold the farm and heeded the call of the Union Carbide and Carbon Company. Established in Ashtabula with his own home and family, Ross invited his nephew to come see "The Best Location in the Nation." "I hadn't seen Ross since I went in the service, so I came up to see him," Lou said. Lou didn't have a driver's license or car, so he took the train to Ashtabula. "I just came up to visit him, but he said they were building a new plant over on Benefit Avenue and suggested I go there and apply if I was looking for a job. So I did and got hired. They sent me to Cleveland for a couple months for training before coming out here to start work." The new factory was Reliance Electric Company, and Lou would become one of the select group of men and women known as the "Seven-Seven," the nucleus workforce hired on July 7, 1947. "I thought I'd work a couple years, save some money, and go somewhere else," he said.

But the strong presence of baseball and table tennis in the community, combined with a budding romance and good-paying job, provided fertile soil in which a Ten Mile transplant could take root. "I started playing baseball with the Knights of Columbus," he said. "I didn't know they were a Catholic organization, there were very few Catholics where I'd come from. One Sunday, this guy on the team asked me if I'd been to mass and I told him I wasn't

Catholic and was not accustomed to the Catholic church. He told me that was O.K., I could join because they needed all the money they could get. . . . I had a terrific year that year," he continued. "I felt like I got along with a lot of the athletes all over the county and felt like I was at home." Lou also played table tennis and handball at the YMCA. His skill and interest in athletics provided a common ground that precluded any discrimination because of his slow mountain drawl. And if anyone called him a "hillbilly," it was no big deal. "One fella, to this day, if he sees me at the mall will say, 'Hey Ten Mile,' then he'll laugh. . . . I never felt offended by it," he said.

Cold Walk to Work

But Loye Wilfong found the flat lands to be hostile at times. Loye returned to Ten Mile from the Army in 1946 with an aversion to mining and little hope for a good-paying job in the mountains. "I could never get up enough guts to go back into that hole," he said. "I'd go back until the light would get down to just a little hole, then I'd turn around and get out of there in a hurry." He turned to his other employment option, the logging industry. "When I came back, I started driving truck," he said. "I drove truck [delivering lumber to the mines] until the timber and sawmills went away." He was left with the welfare option, an unacceptable alternative to a man accustomed to working hard for his food. "I didn't want that for my family," he said.

The bleak outlook in Ten Mile and Buckhannon made the newspaper ads he'd been reading all the more interesting. Industries in northeast Ohio were advertising in local papers and begging for workers. Weary from trying to support a family on the few dollars that could be made doing odd jobs around Ten Mile, Loye, his brother-in-law, Zeward "Zeke" Copelan, and a buddy piled into Zeke's car and headed north in January 1951. "The one, he didn't like it up here," Loye said of his buddy. "He went back in a few days. He didn't like it here at all." Zeward and Loye stayed on, however, despite a shortage of housing and prejudice toward southern migrants.

"I came up here and it was kind of hard to get a place to live," Loye said. "I finally found a place to live on Fox Drive. Then [his wife's sister] and her husband came up here and went to work at Reliance. But they wouldn't hire me there because I didn't have a high school education and I wouldn't lie

Loye and Jean Wilfong in their Merry Drive home in Ashtabula, Ohio.
Photo by Carl E. Feather

about it. I talked to people and they told me the places that were hiring. I wrote them down. They were desperate for people at Lake City Malleable." Loye was hired at Lake City Malleable as a grinder. It was a hard, dirty job, but he liked it. It was piece work pay, and Loye, accustomed to working diligently, set a smart pace and earned a good living. But the lack of transportation made his early days in the flat lands difficult. He had to walk to work from the west side of town to East Twenty-first Street, about four miles. "I'd walk that in the winter—snow and cold," he said. "The worst part was walking across that [Spring Street] bridge. The wind coming across that bridge was freezing. I would walk that day in and day out and not a soul would give me a ride. There would be only one person in that car and they wouldn't give me a ride."

Transportation was not as big a problem for Lou, who depended upon his baseball teammates to get him to appointments. Besides, he didn't have a driver's license and his room with Ross on Fassett Drive put him within walking distance of the factory. But in October 1947, he bought his first car, a 1941 Ford that had been stored almost since the day it was purchased.

Going Home

That car would make many trips back to Ten Mile in the years that followed. Seldom was the trip made alone—other cousins, siblings, or former neighbors who had followed their pioneering family northward hitched a ride back home. It was 260 miles one way, and because Lou worked the night shift, the gang wouldn't depart until midnight or later. "We'd get there in time for breakfast, if they were having it late," he said. Loye Wilfong and Zeke Copelan made a trip back to Ten Mile as soon as they got their first paychecks, four weeks after they arrived in Ashtabula. "We were all broke when we went," he said. "We had just enough for gas money." Loye moved his family, Jean and daughter Cheryl, to Ohio two months after getting his job. His first major purchase was a car. "The first car I had up here was a Chevy," he said. "We went home every payday. Most of the time, it would take eight to twelve hours to get there."

The Tenneys made trips back home as frequently as every two or three weekends. Vacations were also spent back in Ten Mile. Despite the economic bleakness of West Virginia and prosperity at the other end of the concrete rainbow, leaving was hard. "I hated to go on a visit and have to leave," he said. "Everybody would be crying, that would be real hard for me." In time, the expanding community of Ten Mile natives in Ashtabula made coming back a little easier.

Transplanted Romance

Avalon Hollen followed the Ten Mile migration path in August 1947. She had spent her early childhood in Weston, where her father worked on the railroad until the stock market crash. He lost his job and went back to the hollow where the family had a house on an acre fronting Ten Mile Road. After graduation she worked in a clothing factory in Buckhannon. "His cousin wanted me to come up here with him and get a job in one of those plants where we could double our money. So we did," she said. Her father loaned them the car to make the trip. Their first night in Ashtabula was spent in Ross and Dale Tenney's home. Avalon found a job at Nelson Machine, where she worked five years. Her apartment on Fox Drive put her near all the services she needed without having to purchase a car. "Things were different then. You could walk down to the city and get anything you wanted. There was a bus that ran to Nelson Machine from the Shea Theater on Main Street," she said. Avalon had no trouble adjusting to the lifestyle in Ashtabula. "We were young and accepted everything," she said. "But I often wish I'd never left down there, because you leave all your family behind. But eventually it didn't make any difference, because they all left, too."

Lou took notice of the latest arrival from Ten Mile, whom he had remembered as "a mean little girl." Now Avalon's beauty attracted him and they dated at ball games, which helped acclimate Avalon to the community. Lou continued to live with Ross for two years, until Avalon and Lou were married, December 26, 1950. Avalon left Nelson Machine after five years to start a family. The Tenneys' first daughter, Rhonda, was born in 1954. A second daughter, Gina, was born in 1966. She was murdered December 28, 1985, in Youngstown, while a student at Youngstown State University.

The couple's first home was on East Twenty-ninth Street. In April 1963 they moved to their brick house on Edgemere Drive. Surrounding it are those things reminiscent of home and Lou's love for sports. Across the street from the house is the Ashtabula River, just as the Buckhannon River flowed by their home in Ten Mile. A Little League park is situated on the flood plain. There are woods around the field and across the road from their house, and there is a mountain of sorts, the ridge upon which their home is built.

There is also a hint of mountain topography on the Merry Drive property that Loye and Jean Wilfong purchased in 1956, the same year he lost his job at Lake City Malleable. The one-story home is modest, built by years of hard work interrupted by job losses and lay-offs. It is surrounded by woods and some of the richest dirt in Ashtabula County. Loye has built and enriched it with composted leaves, creating soil known to nurture onions that weigh in at two and one-half pounds. He has gained a reputation for his generosity, as well, sharing truckloads of vegetables with the community's poor. His other love is fishing, especially in the mountains of Pennsylvania.

Lou continued to play baseball until he was thirty-nine, then coached for ten years. He gave up table tennis as his work schedule at Reliance and home life placed more demands upon his time. But his love for sports and developing young talent remains to this day. He recalls bringing a hopeful from Ten Mile to try out for the minor leagues. The teen-age ball player had talent, but was inconsistent in his playing. But the recruiter showed an interest in Lou, who at twenty-eight struck out twenty-three batters in one game. The scout offered to send him to the minors, but Lou figured it would take at least two years to get into the majors, and he would have only a couple years to play once he made it. He played it safe and stayed at home base.

Sweet Dreams

As the years passed the trips back to Ten Mile became less frequent for both the Tenneys and the Wilfongs. Loye last visited there in 1992. Riding in the car makes him ill, and he doubts if he will ever see that deep hollow filled to the rim with sweet memories. Indeed, Loye says there is little to see there any more, for Ten Mile began to die when his father passed away in 1963. "He was the life of Ten Mile," Loye said. "When he passed away, that little town died."

The Tenneys return only for funerals. Lou's father died in 1991, at the age of 92. Ross, who had become like a father to Lou, also died that year. Avis Smallridge, Lou's sister, lives on her father's old home place. His brother

Vernon also lives in Ten Mile. But Ten Mile is just a sweet memory reflected in the Buckhannon River for most of those who grew up there during the Depression. "I miss the life I had back there," Loye says. "We were poor people, but we were happy. You didn't have to worry about nothing. I dream about the places and my life back there."

8 the virginians

national carbide: a link for virginia migrant workers

WEST VIRGINIA was not the only state providing Ashtabula County with migrant workers, although certainly the majority were from the Mountain State. Among other Appalachian regions represented, Virginia supplied both white and black migrant workers. From the deep hollows of Kentucky, strong, hungry men made their way north with families in tow. And the coal mines of western Maryland and southwestern Pennsylvania provided a few migrants, as well. Like their West Virginia mountaineer brothers, they came for the same reason and experienced the same loss of kin and home. Only the names were different.

Lookin' for Sang

David M. Alley and his Cherokee grandmother "Ma Miller" haven't gathered herbs from the woodlands of southwestern Virginia since the 1930s. But take Dave into the woods on an autumn day and he can still locate the ginseng, goldenseal, crow's foot, and other herbs that were the foundation of healing in his mountain home of Ivanhoe.

Scouring the Ashtabula County woodlands for ginseng is a September ritual for Dave and his "sanging" partners Dempsey Hamilton and Paul Collins, both migrants from Kentucky. The root of the plant is what they're after. Shaped like a man, the ginseng or "sang" root is revered by the Chinese as a source of energy and virility. Increasingly, U.S. alternative medicine devotees are purchasing ginseng products as well, providing a steady market for the root.

Many a mountaineer has put cash in his pocket through the sale of moonshine and sang, perhaps the two greatest cash crops of the Appalachian Mountains. But finding the root growing in Ashtabula County came as a surprise to Dave, who made his first harvest in 1952. "I never gave it a thought that there would be ginseng in this part of the world, as cold as it was," Dave said. He found the sang growing along the rich bottoms of Conneaut Creek and the Ashtabula and Grand Rivers. The following spring, he and his partners returned to Virginia with eleven pounds of dried Ashtabula County sang. A fur dealer snatched it up at eleven dollars a pound. Never again would they collect such a large harvest of sang from the Ashtabula County flood plains.

Ginseng is found most easily in September, when the red berries and gold leaves distinguish it from the rest of the woodland foliage. There is both art and a concern for conservation in digging it. "You got to put the seed back where you got it from so it will always be on this Earth," Dave said. "If you destroy the seed, you destroy the plant." Even so, the plant is losing ground in Ashtabula County. The trio of sang collectors can muster only three to four pounds a year among them. "It's more for exercise than anything else," said Dave, who also questions the root's alleged properties. "I don't know if it does you any good thing or not." Nevertheless, he chews on the root, which is supposed to impart energy and stamina to the user.

Dave does know that yellowroot works on a sore throat. He cuts a sliver from a dried root and dissolves it on his tongue to dispel the pain and fight the infection. But nothing works against a cold like the fall tonic his grandmother prepared. Dave and his grandfather searched the woods every autumn, equipped with a basket and a handful of colored ribbons, to dig the roots for the tonic. The ribbons identified each root as it was dug: mayapple, yellowroot (goldenseal), bloodroot, crowfoot, ginseng, hall bark, and pawpaw bark and seed. Cherry bark and honey flavored the concoction, which was cooked on the stove in an iron pot. "They would give us this every fall and we never had a cold," he said. "They would line us up and give us each a teaspoon full . . . the whole family took it and everybody around you. They liked it, because they never got sick."

Dave no longer wards off colds with his grandmother's woodlands syrup or spreads a salve of wild onions, ginseng, and skunk cabbage roots on his chest to loosen a cough and congestion. But his memories of the woman who gave him this love and respect for nature have not diminished with time or over-the-counter cold medications.

Indian Heritage

Dave Alley was born on New River, Virginia, April 11, 1930, the third of ten children born to Kyle and Leota (Williams) Alley. Dave's maternal grandparents, Pappy and Ma Miller, were full-bloodied Cherokees. His father's family came from Burning Springs, Virginia. Dave's been told his last name came from the occupation of his great-grandfather, a blacksmith who practiced in an alley. Whatever the occupations of his ancestors, Dave was destined to farm. When he was six, his father moved the family to a 190-acre farm on the New River flood plain at Ivanhoe. It was seventeen miles from the Blue Ridge Mountains, good farming land leased for just two dollars a month. When his father eventually purchased the land, he paid fifty cents an acre for it. The land's bargain price was mitigated by the lack of labor. Farm labor was provided by several teams of horses, Dave, his brothers, and neighbors willing to work for food. His father was often away from the farm, constructing the National Carbide Corporation plant at Ivanhoe.

Dave went to school sporadically until he was nine, but the two-mile walk and heavy load of farm chores became too discouraging. "I tried to go to school," he said. "I made it through the first grade, then I never returned. Staying home farming was more important than going to school." He quit and received his education from the Earth, his mother, and Mammy Washington. Mammy was a black servant who lived in the log house section of their eight-bedroom farmhouse. "She cooked, washed clothes, helped take care of the farm. If it hadn't been for her, I don't think we would have made it," Dave said. She lived there fourteen years and took only her room and board for pay. "She was a person just like one of our family," Dave said. "She was colored, but she was family. She was our judge and jury . . . she was a fine lady."

Kyle Alley got a job at National Carbide, earning $7.03 a week working ten hours a day, six days a week. Much of the pay was in scrip, good only at the company store. With thirteen mouths to feed, the farm was a necessity.

On it they raised corn for the livestock troughs and vegetables for the family dinner table. Dave worked outside the farm driving his father's team of horses for a limestone quarry's owner. He was ten years old and earning two dollars a day. "I was doing the same work of the other men driving teams, but I didn't get paid because I was a boy. I worked like that all winter . . . then I just quit. I wouldn't go back. Daddy told the man I was doing the same work as a man, but he wouldn't pay me."

Dave liked working on the farm, but the pay was poor. There was great hardship, as well—hardship that the family never completely recovered from. It came in 1943, when the New River flooded and took out virtually all the crops. The family lost not only its investment of seed, but the food that would have fed them in the year to come. Further, World War II was draining male help from the farm. Nineteen men left the Alley family to fight in the conflict, but only eighteen returned.

Among those who went was Dave's older brother Bill, who, like his father, had a job at National Carbide. After the war Bill was approached by a National Carbide foreman, Sam Pope, about taking a job in Ashtabula. The company had built a defense plant there during the war and needed help converting it to peacetime use. Bill did one better, he also recruited his younger brother. "Bill came up here and he came home and had this 1939 Chevy," Dave said. "He brought me up here and got ten dollars for bringing me to work there."

The men left for Ashtabula on a weekend in October 1949. Dave's father gave him ten dollars traveling money. "That was the first time I'd ever left home for more than an hour or so and back," he said. "It took us eighteen hours to get here . . . the car could go only thirty-five miles per hour." Dave confesses that he was scared to death of Ashtabula when he first arrived. Being in a city was an entirely new experience for him. Further, neither he nor his brother had transportation—the 1939 Chevy was borrowed from Herb Fetters. John and Herb, also Appalachian migrants (introduced in chapter 1), were among the first friends Dave made in Ashtabula.

Dave rented a room for a dollar a week from Pearl D. Atlas on West Ninth Street in Ashtabula. He immediately landed a job at Union Carbide, which leased National Carbide from the government after the war. He made eighty-one cents an hour, good money until Uncle Sam summoned him to the marines, January 2, 1950. Dave was discharged April 1952 and returned to Ashtabula without giving Virginia a second thought. After Dave left, his father sold the last team of horses and let the farm return to the Earth. Their children migrated throughout the eastern United States, but Kyle and Leota lived out their lives on the farm. "Money, boy, money," Dave said. "There was nothing down there. National Carbide was way down. It was just farming."

Car Ferry Days

Dave didn't go back to Electromet when he returned to Ashtabula from the marines. Instead, he found work with the *Car Ferry Ashtabula*, a railroad-car ferry that made daily trips from Ashtabula to Ontario with carloads of coal. The car ferry was as much a part of Ashtabula daily life in the 1950s as the lift bridge, belching smokestacks, and Lake Shore Park. Watches could be set by its departure and arrival; youngsters and grandparents gathered on the bluff in the evening to await its return.

Dave's assignment, forward-end deck hand, was "a lazy man's job," Dave said. He had a room on the boat and received three meals a day. The job paid fifty-two cents an hour, less than Electromet, but it paid twenty-four hours a day, plus his room and board. "Now, that was real good pay," Dave said. The downside was living on the boat from April to February. The one month he had off, Dave headed back to Virginia to visit his parents and siblings. He also found time, while the boat was in home port, to fall in love. He met Betty Pananen in 1952 through Betty's girlfriend, whom he had been dating. They were married December 21, 1954, in Indiana. They had to leave the state to get hitched because Betty's father was a first-generation Finnish immigrant and had no use for hillbillies, especially as son-in-law material. "A hillbilly moving into a Finnish family," Dave said. "Oh boy, it just didn't work. Her dad, brothers, uncles, did not like me. It took her dad two years before he would even speak to me after I married her." "My father didn't like him," Betty confirmed. "He thought the hillbillies never worked well." Her father's prejudice wasn't directed toward mountaineers alone. "I wasn't allowed to talk to Italians, either," she said.

Dave said there was a general feeling of mistrust toward the mountaineers —at first. Many felt as if the southern migrants had come to take their jobs away. "The Finnish and Italians would talk about you in their own language," he said. "You couldn't tell what they were saying, but you could tell they didn't like you." In time, each group came to trust the other. Dave's in-laws warmed up to him and eventually welcomed him as one of the family. He made many friends through fishing and work—friends from West Virginia and Italy; Kentucky and Finland. In the end, they discovered a common thread united their lives: they had come to Ashtabula for job opportunities that simply did not exist in their native land or state.

The newlyweds set up housekeeping in a rented house on Michigan and West Fourteenth. Dave went back to the car ferry to finish out the 1952–53 season. Two years later, he quit the sailing life. It was a wise move: the car ferry sank the following year, ending an era in Ashtabula maritime history. He purchased a sanitation business in Geneva and ran it until 1961, when federal environmental regulations became too burdensome for a small hauler. Dave then went to work for the Ashtabula Bow Socket. He fondly recalls his twenty-three years at the forge as the best of his working life. "It was one of the finest places a person would want to work," he said. Dave learned the trade quickly and moved up to first-class hammer man after one year on the job. For more than a decade, he hammered bicycle forks destined for the Schwinn Bicycle Company. Then the Bow Socket's hammers were forever silenced, and Dave retired in 1984.

His leisure time is spent on Lake Erie searching for trophy walleye and perch. Dave teams up with other great mountaineer fishermen like Lester "Red" Herron and Arvin Rumer to win numerous fishing tournaments. Every fall, he returns to Virginia to hunt turkey and deer; his Ashtabula Township living room displays the trophies of those hunts. And every September, Dave, Dempsey, and Paul return to the woods to look for sang.

Dave Alley has only a first-grade education—formally speaking. But growing up in the mountains with Ma Miller gave Dave an education in survival that he transferred to the Marines, a car ferry, hostile in-laws, and forge. As the twentieth century comes to a close, opportunities like these simply do not exist for one without an education. But the timing was right for this generation of mountaineers, a generation that could survive, no matter where they landed, as long as it wasn't home. "I didn't want to go, but sooner or later, I knew I had to do something," he said. "It wasn't working out, you just couldn't make a living on farming. Things were changing. People used to be willing to work on the farm just for something to eat. But they wouldn't work like that any more."

Lawrence Elmo Brown, a migrant from Wytheville, Virginia, found the realization of his dreams in Ashtabula County. Larry built this Kingsville Township home and presented it to his family as a Christmas gift. *Photo by Carl E. Feather*

The Black Experience

Many others came to Ashtabula from the Ivanhoe area through National Carbide/Union Carbide. They included brothers Raymond, Roy Lee, and David Jackson; John, Henry, and Ted Shinault; several Crocketts; and Lawrence Elmo Brown of Wytheville. Several of them, including Larry Brown, were black migrants who faced double prejudice in the flatlands.

Larry was born June 4, 1933, in a black farming community near Wytheville in the Blue Ridge Mountains. He was the sixteenth child of his father, George Bud Brown, and tenth child of his mother, Minnie Elizabeth. His father's first wife, Kelly Jones, died after bearing six children. Larry's grandfather, John, had been a slave. John Brown's labors had purchased the farmland on which George and Minnie made their living. Minnie kept 250 to 300 chickens and George raised eight butchering hogs every year. Apple and cherry trees provided fruit; large gardens kept the family well fed.

Minnie taught her children how to work. Larry did housework at seven, field work at eleven. She insisted they do a job right; second-best was not acceptable. Larry bucked an educational system that favored white students and penalized the black. To get his high school diploma, he had to rise shortly after four every morning, do his farm chores, get dressed, and meet the work bus for Wytheville by six. Black children couldn't ride the public school buses or attend the high school. They went to the Wytheville Training School. "I started paying for riding the bus, twenty cents one way and twenty cents back," Larry said. "Someone found out, I think it was the principal, and went to the school board and they said they would pay for it."

He earned fifty cents an hour by working for wealthy white families. Larry graduated from high school May 3, 1950, and wanted to go to college. But there was no money, so he went into the army. He was wounded in Korea and spent four months in the hospital. Larry married in 1952; he and his wife Dorothy, a native of North Carolina, had $6.75 between them on their wedding day. After his discharge from the Army in 1953, he lived in Wytheville, trying to get by on fifty-cents-an-hour jobs. "I cooked in restaurants and cleaned," Dorothy Brown said. "He cleaned houses and tried to get by. That's why we had to leave. There were no jobs for blacks there. Only cooking in restaurants and cleaning homes. We used to work all day, stop at the store and buy for our daughter, and when we got home we had nothing."

Larry and Dorothy went to Detroit where they worked for several months before accepting the invitation of Larry's uncle, who worked at an Ashtabula tannery. Larry said the tannery, Lake City Malleable, and Electromet were the only Ashtabula companies that would hire blacks in the mid-1950s. Electromet hired him January 14, 1956. But when it came to housing, the atmosphere was much more discriminatory. Larry said very few Ashtabula landlords would rent to black migrant families. A September 15, 1953, *Star Beacon* story tells of nine members of a black family being forced to live in a four-room apartment, which rented for $40 a month. In other examples of overcrowding, forty blacks were living in a twelve-room house, and seven were sharing one room of a duplex for $22.25 a month. Larry and Dorothy found housing at the Top Hat Hotel in Ashtabula Harbor. Rent was ten dollars a week and the tenants shared one kitchen and one bathroom. They graduated to an apartment on Lake Avenue and saved their money until they could put $800 down on a house in Conneaut. Eventually, they moved to Kingsville, where he built a new house for his family on an acre of land.

They moved in December 26, 1976. It was Larry Brown's Christmas present to his family and the fulfillment of a lifelong dream.

Larry said that when he was scrubbing floors in rich folks' homes, he asked the Lord for three things: a good education, nice family, and new home. Fifty years later, his prayer—and that of many other Appalachian migrants —was answered in Ashtabula County.

9 a singin' man's family

kentucky's gift of mountain music

Farming in Floyd County

HE WAS THE MOSES of eastern Kentucky, leading his people from the poverty of Floyd County to the wealth of Ashtabula.

He was Joseph, too, preparing a storehouse of hospitality where his kin might weather the years of famine.

And he was David, a singing, praising man tried by years of hardship and pain, but strong of voice and spirit, nonetheless.

Herschel Blevins was born September 16, 1931, in that land of coal fields and farms, dark hollows and stills, Floyd County, Kentucky. His father was Everett Blevins; his mother Nerva Jane Paige. Everett left the family when Herschel was twenty-two months old. Herschel's vague memories of his father are of a man playing a guitar. Everett continued to play music after he left his family—for the State of Kentucky, behind prison bars.

Unable to care for the children, Nerva Blevins passed the responsibility to her parents, William and Alice Paige. Some might say Herschel had a tough childhood, being abandoned by his parents, but he considers it one of the greatest things that happened to him. "I believe my father did me a great service by not being there," he said. "I believe I had a purpose in life, and my father was not capable of helping me take care of meeting it." He learned to call his grandparents "Mom" and "Poppa." To this day, he regards William Paige as the most righteous man he has ever known. "If there is anyone better, I don't know him," he said. "If there is anyone better, it's Christ himself."

They were sharecroppers, poor people working for a landlord so tight "he'd skin a flea for his hide." The farm was between five hundred and a thousand acres, but it was all mountain terrain and difficult to farm. Mules were the only farm animals available to ease the labor. There were a half-dozen homes on the plantation, uncles and aunts mostly, laboring side-by-side to grow enough corn, potatoes, beans, and grain to feed their families and give the landowner his third. Coffee was one of the few items purchased from the store, and it was rationed among the family members. Herschel loved it. "I would actually eat coffee grounds," he said. "I'd chew on them."

If the family wanted meat on the table, they had to do additional work for the landlord, who traded them a hog for their labor. Hunting for meat was an easier and more relaxing option. "We ate everything we could get our hands on," he said. "Groundhog Day was one of the sweetest days in history. Everybody took off on that day to go hunting." Rabbit, opossum, and wild turkey meat have slid down Herschel's gullet. "Never did eat no bad meat," he said. "I was hungry and it was all good."

Two Blessings

Two wonderful things happened to Herschel when he was young, things that would bless his life forever. The first was his teacher, Verbal Hamilton of Betsy Layne. "She was a real wonderful lady," he said. "So sweet, she could just make a kid love her." Herschel said his teacher's leading and inspiration gave him an intense desire to learn. Poor eyesight and familial economic demands forced him to terminate his education at the fifth grade. "But my fifth-grade education would be equal to some of the college educations you get now," he said.

The second great blessing was the day his aunt purchased a banjo. "We got hold of a pig and sold it for six dollars," he said. "This man had a banjo he was selling for $6.50, and somehow we got the other 50 cents and bought it." The banjo was his aunt's possession and it was she who took lessons. But Herschel was the musician in the family; the Paige family just didn't have the gift like he did. Although Everett Blevins had abandoned his son at an early age, he passed a gift to Herschel that would bless future generations. "These things are a gift," Herschel said, lightly pounding the kitchen table to make his point. "If you do something like that, it's a gift."

In his earliest memories of this love affair, Herschel sees himself walking about the field banging a tobacco can with a stick, imitating the melodies and tempos of the mountain music he heard on the radio or at a local talent show. "I got it in my head and I just couldn't get it out," he said. Miss Hamilton took pride in her student's vocal ability and showed him off at other schools. He also sang at the Old Order Baptist Church, but they didn't allow musical instruments. It was a capella, and there was but one hymnal, the song leader's. It didn't matter; most of the parishioners were illiterate. Regardless of the church's stance on instrumental music, God's will for Herschel was to praise Him on the stringed instrument. When the banjo came to rest in a corner of their home, it was as if God had sent a poor man's harp as a sign of acceptance. "You can't imagine desiring something so bad, and then all at once, there it is," he said, his delivery like that of a child telling his discovery of Santa's gifts on Christmas morning.

Herschel was between ten and twelve when the banjo came to his house. He quickly learned the instrument by imitating what he heard played on the radio and picked by old timers on the plantation: "Jesse James," "Pretty Polly," "When the Roll is Called up Yonder." It was mountain music and gospel at first, then bluegrass and country. By the time he was a teenager, Herschel was playing and singing at area talent shows before audiences of 100 to 150 people. His first radio show appearance was on WLSI, Pikeville, Kentucky, at the age of nineteen. Herschel developed the ability to imitate the voices of many Grand Ole Opry and bluegrass stars. While this allowed him to entertain the crowds with a variety of music, it also kept him from developing a unique style of his own. Eventually he learned to imitate Lester Flatt and Earl Scruggs and sing the songs his father wrote from prison for the popular bluegrass duo.

Coal and Moonshine

But singing and picking don't keep the weeds from growing, hogs from starving, or landlord from evicting. To make extra money, Herschel and his grandfather cut prop posts, used to support the ceilings in the coal mines. The work was done by hand—crosscutting and splitting the timber, then hauling it out to the mines. They were paid six to ten cents per post, depending on the length, and could split up to five hundred a day. "By the time I was fifteen years old, I had $40 to $100," he said. "That was big money back then. I made more money on the outside of the mines than I did on the inside."

Herschel is still in the red from his solitary day in a coal mine. "I worked in a mine a half day and said there has got to be something better than this," he said. "I sold my lamp and knee pads to another guy on credit and never got paid for them. They cost me six or eight dollars, and that was forty-five years ago and the guy is dead, so it looks like I won't be getting paid. I never got paid by the coal company, either."

The other source of income in the eastern Kentucky hills was illegal, but very popular and prosperous. "I know people who bought big farms from raising moonshine," he said. Herschel never made it himself, but he has many stories about those who did. Some of them stretch the imagination, like the one about moonshine watermelons: The output of the still was fed into the watermelon vine; when the fruit was ripe, it brought four dollars a slice. Moonshining was a way of life that Herschel neither condemns nor condones. Neighbors drank it together and considered it an insult if their host did not put a jug on the table. Even preachers imbibed every now and then. And it had great medicinal value. "Shine, hot water, sugar, and ginger mixed together to make a tea," Herschel said. "Made us sweat off our colds. 'Course, a lot of people liked to get sick." Shine made in the eastern Kentucky hills was exported to West Virginia, Maryland, Virginia, and Ohio. To make it look like store-bought liquor, a red dye derived from tree bark was added to the drink. Federal Revenue agents kept a close watch on the operations, and many of them died doing it. Herschel said only one revenue agent assigned to Floyd County lived to retire. One rookie agent got his middle finger shot off and quit before the bullets moved up his arm.

Concealing moonshine on its way to market was the biggest challenge. The liquor was hidden in saddle bags and taken out of the hills on horseback. Jugs were painted white to make it look like there was milk inside. "The more open you were with it, the less likely you were to get caught," he said. One of his favorite stories is about the revenue agent who stopped in a general store to buy a half-gallon of liquor. A boy standing in the store with a shoe box in his arms told the agent he could get him a bottle for ten dollars. "He gave the kid ten dollars and the boy left the box with the agent," Herschel said. "The boy never came back and [the agent] got to wondering what was in the box the kid had left with him. When he opened it up, there was the moonshine."

Railroading in the North

Love came into Herschel's life at the age of nineteen. His bride, Magaline Hall, was seventeen. They were married May 25, 1950, after a courtship of one month and five days. "I seen her and fell in love with her," he said. "And she fell in love with me. I was kind of bashful, it took me a week before I asked her to marry me." Herschel left his grandfather's farm and worked the farm owned by his wife's family. It was 125 to 150 acres, and Herschel soon grew tired of dead-end subsistence farming. Further, the economic pressures of post–World War II America were becoming unbearable for the small Appalachian farmer. Other young men from the hollows were heading north, finding jobs, and returning home driving fine cars. But Herschel was still riding a horse, two hours in the morning and two at night, to get to a lumber camp job that paid only four dollars a day. "I just got tired," he said. "Everybody was going outside to get work. I wanted to go like everybody else was." Herschel saved his pay for a week and bought a Greyhound bus ticket to Ashtabula for $10.25. "We had no relatives here," he said. "But my stepfather, Robert Hamilton, was here. Back then, everybody was helping everybody else." Herschel's mother had died in 1946 and Robert moved north after that with his three boys, Dempsey, Charles, and Robert Jr.

Herschel arrived in Ashtabula November 9, 1952, and went to work on the New York Central Railroad three days later. "I was just looking around trying to figure out the lay of the place," he said. "The first place I looked was the railroad. It sounded good to me and I asked the boss if he would hire me. He told me to come to work in the morning. Never even turned around and looked at me." A friend from Floyd County, Irving Tackett, was living on West Fifth Street and worked at the New York Central Railroad Reclamation Plant. Herschel moved in with Irving until he got a paycheck and could rent his own place. His first check for two weeks' work was $92, the most money Herschel Blevins had ever received at one time in his life. "With that check, I was able to rent a house, buy furniture, and hire a guy to take me back to Kentucky to get my wife and son," he said.

Their first son, James, was born in Kentucky in 1951. Four more children were born in Ohio: Burchel, Clyde, Clounia, and Herschel Jr. Herschel and Magaline set up housekeeping on East Sixth Street, which was close to the railroad yards where he worked. They did not own a car and Herschel often walked long distances to get to his assignment. His first car, a 1936 Ford purchased for fifty dollars, came after he'd been in Ohio a year. "Talk about driving," he said. "I wore it out." The second car was a 1939 Pontiac, which became the family's ticket back to Kentucky on weekends, holidays, and vacations—five hundred miles one way.

Pickin' and Singin'

Trips became less frequent as the family grew and their circle of friends in Ashtabula expanded. Herschel teamed up with other musicians to form the Northeast Ohio Coon Hunters. They played bluegrass and country music around the state. Herschel's sons inherited their father's natural musical talent and he taught them how to pick and strum as soon as they were big enough to hold an instrument. Burchel learned to play bass on a homemade instrument—a stick, piece of string, and old washtub—assembled by his father. He convinced his father of his talent, and Hershel bought him a real bass. He was playing it at the age of six and gave his first public performance with the aid of a stool his father made so he could reach the strings. Clyde started on a set of drums and gave his first performance in kindergarten. But he busted the drums by banging on them too hard and ended up playing the mandolin. In 1962 eleven-year-old James played banjo with his father on Ashtabula AM radio station WREO. By the time James was fourteen, he, his ten-year-old brother Burchel, and seven-year-old brother Clyde had appeared with their father and the Stanley Brothers, a nationally known bluegrass band. The Blevins Band became well known throughout the state, playing coon-hunters clubs, fairs, talent shows, and contests in the 1960s and 1970s.

The family moved several times before buying their small farm on Garrison Road in Plymouth Township. With skills gained as a subsistence farmer, Herschel could have survived off his twenty acres. But the railroad provided him with a comfortable income and a job that he loved. "It was nothing to me, I didn't even call it work. It was actually a pleasure to work there," he said. Herschel did not view his blessings in the flatlands as something to hoard. The Blevins household became a hotel for east Kentucky refugees making the transition to a better life. Herschel and Magaline provided many a relative and friend with meals, lodging, and direction in finding work. Some of them found jobs and stayed. Others became homesick or did not find the work to their liking and went back. "If they didn't like it, I always made sure

Linda and Herschel Blevins picking out a tune together. *Photo by Carl E. Feather*

they went back with some money," he said. "I'd be a rich man if I'd saved the money I've given to people. I tried to help other people have all the things I didn't get. I just love people." Herschel views his ability to help others as a divine gift and responsibility. He credits love for others as one reason he had no trouble adjusting to the culture and customs of northeast Ohio. Further, he sees his being here as part of a divine plan to help his people.

Trials and Blessings

Herschel's faith has been tested many times. In 1968 a back injury put him on disability and ended his railroading career. His beloved Magaline died May 25, 1994. Her death devastated the boys, who have not performed together since. Troubled with poor eyesight and arthritis, Herschel believed his days of joy had passed. Then he came across an old acquaintance and West Virginia migrant, Linda Wright, at a bluegrass concert. Herschel, in his easygoing, practical-joker way, planted a kiss on Linda's jaw. A bystander with a camera caught Herschel in the act. "I grabbed her again and kissed her, and

I said, 'Would you marry me?' And she said, 'Yeah.'" It was all in fun, but also prophetic. Two weeks later Herschel showed up at Linda's door to take her on a date—a gospel music sing and something to eat afterwards. That was in February, and they were married July 20, 1995.

Herschel returned to the gospel music stage, singing with Linda at his side. He says he's passing his time until the Lord calls him home, and he's looking forward to that day. In the meantime, he will keep on loving people and his God, like any Moses, Joseph, or David must do. "I believe with all my heart it was just put in my heart to love people," he says. "It's a gift of God. I never had no hatred toward anybody. God always was the leader. I'd go where He led me. It was like I was led by a spirit to meet people who needed me. My desire was to help them."

10 death of a mining town

from kempton, maryland, to a new life in conneaut

At midnight April 15, 1950, the Buxton & Landstreet Company store and the Davis Coal & Coke Company's Mine Forty-two at Kempton, Maryland, ceased operations. Kempton was mortally wounded that night and died forty-two days later when its economic lifeblood, the company scrip—now worthless—was collected and tossed down the 480-foot mineshaft. Black earth was bulldozed over the opening and the town dump erected above it as a tombstone. The token profits reaped by the company store were returned to their source.

Except for what Harry Brown kept.

Son of a Union Organizer

Harry had lived in Kempton as an infant, but because his father was a union organizer for the coal mines, the family never stayed in one town very long. Fate would, however, eventually bring him back to this valley mining town on the West Virginia border one last time—to get married. "My father was a union organizer for John L. Lewis and we used to move approximately every six months to a year—when he either successfully organized the coal mine or the coal company found he was an organizer and they fired him," Harry said.

His parents had met in Pierce, West Virginia, where Harry's father, Harry R., worked in the mines. For the next decade, the couple hopscotched across the mountains of West Virginia, Maryland, and Pennsylvania: Bellslow, West Virginia, where Harry was born; Junior and Scott's Run, West Virginia; Richeyville, Pennsylvania; and McKeefree, West Virginia, where Harry R. owned a couple of small mines. He lost them in the Depression, and the family moved to Lonaconing, Maryland, where Harry spent most of his later childhood and youth. After his parents divorced in the early 1930s, Harry quit school and went to work cutting and laying stone for the National Youth Administration. The pay was $16.50 a month, working one week on, one week off.

One-Street Town

While Harry was getting a tour of Appalachian coal fields, Norma Lantz was growing up in Kempton in the relative seclusion of a one-street town. The town's only claim to fame was the headstream of the Potomac River, which entered the community pristine and left defiled by the high-sulphur coal. "At the foot of their backyard, there was a stream that you could step across and that was the very beginning of the Potomac River," Harry said. "You could see the native trout swimming around in the water. But if you went down the stream a quarter of a mile, where the sulphur bled into that stream, there was no fish in it. The sulphur killed them."

The next-to-the-youngest of five children, Norma was born June 12, 1926, to Alvin and Della Mae (Welch) Lantz. She had a sister, Marion, and three brothers: Clifton, nicknamed "Swifty," because he was so slow; Darrel, also known as "Fatty," because he was never that fat; and Alvin Jr., also known as "Jun." All three are deceased.

Norma's family came to Kempton in 1923. Her father had worked in logging, but by the early 1920s the lumber business was kaput and Alvin went to work in the coal mines. Kempton's mine was so new that a road had not yet been built to the community that would spring up around it. Families moved to Kempton by loading their furniture on a flatcar and taking the Western Maryland Railroad to the Kempton siding. A dirt road finally came to the town in 1928, and remains the only way in and out of the hamlet. It leaves Route 219 near the Fairfax Sand and Crushed Stone Company, rambles through the forest for three miles, then opens upon Kempton, a wide spot in the road.

Kempton, Maryland, 1995. *Photo by Carl E. Feather*

Boom Days in Kempton

Kempton started as a lumber town in the early 1900s and had a school by 1902. Mine Forty-two was opened in 1915 by the Davis Coal & Coke Company, which held a virtual monopoly on a hundred thousand acres of coal lands in Mineral, Grant, Tucker, Randolph, Barbour, and Taylor Counties of West Virginia. At Kempton's peak some two hundred miners and their families lived in the community. The mine company owned the land and the houses that clung to the side of the mountain. The locals called it "Double Row," a double row of double houses on the top of the hill. "Ours was right beside the railroad tracks," Norma said. "We had to crawl under the [railroad] cars to get home for lunch and stuff like that. It was either that or walk all the way up to the store and walk back. And there wasn't time for that. But we were used to it. That was life."

The Lantz home was small, with only two bedrooms, but Norma's mother found room to accommodate at least two boarders. "I can remember every night we'd sit down to eat supper and the conversation with the boarders was 'How many did you load today?' That was the conversation every night,"

Norma said. One of the regulars was a mine safety man. "He came once a month. Mother cooked him beans and cornbread for fifty cents," Norma said. Boarders provided the family the only cash for purchases that could be made outside the community. The Buxton & Landstreet Company provided company stores wherever the Davis Coal & Coke Company operated mines; it was Kempton's only store, and although it was not owned by the mine company, it traded in scrip. "At any time, if you went to town and bought groceries, [the mine] would fire you," Harry said.

A community building stood on the outskirts of town, a stone's throw over the Maryland border into West Virginia. It contained a restaurant, barber shop, pool room, and theater. Norma remembers watching silent movies at the theater. But to see a sound film, she had to travel to Thomas, where the Sutton Theater entertained miners and their families with a different show almost every night. It was a special treat for Norma and the other youngsters to go to Thomas and see a movie. "When they had the matinees on Saturday afternoon, we would walk clear up the hill and catch the train," she said. "It was a mile up the side of the mountain to that little old shanty up there in the woods. . . . The Western Maryland would go through and it would stop at every little mail box along that route. We'd go to the matinee, then Mom and Dad would come to Thomas and pick us up. They wouldn't make two trips to town to take us to the movies." "I remember old Dad Lantz would get himself a big bag of peanuts at Nick's and sit in that '41 Chrysler and eat those peanuts and throw the shells in the street, waiting for the kids to come out of the show," Harry added. Norma earned spending money doing housecleaning chores for the owner of the company store. "I got a quarter for working all day Saturday. When they raised the show in Thomas up to thirty-five cents, I asked her for a raise and she wouldn't give it to me. So I quit," Norma said.

All in all, there wasn't much to do in Kempton. "We had the schoolhouse and it served as the church," Norma said. "We had Sunday school in it. The schoolhouse had about two or three classes in each room and they had one teacher for each class. There were five or six grades in there. The downstairs was the high school." As was the case with most of the homes in Kempton, there were no indoor toilets at school, although an underground dam provided running water to the community. Only three homes were blessed with running water and indoor plumbing: the doctor's, the mine superintendent's, and the store operator's. "The old honey dippers used to come around at night [to clean the outdoor toilets]," Norma said. "We weren't allowed to stay up and watch them, but they'd come around while we were in bed." Children invented recreation using the meager resources the town had to offer. "Our playground was the slate dump from the coal mines," Norma said. "I still got coal dust in my knees—I really do. Of course, we didn't have no playground swings or anything like that. We just went out and entertained ourselves and sneaked out and smoked. We walked up and down the streets for entertainment, and we'd sit on the steps at the company store or play tag on the coal cars. In the wintertime, when the cars would fill up with snow, we'd get in there and slide down in them. My mom and dad never knew that."

Like any small town, Kempton had its cast of characters that provided fodder for gossip and memories. "This Tom Day would go in the store and buy ten cents worth of candy and he'd hide it so the kids wouldn't mooch it off him," Norma said. Whenever Harry tries to keep something for himself, Norma still accuses him of being a "Tom Day." And there was "Gracie," who, as the gossip went, spent a great deal of time at the bachelors' end of town taking care of the gentlemen's carnal needs. "We watched her going up the road—all the windows faced the walk she'd go up—and she'd take a couple of steps, then she'd stop and look back to see if her seams were straight," Norma said. "We were in high school and we got a big kick out of it because we knew what she was and everybody told us what she was."

The common thread and experience of the townsfolk was the black vein of coal that ran beneath their homes, school, and community. The union wove that thread into a strong fabric that provided the miner with his only security in a dangerous world. It was a fabric so strong that it also created walls between immediate family members. Norma's home was no different. "When you walked in that house, on the left wall would be a picture of President Roosevelt and on the right wall was John L. Lewis," Harry said. "And if you wasn't a Democrat, don't come in. And yet they sold their vote for a miniature [1.5-ounce bottle] of whiskey. They'd walk along the line and the guy would hand them a miniature. They'd walk in and put an 'X' under Democrat and walk out. That's the way they done it. [Norma's maternal] grandfather worked a scab mine in Crelin, Maryland. If our mines were on strike, Norma's father would not take her mother over to see her mom and dad. And they would not sit at the same table and eat a meal with them while they were on strike. They were union."

There was only one other loom that wove the threads more tightly, and that was the solidarity of spirit awakened by the siren that alerted the community to a mining accident. "When anybody got hurt in the mines, they'd put that big old siren on and when that thing blew, everyone would take off and go to the mines," Norma said. There were no phones or anything. Everybody took off to the mines to see who was hurt. We'd go down to the mine and wait for them to bring the elevator up. . . . It wasn't something that happened too often. But when it did, it was a bad one." Norma's family never lost a member to a mining accident. But two men who worked with Harry's father died when the ceiling collapsed on them at Richeyville.

Danger Below—Death Above

Coal is mined in one of two ways: strip mining, used when the coal seam is close to the surface and can be quarried; and deep mining, which requires either a vertical (shaft) or horizontal (drift) approach. Drift mines were common on family farms where the seam could be accessed by digging into the side of the mountain. Small, independent mines were often of this nature; the coal was extracted in small quantities using pick and shovel. A pony or mule was frequently used to pull the car from the tunnel.

Larger mines, such as those at Kempton, Maryland, and Thomas, Pierce, and Davis, West Virginia, used vertical shafts to deliver men to the coal seam, provide fresh air, and remove the coal and rock. Horizontal shafts branched from the bottom of the vertical shaft as they followed the coal deposit or seam, usually marked out in rooms, or chambers. Dave Losh, a Chardon resident who worked in the Davis Coal & Coke Company's Pierce Thirty-nine Mine in the mid-1940s, said the Pierce shaft dropped 438 feet. Miners reached the bottom by riding five or six at a time in a metal cage. Dave said the cage he was riding in went into a free fall one day and dropped 237 feet before a safety mechanism engaged and arrested the death plunge.

Once they reached the bottom of the vertical shaft, miners rode to their work site, or "place," in coal cars powered by an electric motor. Several cars attached in a chain and driven by a single motor comprised a "man trip." It took forty-five minutes just to get from the top of the Pierce mine to the place. Dave said a crew of three or four—a machine operator, timber setter, and one or two helpers, or "buddies"—worked each face of the coal seam. The first step was to undercut the face at floor level with a six- to nine-foot

Davis Coal and Coke Company mine in Kempton, Maryland.
Photo courtesy of Norma Brown

saw blade and drill holes near the top for blasting charges. The cut on the face was generally fourteen to sixteen feet wide, six feet deep, and as tall as the seam, usually four to six feet. Dave had an electric drill to make the dynamite holes, but his father, who worked in the mines forty-three years and helped Dave get his job, had to use a hand-powered auger. "In the old days they had a breast plate, a metal plate that you wore on your chest, and you drilled by hand," Dave said. "It was you against the drill."

A blasting charge was tamped into the hole and sealed with rock dust. The men walked forty to fifty feet away from the face and triggered the explosion using a lantern battery (the lanterns were worn in the miners' helmets). The explosion released the coal, which could then be loaded into cars. Mechanized loaders were introduced beginning in the 1920s, but full-scale mechanization, with an accompanying loss of jobs, did not occur until the late 1940s. Coal was still being hand-loaded at the Kempton mine when Joseph "Sappo" Turek of Davis, West Virginia, went to work in the mid-1940s, at the age of twenty-one. Joe said the mine was about 360 feet deep; it took about fifteen minutes on the man trip to reach the place. The seam at Kempton was up to twelve feet thick, but was also cursed by "Big Joe," a layer of shale several feet thick that divided the seam. Big Joe had to be drilled and blasted just like the coal face, and the rock had to be shoveled out and carried up the rock chute to the "picking table," where coal was separated from the slate. The rock was discarded on the gob dump. Joe said miners despised rock seams like Big Joe because mine companies didn't pay to load rock. And in the early days of the Kempton Mine, miners received only ten cents for each ton of coal shoveled into a car. Joe shoveled with a Number Two shovel, and he figures a shovelful was about ten or fifteen pounds of coal. A robust miner could also use a Number Four shovel and get more coal, and fatigue, per bite.

Shoveling was made all the more difficult if the seam was low—some seams ran only three or four feet deep—forcing the miner to work in a stooped position. Compounding the discomfort was the darkness, psychological stress of confinement, and constant threat of firedamp or methane, which could cause an explosion, and blackdamp, a carbon dioxide and nitrogen mixture that would asphyxiate miners without warning. The coal dust, released from the blasting, was yet another explosion hazard.[1] Moisture was a nuisance in some mines. Joe said the Kempton mine had an ongoing water problem and required a large pump system to keep it under control. The pump foreman worked even when the miners were on strike; to abandon the pumps would have meant losing the mine to water.

Harry Brown said miners worked in constant danger, but the risks were greatest during and immediately following blasting, when the ceiling could come crashing down. Homer Floyd Fansler's *History of Tucker County* notes that an average of five miners died every year, mostly by falling slate, in the Fairfax District, which included Thomas.[2] Timbering, reinforcing the ceiling with wooden beams and posts, was essential to prevent cave-ins. A timber measuring anywhere from five to twelve inches square and twelve to twenty-two feet in length was placed across the ceiling perpendicular to the shaft wall. Harry Brown's father used a buck saw to cut the timbers to the right length. Two miners, or "buddies," raised the timber to the ceiling and set the support posts under it. Darald Spangler, who worked in mines near Morgantown, West Virginia, said his crew used a jack to raise the timber to the ceiling and hold it in place while the props were set. "That's why a lot of us had bad backs," he said, recalling the heavy timbers. "Green timbers, they were the worst. They'd kill you."

The timbers and props, usually set on four-foot centers, were not failproof insurance. "A lot of people got killed in slate falls," Darald said. "My brother-in-law was laid up one winter on account of a slate fall. What happened, a piece of slate fell on his head he walked around that mine and didn't even know where he was." Darald witnessed a piece of rock measuring twenty-two feet across and twenty-seven feet high crashing through timbers to the floor—a "cutter" in miner's jargon. Had a co-worker not told him to run, he probably would have been killed. The collapse closed that section of the mine and furloughed fifteen men, including Darald, who migrated north a couple of years after the closing. Dave Losh also gave up mining and followed kin to Cleveland and factory work after the Pierce mine closed in 1946. But Joe Turek remained a miner for thirty-five years, working mines in Morgantown, Fairmont, and other parts of West Virginia before retiring at the age of fifty-six.

"No opportunity there"

Perhaps it was the danger or the strikes, or simply a father's desire for something better for his son than he had known, but Harry's father insisted his son not work in the mines. The edict fit well with Harry's plans, for he had no desire to be a miner. Nor did he care to live the rest of his life in Lonaconing. "I like Maryland," he said. "It was a good place to grow up. You could walk out and go fishing in the trout streams. But like Norma said, when nine o'clock came, they rolled up the streets and went to bed. I knew there was more to the United States than where I was raised, and we were raised in poverty. Let's face it, it was during the Depression. And I thought I could do better because I was willing to work. . . . There was no opportunity there, and there still isn't."

On his eighteenth birthday, Harry Brown signed his ticket out of Lonaconing. He enlisted in the U.S. Marines Corps. "I wanted it," he said. "I lived my life wanting to go in the Marine Corps. It didn't take the war to get me into the Marine Corps. I knew I was going to get out of Lonaconing. That wasn't where I wanted to spend my life. It was the first time I'd ever been out of the mountains of Maryland. I used to cry myself to sleep lying there in boot camp. Man, that was tough for someone who wasn't used to that kind of stuff. I cried myself to sleep a few times."

Times were changing in Kempton, as well. A prolonged strike at the mine sent Norma's father in search of work outside the community. His sister's husband was working in Akron, Ohio, at the Goodyear plant, and he as-

Kempton, Maryland, in the 1920s or 1930s, when it was a booming mine town.
Photo courtesy of Norma Brown

sured Alvin that he could get him a job there. Norma accompanied her father to Akron for the job interview. But Alvin didn't pass the physical and
went back to Kempton to wait out the strike. "Meantime, I got in at the
Goodyear Aircraft," Norma said. "I went up with my Dad and we were going
to work and do what we had to do to make out. But he had to go back home
and I stayed with my aunt. I worked up there a year until I got laid off."
Norma was eighteen when she left Kempton to build bombers and fighter
planes in Akron. The big city was a fascinating change of life for a girl raised
between two mountains. "Big city, you know," she said. "I met a real nice girl
who really helped me out. She had polio and was crippled up really bad. No
one else fooled with her. Kleta Keyser, that was her name. I don't know what
I would have done without her."

Young women from all over the country, many of them from Appalachia,
had come to Akron to work in the war plant. Therefore, Norma did not experience the prejudice some Appalachian migrants encountered in the North.
Further, there was a large population of Appalachian workers in Akron from
the World War I emergency. The Ohio Industrial Commission in 1917 recruited workers to work in the "gum mills." Akron gained 144,000 new residents from 1910 to 1920, many of them Appalachian migrants who stayed
on and established beachheads for the next generation.

Silver Lake Romance

After the war, Norma returned to Kempton and became engaged to a local
boy. Harry, home from the Pacific Theater, came to Thomas with his cousin
on a twenty-day convalescent leave. They ended up at a birthday party at
Silver Lake Park, a small West Virginia resort near Kempton. Harry and
Norma met at Silver Lake that night. "I sat outside on the swing and Norma
came out and sat down beside me," Harry said. "We sat there and talked a
while. Next day, she come up and got me and we went for a ride in her father's
'41 Chrysler. We had a flat tire, naturally, because there wasn't no tires in those
days. I knew her three days and when I left there, I gave her my Marine Corps
ring. She had it on a string around her neck. And my cousin and I got on the
train to go back to Cumberland, and I told him, 'I'm going to marry that
girl.' And he laughed at me. He said, 'You're stupid, you shouldn't have left
your Marine Corps ring up there. That thing cost money.' I went back to the

hospital and I got a weekend pass," he continued. "Some guy gave me a ride into Baltimore, and I hitchhiked that lonely road, Route 50, right up through them mountains. I got as far as Red House, Maryland, and I hired a cab to take me into Kempton. I got there about one o'clock in the morning and me and Norma set up all night and talked. At seven o'clock, she took her Dad's car, took me out to Red House, and gave me a pack of cigarettes. I started thumbing my way back to Portsmouth Naval Hospital. And the next time I saw her, I was discharged. I stayed one night at her house and we were married the next evening. They said it would never last. We couldn't have any children for the first year, because everybody thought she was pregnant. Our first boy was born eighteen months after we got married."

Harry and Norma were married November 17, 1945, in Oakland, Maryland. Despite Harry's eagerness to get out of Lonaconing, he returned there and found work in the textile mill threading bobbins. But Lonaconing was a town in decline and Harry wanted something better for his family than the $1.07 an hour he made at the Celanese Rayon mill. In June 1948 he took his Aunt Annie to visit Conneaut, Ohio, where his uncle and aunt, John and Lela Brown (parents of Berdell Seibert from chapter 2), were already established. They owned Brown's Cash Grocery Store at the corner of Sixteenth and Mill Streets. "I stayed here a week with Aunt Annie and went home and worked three days in that textile mill and left, quit," he said.

Fishing for Work

On July 3, 1948, Harry Brown said good-bye to Lonaconing for good. "I had no job, just a '33 Plymouth, my clothes, and a twenty-dollar bill when I left Cumberland, Maryland," Harry said. "And Norma was living there with two kids. I came up here and seen old Meig Grow up here at the harbor. I said, 'Mr. Grow, I'm looking for a job.' I'll never forget what that man asked me. He said, 'You ever do a day's work in your life?' And I said, 'No sir, not to my knowledge.' He said, 'I think you're being truthful. I'm going to hire you.'" He was given the job of stern man on a fishing boat. He'd never been on a boat in his life, but he loved fishing and loved the pay. "That paid big money," he said. "I went from $1.07 an hour to $1.39 and all the overtime you can handle, guaranteed six days a week. The first year I worked for him, I worked eighteen weeks without a day off."

Harry went back to Maryland and brought his wife and two kids to Conneaut. They lived in an apartment on Madison Street, near the railroad tracks. Norma said she was afraid of hobos getting into her house and secured the back door by rolling the wringer washing machine in front of it. But she liked Conneaut and made friends easily. "I loved Conneaut from the time we came up here," Norma said. "I was fascinated by the lake."

Norma and Harry became very good friends with Roland and Betty Stewart. "He and I been closer than any two brothers," Harry said. Betty said it took some time to adjust to Norma's hill vocabulary. "Betty Stewart would call me up and say, 'What are you doing?' And I'd say, 'I'm dressin' the bed.' And she'd say, 'What do you mean, "dressin'" the bed?' When you changed the sheets and pillowcases, that was dressin' the bed. When you just made it up every day, that was 'making the bed.'" Norma also had trouble with store clerks who couldn't understand what she wanted when she asked for a bottle of "tonic," a generic term for soda pop. "We were hillbillies," Harry said. "I mean out-of-the-mountains hillbillies." Norma recalls being invited to meet another couple for dinner at the Sugar Bowl restaurant in Conneaut. The lady had not met Norma and Harry in person and was apprehensive about how these hillbillies might be dressed. She was surprised when Norma showed up in a sharp red suit. "I guess she thought I was going to come in overalls," Norma said.

Harry eventually got a job at the RMI Sodium Plant in Ashtabula Township and worked there thirty years. The friendship between the Browns and Stewarts grew strong. The common bond was a mutual interest in stock car racing. "I had a '37 Lincoln Coupe," Harry said. "I knew nothing about a car and I didn't know where the starter was at, let alone working on one. And they looked at that big old '37 Lincoln Coupe and decided it would make a nice stock car." The men towed their cars up to five hundred miles each weekend traveling between race tracks. "That was our life," Harry said.

Interspersed with racing events were periodic visits back to Maryland and West Virginia. "I'd take the boys and drive back by myself," Norma said. "It would scare my mother to death driving those old jalopy cars." Neither Harry nor Norma had any problem heading back north when it came time to leave. "Two to three days back there and we were always ready to go back to Ohio," Harry said. "Even today, I guess I'd say Conneaut is still my home, and we've been in Texas fifteen years."

Half a century has passed since Norma lived in Kempton. Her parents, and most everyone else, moved out after the mine closed. The company houses were sold and moved out of the town. Today, about a dozen homes, including a couple of new ones, comprise the town of Kempton. Remains of the old mine and several community buildings can still be seen. The town dump hides behind a slate heap. There is only one road into and out of the town. Harry keeps a few Buxton and Langstreet coins in his safe deposit box as reminders of childhood days when coal was king and scrip the queen of his dirty dominion. He and Norma have no regrets about leaving the depressed economy of Maryland's western panhandle. But Betty and Roland Stewart recognized early in their friendship that regardless of the Browns' negative view of the region's economy, their childhood home continued to tug at their hearts.

"I noticed every trip we ever took with them, we ended up in West Virginia before we came home," Betty said. "The first trip they took back there with us, I fell in love with those mountains. And I said to Harry, 'If you lived here in this, why in the world would you move to Ohio?' And he said, 'Because I wanted to eat.'"

Notes

1. Homer Floyd Fansler, *History of Tucker County, West Virginia* (Parsons, W. Va.: McClain Printing, 1962), 565. Seventy-one miners were entombed in the 427-foot shaft at the Davis Coal & Coke Company's Kempton mine February 29, 1916, the result of a dust explosion. Fifteen of the miners were killed, the rest rescued.

2. Ibid., 563. The author notes that the actual figure was probably higher because many such deaths were not reported to the county recorder. He cites one example: twenty-five miners were killed in an explosion at Mine Twenty-five in Thomas on February 4, 1907, but only sixteen deaths were on record. In the aforementioned Kempton explosion, only eight of the deaths were recorded in Tucker County. In general, many of the West Virginia miners at the turn of the century were European immigrants with low social status and seldom any relatives in the United States to keep track of their well-being—or death.

11 the boys from belva

backwoods culture

MOUNTAIN COAL MINERS were not alone in their struggle to find enough work to feed themselves and their families. By the end of the 1940s, many West Virginia farm families were hard pressed to produce enough income from their rocky hillsides to meet the expanded economic demands of post-war life. Their sons, returning from World War II, had seen another side of life that offered more excitement, material possessions, and opportunities than their allocation of hill country could provide. Many stayed only long enough to get a home-cooked meal, check in with childhood friends, and peruse the "Help Wanted" ads. Most ads were for insurance and vacuum sweeper salesmen or low-paying laborers' positions. But in 1951 Wally Morris of Belva, West Virginia, found a gem among the dross—Electro Metallurgical in Ashtabula was hiring, and no experience was necessary. Wally and his brother Lloyd headed toward Ashtabula County's bright lights and big bucks to raise some cash—and a little Cain—in the flatlands.

Movin' On

The drive to keep moving on in search of a better life is in the Morris blood. It brought Henry Morris, an English immigrant, to the western frontier of Virginia in 1776. And in 1951, it sent Morris's great-great-great-grandsons, Lloyd and Wallace Jr. "Wally," north to the shores of Lake Erie.

Henry Morris settled in what is now Richwood, West Virginia, though it was the remote wilderness of Virginia back then. When West Virginia became a state in 1863, the late Morris earned the posthumous distinction of being one of its earliest settlers. Near Summersville on State Route 39 is a monument to Henry Morris's two daughters, Peggy and Betsy, whose lives ended tragically young. They were scalped by Indians in 1792. According to Lloyd Morris, who loves to share the histories of his family tree, the story begins with Simon Girty, a Pennsylvanian frontiersman and spokesman for Native Americans who was adopted into the Shawnee tribe and became the stuff of legends, many of them unfavorable. (Girty appears in Zane Grey's first book, the historically based *Betty Zane*.) Girty was declared a traitor after his Indian sympathies led him to desert from the Revolutionary forces to the English in 1778; he led the attack on Dunlap's Station and Fort Jefferson in 1791. As Lloyd Morris recounts the family history, Simon Girty was a casual acquaintance whom Henry Morris took into his care one winter. While away on a trip, Henry heard others describing this man, who had a big scar over his right eye. "They told him, 'You watch out. He's a traitor. Whoever gives him the best deal, Indian or white man, that's who he's for. You'll be sorry you kept him and fed him,'" said Lloyd. When John Henry returned to his cabin, he told Simon Girty to hit the trail. According to family legend, Girty conspired with the Indians to get revenge by murdering Morris's two daughters, ages twelve and fourteen, while they were tending the family's cattle. Henry Morris and his brother-in-law, John Young, found Peggy about sixty yards from the house. She had been scalped, tomahawked, and had a broken back. She told her father that an Indian killed Betsy. Peggy had tried to escape, but her dress got caught on a briar and Girty caught up with her. They found Betsy with four knife wounds completely through her body. Peggy died at midnight. After burying his beloved daughters, Henry Morris went looking for the murderers. His search led him to an aged squaw who said she had been abandoned by the tribe, which had moved beyond the Ohio River. Henry returned home to mourn his loss.

Ten years after the massacre, Henry's brother Ben was at Kelley's Creek when he heard the bragging of a old Native American whose tongue had been loosened by whiskey. The man boasted of killing a paleface and taking his only red-haired scalp from another victim near the murder scene. When the man fell asleep, Ben Morris told his companions that he intended to kill him. They prevailed upon him to abandon the plan—or so they thought. The next morning a shot rang out at Kelley's Creek. Despite the retribution exacted by his brother, it is said that Henry Morris despised Native Americans until his dying day in 1824. He was buried next to his precious daughters, at Peter's Creek.

Makin' Do

All traces of the Native American population had disappeared by the time Henry's great-great-grandson, Wallace Richmond Morris, started his family in these hollows more than a hundred years later. But in many ways, life was not much easier for Wallace and his wife Belva Lorraine than it had been for his father or grandfather. Electricity would not come to the Morris homestead until the 1950s. Farm work was still performed by teams of horses and strong-backed men. A fireplace warmed the drafty house made of irregular timbers covered with a patchwork of roofing paper scraps. Both the toilet and well were "out back."

Fifteen children were born into this environment of inconvenience. Wally, born July 21, 1924, was the first; Lloyd, born May 5, 1932, was fourth. Fire destroyed the family's first home and Wallace hastily erected a make-do shelter. Their next home was a four-room house on twenty-five acres of farmland in Belva. Rent was twenty-four dollars a year. Wallace Richmond Morris lived there until his death. The house had two downstairs bedrooms that shared a central fireplace. Upstairs were two more rooms, one for beds, another for drying onions and storing staples. "We would sleep three or four to a bed upstairs," Lloyd said. "The only heat you got in the winter time was from the fireplace downstairs . . . you'd have so many covers on you, you could hardly breathe."

A railroad sideline, and in later years a road, ran in front of the house. But in Wally's early childhood, the road passed just eight feet behind the house. Beyond that was Twenty-Mile Creek, which periodically overflowed its banks, washed out the road, and invaded the Morris family's kitchen. The highway workers got tired of rebuilding the road and moved it across the tracks. The house stayed. The dirt road and railroad sideline were the family's lifelines to the outside world. The closest neighbor was about a half mile away. Family members were a day's journey on horseback up the mountain, across the ridge, and into the next hollow, known as Blue Creek. Wally said his grandparents came out of the hollow only once a month, to purchase their staples.

Their lives and culture were secluded and protected by the mountains. "That's where our Grandma and Grandpa Morris originally lived," Lloyd said. "We'd walk over there on a Saturday night; it would take us five or six hours to take groceries over to them. Then we'd stay for maybe half a night. You'd be a kid, maybe ten or twelve years old, and come back at night. You'd walk while you were sleeping, sleep while you were walking." "I got lost over there one time in broad daylight—for four hours," Wally added. "Couldn't see the sky, didn't know where I was at. I got off on a bad path . . . those were great days."

It was a three-mile walk to the school Wally and Lloyd attended. "I went to school at Victor School," Lloyd said. "A little one-room school." "With a little four-foot teacher, Ethel Legg, who could whip those farm boys," Wally added. Education was scheduled around planting, plowing, and harvesting. Lloyd guesses that he went to school part of the year for about seven years. Wally has about three years of public education. "I went more in the year that it was made compulsory than I did all the other years," Wally said. "I would say we got three or four years of education apiece," Lloyd said. "We're not no smart people, but we're not no dummies. There are people that went to college that can't read or write. We can read and write and we got pretty good sense, we got a lot of common sense. What we did, we are really self-educated. Common sense and self-educated. The deal would be to learn everything that you could learn."

The family farm was the boys' real-world schoolhouse. Lloyd estimates that they farmed thirty to forty rented acres. Most of what they raised was food for the family and livestock; surplus was sold to produce buyers from Charleston, about fifty miles to the west. The family also sold eggs, hogs, and chickens to raise money. "The most we ever had was about sixty head of hogs, four to six head of cattle, several horses. I guess we had three hundred to four hundred chickens all the time. Ducks and geese would run loose around the place all the time," Lloyd said. The chickens were an easy-to-steal commodity. Wally recalls forty of them disappearing overnight. "We had one guy down there that would throw a fishing line with a worm on it over the chicken coop wall," Wally said. "The chicken would swallow the hook and the guy would steal it just like that."

Barbed wire kept the four-footed livestock from straying beyond the Morris family's control. "All this property we circled with four-point, four-strand barbed wire," Wally said. "I would say this barbed wire went straight up the hill five miles, then around, then back down," Lloyd added. "We'd put locust posts in the ground . . . everything was by hand. Anybody who lived on a farm knows there was no time for anything else. The only time we had to play once in a while, when we was kids, was on a Sunday."

Crops included corn, oats, sorghum (for molasses), peanuts, soybeans, potatoes, and all manner of root vegetables and legumes. It required the labor of every family member to grow enough to feed the family. A typical day of working the fields began at six in the morning and ended with sunset. All work was done with horses and strong human backs and arms. "We made like haystacks out in the field," Lloyd said. "You'd make a platform on the ground [to isolate the hay from the dampness], and you'd put a big pole in the ground and stack hay like thirty-foot wide up that pole until you got to the top—thirty feet high. And you'd put a big pile of straw below you and jump off. Always a kid would do that, you'd jump off in the straw so you wouldn't get hurt. You couldn't leave a rope [at the top of the pole]. If you had four or five stacks of hay, you'd have to have a rope for every one that you let yourself down on, and you'd be using too much of your money on rope."

Grains were hauled to the mill, ten miles away, on the back of a horse or a human-powered railroad section car. The car had four handles on it, one on each corner, so it could pushed along the track. Three or four boys would run alongside the car, get it moving, then jump on. A stick held to the wheel served as a brake. The car was shared by folks who lived along the railroad tracks. "We would take maybe ten to fifteen bushels of corn up to this mill and have them crush it into cracked corn," Wally said. "We'd set this thing on the track, go up there, and have to set it off again. The train only ran once a day, but sometimes they would come and catch us on there. One time we had to unload it quite quick. Usually, if we would shine the light, they knew what we were doing. They were real nice about it, they would stop until you took everything off." The most dangerous trip was to the store in Jamocha, about twelve miles away by rail. On that route there was a half-mile-long bridge. "If you ever got caught on that bridge with a train on it, it would have been the end of you," Lloyd said.

Trips to the larger communities and store were rare, however, for there was little money to spend there. Most cash went for farming supplies and clothing. Almost everything the family needed in the way of food was raised on the farm. Sugar and coffee were the only two staples that had to be purchased. "We wasn't what you'd call poor," Lloyd said. "My dad provided for us pretty good. And he worked in the winter for money. We raised a lot, we had our meat and stuff. We would raise turnips, carrots, potatoes, and hole them up in the ground. We'd dig them, then we'd put them back in the ground in big holes in straw, like thirty bushels to a hole. You'd go in there of the wintertime and you'd dig in a hole and get maybe two or three bushels at a time. . . . We had three good meals every day, and it would take three skillets of potatoes and my mother would make a big pan of gravy. You'd have bacon or you'd have ham, whatever. We never starved or anything."

Food that could not be preserved by burying was canned. Every spring Belva Lorraine and the girls picked and preserved three to four hundred half-gallon jars of wild greens. In the fall, they pickled two or three barrels each of sauerkraut, beans, and corn. Butchering was done around Thanksgiving, after it was cold enough to leave the meat to hang without spoiling. Much of the meat was put up in glass jars for consumption during the summer months.

The noon meal was unlikely to include meat, particularly for lunches taken to school. "For lunch, we used to take biscuits and fried potatoes or lard with salt and pepper in it," Wally said. "We used to go to school and take a potato sandwich—fried potato sandwich or mashed potato sandwich or mashed bean sandwich—and those kids that were well-to-do would fight you over it and trade you fancy lunches for it."

The well-off youngsters were not likely to have traded for the boys' clothing. Wally can remember having to stay in bed under the covers while his mother mended the only pair of pants he owned. "We wore shoes and clothes from the second-hand and Outdoor Army-Navy surplus that we ordered through the mail," Lloyd said. Their father repaired the soles and heels of the family's shoes until the tops disintegrated.

The boys had no toys when they were growing up and never knew what it was like to receive a Christmas or birthday present. "We never fooled with presents or trees," Wally said. "All Christmas meant to me was a holiday we'd put off firecrackers and if you wanted to drink, you could get polluted, you could get soused." Lloyd recalls getting a bushel of apples and a bushel of oranges for Christmas from the city people who bought produce from the family. Wally doesn't recall such extravagant Christmases, however. "I never saw no bushel of apples," he said. "The only thing I'd seen was a piece of hard candy and a couple of nuts and an orange, which was a big deal. I think things got better after I left. Of course, back then, a bushel of apples was only a quarter." The big holidays were the Fourth of July and Easter. "Not because of what Easter meant," Wally said. "It was a time we could eat all the fried or boiled eggs we wanted. And I used to put away six or eight of them, fried."

Makin' Trouble

Without toys or school to occupy their free time, the boys often ended up sticking their noses into other folks' business. One of Wally's favorite pastimes was to heckle camp meeting worshipers. "I would sit in the back seat and spit tobacco juice on the floor," he confessed. "We'd disturb the people in worshiping, and that was a major crime. They'd have church up to that Bentree Church. We'd go there and rock the people who came. We'd throw rocks on top of the church, it had a metal roof."

"Halloween, us five boys would go out and we'd turn toilets [outhouses] over," Lloyd said. "That was the big thing. When I was ten or twelve years old, we'd get on a big, high bank—there was a main road that went up from Belva to Bentree, and this bank was almost straight up forty feet above it. We'd get up there and get mud clods and we'd stand up there and see if we could hit windshields. I hit a windshield one time, oh it made the awfulest noise, and here it was the damn highway patrol. We had an uncle with us that was just a little bit off. He crawled up a tree, and they called other cars in and they'd shine the lights all over—and they'd shine the light right over him. And I thought, 'Oh, Gosh!' But we hid in the grass."

"Another pastime we had was going to holy roller churches where they handled fire and snakes," Wally said. "That was a big thing down there. They would handle those coals. They'd talk in those tongues and roll all over the floor and just shake there, like their eyeballs were comin' out. They'd just quiver." "We drilled holes through the buildings so we could watch," Lloyd added. "And guess what we saw inside—they were having sex! They were just a-quivering and going on." "A lot of times the young men would join the things just to get in with the girls, with the families that had beautiful girls," Wally said. "They'd just put on the act."

The boys' father had nothing to do with religion—or the law—in his younger days. The Puritanical doctrines made no accommodations for his moonshining enterprise, which was headquartered a mile or so into the woods behind the family's Blue Creek home. As the eldest son, Wally had the duty of helping his father in the production and concealment of the brew. "The revenue agents would come looking for him and he would bury the stuff under the road where he was working," Wally said. "He'd take it and hide it that night when they were finished working on the road; he'd dig a hole, and put maybe four or five half-gallon jars of moonshine under there. Nobody would find it when they came looking for it." Wally recalls that on one occasion when revenue agents came looking for his father, "He climbed up in a tree and put a stuffed dummy in there, just like a person. The revenuers come looking for him and they thought it was him up in the tree and they told him if he didn't come down, they'd have to shoot him. Finally, he never came down, and they did it, they shot him. That stuffing flew out everywhere. But he'd already gone out the back way." The agents finally caught up with Wallace Richmond Morris, who spent six months in a federal penitentiary. That, and the tragic death of a son in 1935, mellowed him. He took the Blackstone Law Course by mail and learned to type. He ran for justice of the peace and served two terms. Then he watched as his children left the farm for better opportunities in the North.

Workin' Hard

As the boys got older, they came to realize that their options in the land of their ancestors were few and unattractive. By the time Wally was twelve years old, he was working as many hours a day cutting timber. Pay was fifty cents an hour. "At one time we had to walk about four miles just to get to work," Wally said. "Then work ten to twelve hours and walk back. We didn't get paid money—you could get a grocery order at the store, Once in a while maybe you'd get five or ten dollars."

Wally lied about his age and at fifteen entered the Civilian Conservation Corps. But his mother would not sign for him to join the armed forces, so Wally had to wait for World War II to release him from the mountains. He was drafted in 1943 and was in combat before he was twenty. He fought in five major European campaigns, including second wave D-Day and the Battle of the Bulge. But his first battle was one against prejudice. "I had a lot of trouble, being a hillbilly," he said. "Especially people from New England. I really had a tough time. A guy from New York knocked my helmet off in ranks one day. And the drill sergeant said, 'If you want to mess around, you'll just go in the ring.' I'd never been in a ring before. We had sixteen-ounce gloves. This guy was a boxer from the city. And he beat on me until he couldn't move any more. But he didn't knock me out. I could take it because I was good and tough. And then I laid it on him, and he was in the hospital for three weeks . . . and then he became my best friend." Communication also presented its challenges. "That was a dilly," Wally said. "I met a girl from New England on a train going to the service camp. And I had never heard any of those people before, and we couldn't understand each other. And I couldn't understand the English people at all. But you know, I was able to pick up German and Italian. But I couldn't pick up French at all."

Wally came home a decorated war hero. But the economy of central West Virginia could not bestow any blessings upon him for his sacrifices. After working at a few menial jobs, he re-enlisted in the army and spent four more years in Europe. He returned to the mountains and got a job working on the coal tipple, an apparatus for loading into railroad cars the coal and rock as they came out of the mine. It paid more than seven dollars an hour—in scrip. "That was big bucks," he said. "But it was hard, hard work. They had a six-foot seam of coal and there was a four-foot seam of rock between it and we had to pound that rock up and put it in a chute, and a conveyor took it up over the mountain and dumped it. The roof was about ten foot high and that rock would come out fast and we'd have to pile it up. I'd leave, it was shift work, come back and it would still be up to the roof. It was hard . . . I'd get so sick, I'd hang my head out and vomit, take a salt pill, and go back in to work again." Wally couldn't take the strain of the intense labor and went to work at a sawmill, also physically very demanding.

Meanwhile, things were not going all that well for Lloyd, either. He left home in 1949, at the age of seventeen, after having a spat with his father. He went to work at the Webster Hardwood Lumber Company in Dixie, West Virginia, making a dollar an hour. "After I was there three weeks, they gave me a ten-cent raise and put me in charge over everyone else there," Lloyd said. "Then I went from a dollar and ten cents to a dollar and twenty-five cents an hour. I was even boss over the owner's two brothers."

Neither Lloyd nor Wally was interested in spending the rest of his life working at sawmills, regardless of the income or positions to be won. Nor did Lloyd want the kind of lifestyle his parents had known—a large family, subsistence farming, and associated financial insecurity. "We didn't want to live in that environment," Lloyd said. "We wanted to better ourselves. We wanted to go somewhere where there was an opportunity."

Goin' to Town

And so it was with great interest that the brothers read the advertisement in the *Charleston Gazette* about a Union Carbide plant in Ohio that was offering employment to men from Appalachia. Wally and Lloyd traveled to Charleston and met UC recruiter Frank McClintock, who signed them up for work at the plant. Then the brothers got into their 1941 Ford and drove to Ashtabula. They took their physicals and went right to work, although Wally weighed only 132 pounds and the minimum was 135. "They needed people and accepted me. They couldn't get the people here [in Ashtabula] to work," he said.

The men arrived in Ashtabula April 18, 1951, and went to work the next day. The company issued them work gloves, a hard hat, and steel-toed shoes and advanced their rent on a West Fifty-eighth Street apartment. Wally and Lloyd were assigned to the traffic department, taking care of the plant grounds. For two men accustomed to the rigors of farm work, mining, and the sawmills, the job was like taking a vacation. "It was like child's play there," Wally said. Their work ethic irritated local workers who complained about how Wally, Lloyd, and other mountaineer migrants set an industrious precedent. "I couldn't stand not working," Wally said. "The people would say, 'You're going to kill the job for us.' They would get after us." "We used to double over [work two shifts straight]," Lloyd added. "Nobody else would double over. We used to double over three, four, five times a week. And they'd furnish meals from Stan's beer joint. Bologna, ham; an orange or apple; and pie. Free lunch!"

Cain Raisin'

Despite doubling over frequently, the men found time for drink, women, and country music in the county's nightspots. Wally said Appalachian migrants created social centers at certain bars and congregated there after work and on weekends. Country music blared on the jukeboxes and specials like foot-long hot dogs and beer by the pitcher attracted the migrants. Some of the migrant haunts included the Subway Cafe on Lake Avenue, a "raunchy" place known for occasional fights; Stop 91 on Route 46, Plymouth; Crow's Nest on Lake Road near Union Carbide; the Green Lantern on Route 20 West; and the Blue Skies and Rex Cafe on West Avenue.

"We hit them all," Wally said. "A lot of those places belonged to me. I spent a lot of money there." "Stone's Grill," Lloyd said. "We used to go there, and if you'd drink a pitcher of beer down, you'd get a brand new two-dollar bill and the beer free. We'd go in there and drink a pitcher of beer, go across the street to a billiards place, and play pool until the four bucks were gone. Then we'd go back and drink another pitcher, get four bucks, go back, and play more pool. But the third time, the guy says, 'You get out of here or I'll throw you out. You ain't getting any more beer, you're a bunch of pigs!'"

Life was good in Ashtabula for two single young men from the hills, despite an occasional clash of cultures. Echoing the experience Jean Wilfong related earlier (in the introduction to this book), they encountered some resistance in matters of vocabulary: "I used to go in the store and ask for a paper poke," Wally said. "And the store man would say, 'You dumb hillbilly, it's not a paper poke, it's a bag.'" Their wages had started at 96 cents an hour and quickly rose to $1.46. With the overtime, they had plenty of money to spend on nice clothes, food, and drink. But they owned only one car between them, the 1941 Ford they arrived in. "We had some times with that," Lloyd said. "When we both started courting, there was fire on the mountain," Wally added. He recalls an incident that occurred one time he had promised to return the car in time for Lloyd to go on a date. When Wally didn't show up, Lloyd called a cab and went looking for his brother. When he found the car, Lloyd crawled under the dash and cut all the wires. "Wally was going to beat me up," Lloyd said. "I called the police on him." "I didn't speak to him for a week," Wally added. "And we slept in the same bed."

The brothers returned home several times a month during the first year they spent in Ohio. "We'd take Route 7 to Chester, West Virginia, Route 30 to Route 2. It would take ten, eleven, twelve hours of driving as hard as you could," Wally said. They enjoyed their breezy lifestyle but for only a short season. Their looks soon attracted the attention of local ladies. Lloyd met his wife, Ruby Bean, at the skating rink on Jefferson Road. "We were nice-looking guys then, when we were young," Lloyd said. "I'm not bragging, but

Wally Morris found the Lord in this West Fifty-seventh Street church in Ashtabula, December 19, 1953. Since then, he has committed his life to serving God and playing his music on the Dobro. *Photo by Carl E. Feather*

I had curly, wavy hair . . . and I had this leopard coat on. When I walked in the door [of the skating rink], Ruby's friend said to her, 'Look what just walked through the door.' And my wife said, 'Those kind come a dime a dozen.'" They were married in January 1952, to the protests of Ruby's family.

"My father-in-law was the boss at Lake City Malleable, and he had these people from West Virginia and Kentucky working there," Lloyd said. "He said they were nothing but drunks, he didn't want no hillbilly marrying his daughter. They wouldn't let us get married, so we took off to West Virginia and got married. They wanted to annul the marriage, and I said, 'You don't have enough money to annul this marriage.'" Lloyd said that country music provided the common ground with his in-laws. "I was lucky. My brothers-in-law liked country music and foot stomping. After a year or so, they thought as much of me as they did their own sons. . . . I proved myself to them."

Lloyd stayed at Union Carbide five years, then spent a year sailing on a Great Lakes freighter. He went back to Union Carbide, got laid off, and found work at Sheffield Manufacturing, where he worked for twenty-eight and a half years before it went out of business. He and Ruby had three children, built a new house, and lived a comfortable life far from the hills of Lloyd's childhood. Lloyd turned showman and promoter in the 1970s, when he was asked on the spur of the moment to serve as master of ceremonies for a country music show at Play Pen Park in Warren. That launched him on a four-year career as a promoter of country music shows in northeast Ohio. His "Whip-Poor-Will Productions" represented many regional bands, including Marty Licklider and the Missouri Fox Hunters.

Wally married Sonia Haag in August 1952 and the couple had ten children before the marriage ended in divorce. He married his second wife, Thelma Carpenter, in August 1971. He spent thirty-three years with Union Carbide, most of them as a messenger or guard.

A Changed Man

Wally says the most significant result of his coming to Ashtabula was not his marriages or employment, but his spiritual conversion December 19, 1953. Like Saul, converted on the Damascus Road as he pursued Christians to their death, Wally Morris, the young man who taunted Christians in the churches of Bentree, found Jesus Christ in a foreign land. "I promised the Lord in World War II, when I was in a tight place and wounded, if he would get me out of it, I would turn to him," Wally said. "But for eight years I lived more wickedly than I ever did. But then I got to dreaming about falling and never stopping; about burning and everything going wrong. So I went to a Nazarene church at Fifty-seventh and Washington Streets [Ashtabula]. I said, 'I'll just go up and see what it's like.' And I got saved that night."

Combining his newfound faith with the love for music he shared with his brother, Wally performed in many gospel bluegrass bands, including Pete and The West Virginia Boys, led by Hayward "Pete" Ball (who takes a bow in chapter 12). "I've been interested in music all my life," Wally said. " I started off with a flattop guitar when I was about twelve or fifteen, then I got away from it. The instrument I was interested in and I used to hear on the Grand Ole Opry was a Dobro, a steel guitar without electric. I didn't find out what kind of instrument it was until 1968. I had listened to it as a kid

Lloyd Morris remembers when downtown Ashtabula was a hot place to be on a Saturday night. That was the 1950s, when Lloyd and his brother Wally arrived fresh from the hills. Lloyd later turned country and western music promoter and staged many shows in the former Shea's Theater (behind him in this photo) on Main Avenue. *Photo by Carl E. Feather*

over the battery radio, and I was finally able to get one, a learner, for $100."

All of Wally and Lloyd Morris's brothers and sisters followed them to Ashtabula. They stayed with Lloyd or Wally to get their start in the new town, then found jobs at restaurants, factories, and in construction. Most of them moved on to California or Oklahoma; only Wally, Lloyd, and Dennis, a younger brother, stayed in Ashtabula. Lloyd said the hardest part of coming to Ohio was leaving everyone behind. "All your friends and relations that you knew, the favorite kin people you would go visit," he said. "When you come up here, it just all went away, and you'd go back and they'd died off."

Would they consider going back? "I'd like to go back there," Lloyd says. "I'd like to go back there once a year or every five years and live a month the way it was when I was a kid." "Oh no, no, no," Wally interrupts. "I've thought about it a couple times here lately, if I found the right place. Now that I'm retired and don't have to depend on the work I used to have to do. But now,

I have been here so long, that it would be hard to tear up roots. I got more of my own here now than there are in West Virginia. The only thing I missed was the culture. The culture here in this part of the country is different from what it is down there. It's slow paced back there, and it's a fast pace here. But I like the convenience here—the city water, the telephones."

"It's hard to explain," Lloyd adds, surveying the plush carpet, fine furniture, and conveniences of his newer mobile home. "It's a sense of doing better here."

12 farmer's boy

hayward ball: from the farm to lake county industry

LAKE COUNTY, Ashtabula County's neighbor to the west, also provided a better opportunity for Hayward "Pete" Ball, Wally Morris's pickin' and sin-gin' partner. The Chemical Shore brought Hayward to northeast Ohio from Tucker County, West Virginia, but it couldn't keep him in Lake County. Like many factory workers in the 1970s, as employment opportunities declined, Hayward found himself facing the prospect of midlife joblessness. And like many migrant industrial workers, Hayward went back to West Virginia with the hope of finding things better than when he had left.

Tucker County Childhood

West Virginia Route 72 diverges from U.S. Route 50 near Rowlesburg and plunges south through some of the most breathtaking mountain scenery to be found in the state. These are rugged mountains that turn purple and gold in fall and hazy green in summer and spring. Winter snows brushed upon their backs reveal their spiny framework like an x-ray penetrating a fleshy fa-cade of health. Despite their beauty, they remain mountains: barriers to the influx of progress and mechanization, obstacles to a better life, and challenges that demand more than faith to move.

Level ground is in short supply in this region, but its inhabitants have for decades managed to farm what little there is of it. Old barns and family home-steads still appear out of the morning fog that sleeps late and reluctantly releases the landscape to the gray sun. By early afternoon all traces of the fog have evaporated from the verdant pastures where cattle and sheep graze. The presence of livestock is poignant testimony to the mountaineer's determination to tame the land as well as to the animals' ability to fight the constant pull of gravity.

The pastures plunge toward the lovely valley of the Cheat River, a well-fed stream replenished by the drink offerings of the mountain peaks. The locals have given colorful names to the tiny streams and rivulets born in these mountains: Licking Creek and Clover, Minear, Horseshoe, Roaring, and Pleasant Runs. Rising on the north side of Pifer Mountain, Bull Run flows east to deliver its cold waters to the Cheat River between Hannahsville and St. George. The Bull Run region was the childhood home of Hayward Ball, who left the hardships of Tucker County in the mid-1940s for a better life in northeast Ohio.

Hayward was born at the Head of Bull Run November 27, 1927, the first of Isaac and Ruby Ball's four children. Their home was a three-room frame structure: a split bedroom, kitchen, and living room heated by a pot-bellied stove. There was no electricity at Bull Run and running water consisted of Hayward with a bucket in each hand running to the spring. There were few creature comforts in that old home, but lots of memories. "I've woke up with snow on my bed, but as far as I'm concerned, those were the good days," he said. His home was seventeen miles from the nearest town, Parsons, and for the first decade of his life Hayward knew little of the outside world. His father's parents and brother also farmed on the mountain, and some of Hayward's fondest memories revolve around the days he spent at those farms. The farms were the families' only means of support, except for the occasional work Hayward's father might find in the woods. "My daddy used to say, 'If you don't raise it and work for it, you're not going to have it,'" Hayward recalled.

The family raised hay, oats, corn, buckwheat, rye, and wheat on the farm. A large garden provided the potatoes, cabbage, carrots, and other vegetables that were buried for storage throughout the long winters. Coffee, sugar, footwear, and some clothing articles were the only purchased items. Milk, butter, and eggs provided a source of cash or trade credit at the country store. Even so, new shoes were few and far between. "Dad would re-sole, re-heel the shoes," Hayward said. "He used to make soles out of leather, rubber belts. He'd make heels out of hard rubber blocks."

The Bull Run School and Methodist Church formed the nucleus of their community. Both were about one mile from the Ball farm. The family made the trip to worship in a horse-pulled wagon or bobsled. A lean-to on the side of the church building provided shelter for the animals during service. The Ball family attended both Sunday morning and evening services. Chores were held to a minimum on Sundays out of respect for the Lord's Day. "If it wasn't done Monday through Saturday, then it wasn't done unless it absolutely had to be," Hayward said.

School was mandatory for the Ball children, and Hayward completed eight grades under the tutelage of Mr. Williams. While his parents made a requirement of school attendance, they could not afford to let their son sit in a classroom during planting and harvesting times. "A lot of times, Mom and Dad would send a note for me to leave school at two o'clock so I could work," he said. "I'd work until dark and have to take a lantern with me to do my chores—milking, gathering the eggs."

Harvest was a particularly busy time as neighbors pitched in to help each other. Hayward's maternal grandfather owned a portable sorghum mill, which he rented to farms in the region. Sorghum, a type of sugar cane, was harvested from the fields and fed into the mill, which used metal rollers driven by cogs to crush the cane and release the sap. A mule walking in circles and attached to the mill by a pole drove the mechanism. The pulp was returned to the fields for fertilizer, the sap collected and slowly added to evaporator pans heated by wood fires to produce sorghum molasses. As with apple butter, the syrup required both constant stirring to prevent burning and an experienced overseer who could recognize when the molasses had reached optimum density, color, and flavor. Molasses stirs were often communal events that involved kin and neighbors sharing in the labor and camaraderie of harvest. "That was a good time," Hayward said. "Everybody pitched in and helped each other."

His "Bottle of Medicine"

Hayward felt a call early in life to become a pastor, but could not articulate those feelings to a spiritual mentor who might have helped him pursue that calling. "I had a calling, but I didn't understand it until later in life," he said. "I didn't understand what it was all about . . . and didn't do anything about it." Until the time he entered high school he expected that life would be much the same for him as it had been for his father and grandfather: he would marry, settle down on his allocation of family farmland, and raise a family there. After all, practically everything a man needed could be raised on these mountainsides.

But after completing his junior year of high school, Hayward decided to take a year off to earn some money. He found employment in the lumber business—driving a team, cutting timber, and peeling bark for twenty-five to fifty cents a day. The income gave him a taste of the conveniences that could be purchased with payroll dollars and the life that existed beyond subsistence farming. Yet the opportunities for earning that cash in Tucker County were dwindling. Farmers could not afford to pay their help more than a quarter or so a day. Jobs in the mines paid better, but they were scarce, and Hayward wasn't interested in risking his life in one of those holes, anyway. "I worked three days in the mines and quit," he said. "It wasn't my bottle of medicine."

Then he heard about work in Ohio. "Some of the boys in the neighborhood had moved here," he said. "Luther Schaffer, Wilbur and Charlie Shahan." On a whim, Hayward climbed into Virgil Jeffer's '39 Chevy and the two men headed toward Ohio May 30, 1947. "The first place I found work at was Call's Nursery [Madison], driving a team of horses," Hayward said. The job paid twenty-eight cents an hour, nine hours a day. "You spent eight hours in the field, a half-hour each in the morning and afternoon taking care of the horses." He stayed in Perry with Luther Schaffer, who charged Hayward four dollars a week room and board.

Hayward said Ashtabula County and eastern Lake County were not all that dissimilar to rural West Virginia in the mid-1940s. There were many dairy farms and nurseries scattered around the area where housing developments and shopping plazas now stand. The big difference was in the amount of money one could earn on a farm in Ohio—as much in a single hour as an entire day of labor paid in the mountains. Even more lucrative were the factory jobs. Hayward set out to land one shortly after arriving in Lake County. He applied at Diamond Alkali in Painesville July 11, 1947, took his exam the next day, and started work. The pay, thirty-two cents an hour, was only slightly more than what he was making in the fields, but the opportunity for advancement and pay raises was significant.

Hayward moved to Painesville; his room and board increased to five dollars a week but his new lodgings put him closer to work and public transportation. Painesville had a large population of Finnish immigrants, and Hayward occasionally encountered some heckling about his "hillbilly" background. But he had a philosophy about such things that allowed him to handle the chiding. "While they were agitating me, they were leaving someone else alone," he said. "If you got any Christian background about you at all, you know the Good Lord will help you." Harassment was common at work, as well. But hillbillies were a majority and felt no threat from the barbs. "That's like the foreman I used to have," Hayward said. "He'd catch me when I'd be on my lunch break, especially when I was on afternoons. He'd come in the locker room and he'd start in, 'If you hillbillies hadn't come up here, you would have starved to death down there.' But that didn't rile me none, because I knew of the twenty-eight men on our crew, only two were Buckeyes. The rest were from mountain states. Diamond at one time used to send trucks down there to recruit people to bring them to work up here. You could hardly find anybody that was right here from Ohio."

Music and Marriage

The proliferation of mountain folk in the flat land of northeast Ohio brought with it a strong following for country music in the area. Like many mountaineers who grew up with music in their homes, Hayward joined a country band, playing on weekends at bars around the Painesville area.

Three years after moving to Painesville, Hayward met the woman who would become his wife, Mary Frances Adkinson. Mary grew up in Marlington, Pocahontas County, West Virginia. With four brothers, three sisters, and a railroading father, Mary's life in West Virginia was not blessed with material goods or leisure time. Her mother died when Mary was eight. She finished fourth grade and went to work around the home, assuming the role of mother. Her father helped make ends meet by making moonshine. One of his customers, Rodney Buzzard, was a policeman. Mary said her father got away with selling liquor to a policeman until a friend reported him. He was sent to prison. "But there were so many kids, they went around with a petition to let him go because there was no one to take care of us," she said. "After he came back from prison, he went to work on the WPA." Did his prison stay cure him of moonshining? "Not really," Mary said. "He'd get a chance and he'd make more."

Haywood "Pete" Ball at the Pickin' and Singin' concert, Austinburg, Ohio.
Photo by Carl E. Feather

Mary's father retired from the railroad when his World War I benefit check finally came through, giving him enough money to purchase a small farm. But Mary tired of farm work and hill living. "There was too much hard work there," she said. "I used to have to lug a hundred pounds of coal up the side of the hill and carry water. I said it was time to leave." She took her seven dollars of savings and headed to Washington, D.C., in 1942. "I was scared to death there until I found my cousin, Clair Seton," she said. Mary found a job at the Mayflower and Sanico Bakery, a food processing plant where she worked for three and a half years.

Mary experienced some harassment over her mountaineer dialect and ways in the big city. "They'd mock me, copycat off me when I was talking," she said. Eventually, she grew tired of Washington's pace and headed back to Pocahontas County at the end of the war "to see if anything had changed." It hadn't, and Mary hitched a ride to Painesville with two friends from Pocahontas County, Bob and Estelle Bird. Bob had found work at Diamond Alkali and offered housing for Mary until she could find a job. "I went to the basket factory up here and made fifty cents an hour," she said. "I didn't like it here at first. It was the people, mostly. A lot of them I met I couldn't understand. There were a lot of Finnish and Italians."

Mary and Hayward met through the Birds on a blind date to a Mexican restaurant in Cleveland. For Mary, meeting and falling in love with a West Virginia man was not what she was expecting from her move to Ohio. She figured she'd marry an Ohio native. "Got a hillbilly, instead," she said. After a short courtship, they were married October 24, 1950. "He wouldn't let me go," she said. And Hayward explained, "I knew that was what I needed to get my life straightened out."

Hard Times in a New Town

Their wedded bliss was soon interrupted. Eleven months after they were married, Mary almost died from complications of childbirth. The infant could not be saved. In January 1952 Uncle Sam invited Hayward to participate in the Marine Corps. For the next two years and eight months, he served his country while Mary made a home in Painesville. Mary's father came up and stayed with her during her husband's absence, but never for any long stretch. "You couldn't dynamite him out of those hills," Hayward said.

Hayward returned to his home and job in 1954. The couple eventually moved to Madison and adopted two children: Richard and Katherine. Charlotte Sheets, Katherine's half sister, though not adopted by the Balls, they also claim as one of their own. Work at Diamond slowed in the 1970s and by 1976 the signs were clear that the factory would soon shut down. Hayward left in October 1976 because he didn't want to expose himself to the health risks of decommissioning a chlorine plant. "I didn't want to eat all that rotten gas and stuff that would come out of those lines," he said. They headed back to West Virginia to look for work. Mary had an uncle in Beckley who owned a furniture store and needed a delivery truck dispatcher. "I didn't know any more about that than going to the moon," Hayward confessed. Nevertheless, he took the job and made good at it until the hours and demands became too much for him. His next job was selling vacuum cleaners, which lead to a job in a repair shop. But by 1980 the adopted family they had left behind in Ohio was calling them back. They returned in July and Hayward found work as maintenance man for a government housing project. A year later they sold their mobile home in West Virginia. They have considered themselves Ashtabula County residents ever since.

Hayward has not severed his ties to his Appalachian culture, however. His heart turned back to the faith of his childhood following an earthquake in northeast Ohio in 1985. He and several other musicians of mountain heritage —Royce Green, Bob Housel, and Wally Morris (introduced in chapter 11)— formed a gospel music group, The Glory Land Singers. Operating on faith and donations, the group performs at nursing homes, churches, and civic events around northeast Ohio. In 1994 they gave 102 performances, 57 of them at nursing homes. Hayward has even traveled to West Virginia and Alabama to perform as a gospel singer. But when he comes home, it is no longer to Bull Run, West Virginia, but Geneva Township. "This is more like home than West Virginia," he says while sitting at the kitchen table of his mobile home. "Yes, I like to go back, but I'm down there a week or so and then I want to come back."

13 a coal miner's life

darald spangler's life and car get a push in ashtabula county

Deeper in Debt

"Next time you hear that song 'Sixteen Tons,' you think of me," said Darald Spangler as he sat at the dining room table of his Kingsville Township home. "The coal company owned the house, they owned the mine, they owned the store, and they owned you."

Darald has been a free man for nearly a half century, but as he looks back on his youthful days in the New Hill coal camp of West Virginia he sees a way of life more akin to the nineteenth century than twentieth; a system closer to slavery than to freedom. Both Darald and his wife Kathern grew up in coal mining towns of Monongalia County, West Virginia. Their childhood homes were communities on roads that branch off State Route 7, or Scott's Run, as it's known to Morgantown locals. "I knew a man who used to say, 'The farther up Scott's Run you go, the tougher they get,'" Darald said. "Then he'd say, 'I live two houses past the last one.'"

Darald's hometown of New Hill was owned by Consolidated Coal Company and was about a mile up the mountain from Cassville and eight miles west of Morgantown. Kathern grew up in Sabraton, about three miles east of Morgantown. Their childhood experiences mirrored each other in many ways, although a major difference was that Kathern's parents, Harvey Allen and Loretta Uphold, owned their house, which was home to eight children. In New Hill, Consolidated Coal owned the fifty-two houses that comprised the town. "They were all about the same—three bedrooms, a kitchen and dining room combined, a pantry, and an outhouse," Darald said. "And they were all painted yellow." The houses had electric lights, but outlets were adapted from a lightbulb socket. Darald still recalls his mother ironing in the dining room and the overhead light going round and round as the bulb followed the wide arc of the cord plugged into the bulb socket.

There was no running water in the house—water was piped in from Morgantown to a single faucet at the end of the street. All fifty-two families carried their water from that communal spigot. The implications of this arrangement are staggering. There were eight people in the Spangler household, and every drop of water they used had to be toted about an eighth of a mile. Once they got the water to the house, they had to heat it on the kitchen stove for laundry, bathing, or cooking. Family members took their baths in a metal washtub and laundry was done on a scrubboard. Darald still recalls how rough his mother's hands were from the years of scrubbing her miner husband's dirty clothes. "You spent all your time surviving, and that's a fact," Darald said.

The community was built on coal—even the road that ran outside Darald's house was made from coal and slate. Coal dust from the tipple hung in the air and sometimes sparkled like black snowflakes. The mine operated night and day. The percussion of coal cars being dumped into the tipple and the constant rattle and whirl of the conveyor belt were the background music of New Hill. A few hundred yards from the Spangler home, just beyond the baseball diamond, was the gob dump, where the coal company discarded the slate and low-grade coal after extracting the higher-grade coal from the slate (as described in chapter 10). When children weren't hauling water from the communal spigot they were searching the gob dump for usable coal. They hauled the coal home in buckets and on sleds and homemade buggies. Darald said life around the gob dump was survival of the strongest—hunters staked out their territory and had to be willing to defend it if a stronger child came along. Coal from the gob dump was inspected by Darald's father before it went into the coal bin, which was attached to the outhouse. If slate was found in the coal, the youngster could expect big trouble.

The gob dump was usually on fire, spewing foul gases into the community. "When the wind was right, you smelled that stuff all your life," Darald said. "They would just burn and burn, year after year." When the dump couldn't provide a family with enough coal to heat the house, the miner had to purchase fuel from the company. Darald said the mine company sold coal to the families at a reduced rate, but it was ungraded coal straight from the chute—"running mine coal." "You might get real big chunks that would have to be broken up," Darald said. "Or you might get dust or even slate. It looked like something they didn't want."

A pot-bellied stove and a grate vented into a living room fireplace heated the entire single-story house. Darald said the heaters didn't have blowers on them and warmed only a small radius beyond their fires. "You'd burn in the front and freeze in the back," he said. The fires required constant attention and the ashes had to be hauled out regularly. They were spread in the street, and despite the constant traffic of coal, dirt, and ashes through the house, Darald said his mother managed to keep it clean with just soap, water, and hard work. One positive aspect of this austere arrangement was that there was no bathroom to keep clean—the outhouse was cleaned once a year by the honey dippers hired by the mine company for the annual clean out. The children followed the two men around town as they went about their job— that was as exciting as life got in New Hill. "Anything was fascinating back then, even watching the honey dippers," he said.

Youngsters gathered at the ball diamond when there were no chores to do. They had no money for baseballs or bats, so they made their own. Twine wrapped into a ball and covered with black friction tape from the mine company made a good baseball. If one of their sisters had a rubber ball from a jacks set, it was confiscated for the nucleus of a twine ball. Darald said the rubber center gave the homemade baseball extra distance. Discarded shovel handles served as bats. The boys also made their own bow and arrows. Goldenrod stems were used for the arrows; the bow was simply a piece of inner tube pulled back between the thumb and index finger. Their target was each other.

One of the most mischievous games played by the youngsters was "pulling the pocketbook." Darald and his friends tied a long string to the handle of a lady's pocketbook, which was placed in the middle of Route 7 at night. When a motorist stopped and approached the pocketbook, the pranksters, hiding in a culvert, jerked the handbag out of the road. A variation on the game was "throwing the fish plate," the piece of metal that attaches railroad rails together. The plate was tossed onto the concrete road as a motorist passed in the night. The startled driver would think it was a part that had fallen off his car. Darald said the boys always disclosed themselves as the source of the prank and sometimes got chased into the culvert. "That culvert saved a lot of our lives because the big guys couldn't get to us in there," he said. "We didn't hurt anybody. We just made them mad."

Although Morgantown was only eight miles away, Darald made very few trips to the "big city." The family did not own a car and it was a mile's walk to Cassville to catch the bus. Entertainment options included two motion picture theaters in Morgantown: the Morgan, which played westerns; and the Warner, which showed dramas and romantic shows. "We'd hitchhike when we went to the movies," Darald said. But it was easier to stay in town and wait for the movies to come to the school. Darald said a traveling projectionist from the Morgan Theater set up his show in the schoolhouse on Saturdays. Children saved up twelve cents a week to see a show that included a serial to keep them coming back. The price of admission was usually earned by gathering scrap iron and selling it to a man who came to the mine camp once a week. "Back then, you didn't get nothing from your parents per week," Darald said. "Everybody was poor up there and everybody had kids to feed." Darald earned spending money as a teenager hoeing corn. "We got our first bike by working for a dollar a day, my brother and I, hoeing corn," he said. "There were a lot of rocks in those fields. Seems like you'd throw the rocks out and they'd just come back up."

Most provisions were purchased from the company store in Cassville. Darald said his sister used to carry twenty-five-pound sacks of flour home from the store. If it rained on her trip, she was expected to remove her coat and keep the sack of flour dry. All trading was done in scrip and Darald's mother had to be a savvy shopper to keep the family budget in line with her husband's production at the mine. A garden helped stretch that budget, but each lot was only a hundred feet square, hardly enough room for a garden meant to support eight people. They turned to the woodlands where blackberries and blueberries were free for the picking. Darald said he woke up many mornings to a breakfast of milk and blackberries that his mother had canned in half-gallon jars. Clothing was homemade on a sewing machine that Darald still has, a memento of tough times and sweet childhood days, when Darald used to pretend the flywheel on the treadle was the steering wheel of a car.

War and the World beyond Cassville

The family's housing situation improved when Darald was thirteen and the coal company began to sell the houses. Darald's father purchased the house on the end of the road, which included a 1.9-acre lot. The family expanded its garden and bought a couple of cows. A side benefit of having cows was that the cattle feed came in decorative cotton sacks. Ethel Spangler based her selection of the brand of cattle feed on the appeal of the bag, which was turned into dresses for her four girls.

George Spangler paid for his new home in broken bones and pain. Darald said his father had several close calls with death in the coal mine, including a slate fall that pinned his shattered leg under his back. "The shoe from his broken leg was in the middle of his back as he lay there pinned," Darald said. His father suffered a broken neck in another accident. Black lung eventually claimed his life. Kathern's father also suffered many accidents, including one that left him in a body cast for weeks. "I'll tell you, a coal miner suffers," Darald said. "We'd go to town and go to the front of the courthouse, around the square, and you'd see men there playing checkers. And maybe one man would be missing an arm, and another his legs. They'd be all chewed up, and you'd know it was from working in those coal mines."

Darald grew up giving no thought to what his life would be like once he was out of high school. The only job options in Morgantown at that time were the glass factories or coal mines. But World War II changed everything. Darald's patriotic spirit was stirred in 1943 and he dropped out of his junior year of high school to enter the U.S. Navy Seabees. Darald worked with the construction battalion in the South Pacific, building airports on the islands and experiencing the world beyond the mountains. "I was homesick," he said of his days in boot camp. "I thought I was going to die." In addition to the homesickness, there was harassment. "They'd call you a hillbilly, say you got one leg shorter than the other. One guy said he'd went to West Virginia and saw a cow fall out of the lot and through the fence. They'd call you a ridge runner. Oh, it was bad. But after a while, you'd get used to it."

Darald believes that his navy experience conditioned him for the eventual migration. "It gave me a better outlook and helped make me an extrovert," he said. Darald was discharged in April 1947 and returned to West Virginia, where he soon met and fell in love with Kathern. They were married November 22 that year. Darald got a job in the coal mine, difficult work for a man

Darald and Kathern Spangler both grew up in coal mining camps near Morgantown, West Virginia. A job at National Distillers, later known as RMI Sodium,
brought the Spanglers to Ashtabula County in 1954. They are pictured in their
Kingsville Township home. *Photo by Carl E. Feather*

who confesses to be a claustrophobic, but the only kind of work he could find there. After two years of digging coal, raising timbers, and a close escape from a cave-in, Darald quit and went to work for Sterling Faucet Company. But his Christmas present from the company in 1949 was a layoff notice, and Darald began thinking about following his friends north to Ohio.

"My friend, Leo Thomas, had a sister on Lake Erie Street in Conneaut," he said. "She told him they had this good operation at National Distillers and come up here and got a job there. He came back over the holidays and told me about it and I followed him up here." Darald came to Ohio in a 1941 Mercury station wagon with wood side panels. He got hired at National Distillers' sodium plant, later to be known as RMI Sodium, and went to work December 28. Unlike many of the new hires at the plant, Darald was not placed in the cell feeding section, a hard, hellish job at which few men survived more than a day. Cell feeders controlled the flow of salt into the reactors where sodium and chlorine were produced by electrolysis. Darald said the temperature around the cells was 400° and temperatures in the top of the building reached 1,100°. Workers wore insulated underwear and heavy outer garments to protect themselves from the hellish environment, which was tinged with chlorine gas. Burns from metallic sodium presented another danger to workers. "A lot of people got burns in there," Darald said. "I had a friend who got his eye burned out." Cell feeders worked twenty minutes on, forty minutes off, because of the heat. As with the furnace-room work at Electromet, many men simply couldn't handle the conditions and quit after their first day. Darald was fortunate; he was instead assigned to the boiler room, where it seemed as if his life had come full circle. "Now, you want to know what my first job was?" he asks teasingly. "Shoveling coal."

With a job secured in Ohio, Darald found an apartment at Fifteenth and Harbor Streets in Conneaut and went back to West Virginia for his family— Kathern and daughter Linda. Rent was $42.50 a month, and after paying that and the other basic living expenses, there was little money for extras, including car repairs. Darald said his nine-year-old car needed a push to get started. He would prevail upon the owner or customers in the donut shop below his apartment to give him a push to get to work and on his co-workers to do the same at night to get him home. The family had only bedroom and kitchen furniture when they came to Ohio. Darald said one of their first purchases was a maple set—hard maple–frame living room furniture with cushions and end tables. "That was $100, a lot of money," he said.

Tough Times for a Lady

The move was particularly difficult for Kathern, who was stuck in the apartment all day and didn't have the social experience of a job to acclimate her to the new culture. "I was scared to death," she said. "I didn't know anybody." But things were going well for Darald at the new job, where chief engineer Pete Dawson took him under his wing. Dawson's family had come from West Virginia, which may account for his special interest in Darald. Whatever the reason, he encouraged Darald to study for an operator's license so he could rise above the $1.38 hourly starting rate. Kathern helped Darald study for his boiler operator's license. "My wife knew more about boilers than I did," Darald said. The long nights and weekends of study paid off when Darald got his license in May 1951. His pay increased, to $1.64 an hour, and so did his responsibility. Darald pulled as much overtime as possible to earn extra money for his family, which grew to three children. "I never turned down overtime," he said. "One time I worked 104 hours in one week. I was tired, I felt like I was hollow inside. But I needed the money, I was raising a family."

Things didn't improve for Kathern after they purchased their home in Kingsville Township in 1954. Kathern said the community seemed cliquish and it was difficult to make friends. "I got pretty lonesome at times," she said. "In my opinion, I don't think they make friends that well around here. . . . It was lonesome, just me and the kids. I didn't have nothing else to do, so I just cleaned the house and took care of the kids. If you're not in a clique here, you just don't fit in." The warmth and happiness Kathern knew in the company-owned coal town of her childhood outshine the more secure life she has found in the North. For Kathern, northeast Ohio is like the coal mines she left behind—cold, dark, damp, and lonely. But Darald said he found many of the community members willing to extend a helping hand to a family from the hills. The owner of the corner general store, Bob Swanson, made it a point to offer assistance to Darald when the company was on strike in 1954–55. "We didn't have a pot to—" he said. "Bob Swanson and his sister had this store in town, and he came up to me and said, 'If you ever need anything, you come down and get it.' I didn't do it, but I'll never forget his offer. I thought that was quite the thing, because he didn't know me from Adam."

Darald's avenue of assimilation was his love for baseball, a love Kathern did not share. Darald played in the industrial league and, along with several other Kingsville men, helped build the Little League parks in Kingsville and North Kingsville. He repaired baseball equipment in his basement and built a ball diamond in this backyard, where he coached young ballplayers. Darald also worked as an umpire. Kathern became his secretary and answering service. "She got so sick of baseball," Darald said.

Trips back to West Virginia helped break the boredom and loneliness of being a migrant housewife, but they were infrequent, occurring only two or three times a year. Darald said they stopped going back because the trips were too exhausting—their siblings or parents were always asking them to help with chores or setting a hectic visitation schedule for them. "Everybody wanted us to be at their place," he said. "Kathern would come home and she'd be dead tired from running around down there." "It wasn't a vacation," Kathern said. "All we did was work."

Darald hasn't been back to West Virginia since the late 1980s. He can't travel long distances, and the patio on the side of their home is as good as any vacation spot. A fresh breeze blows through there on hot summer afternoons, a breeze free of gob dump gases and coal dust snowing down from the tipple. These days, the air is also free of the industrial pollution that once blew in from the RMI sodium plant, where Darald worked for thirty-seven years. The company closed the plant in the early 1990s.

Looking back on his migration experience and his years in the plant, Darold dismisses it as his effort to "just make a living the only way you knew how." Like many Appalachian migrants, he came with a car and life that needed a little push from the local people and economy. Within a few years he was driving in high gear and never slowed down until retirement. "The ones I knew worked hard because they really knew what hard times was," he said. "My foreman said I was too conscientious about my job. But that's the way I was raised and that's the way my family does it to this day. . . . They were good workers, because you knew where you were coming from and you wanted to make it."

That knowledge helped workers like Darald handle the heckling he got from Buckeye co-workers about his dialect and mountain roots. He said it wasn't unusual to have co-workers call him up on the telephone just to tell him the latest hillbilly joke. But Darald said he always had the last laugh when someone called him a "dumb hillbilly." "We couldn't be too dumb," he says, his face ready to explode with laughter. "We took over Ohio and never fired a shot."

14 reading, writing, and ohio

teachers and migration

One-Room Schoolhouse Teacher

ON HER LAST DAY of high school, Oleta McMillion's father stopped her as she was going to catch the bus and conceded victory to a young mountain girl's dream. "He said, 'If you really want to be a teacher, then I'll find the money. But I think you are making a mistake,'" recalled Oleta McMillion Swaney, now a Kingsville Township resident. The concession came in the spring of 1941, in Pocahontas County, West Virginia, where Oleta lived with her parents Wilton and Gola (Simmons) McMillion on their Droop Mountain farm. A decade earlier, Wilton McMillion had been a teacher, and a good one at that. But Wilton preferred to inscribe his lessons in the furrows of a mountainside rather than on a squeaky chalkboard. Oleta picked up where her father left off and became the teacher in the family.

She was born March 27, 1923, in Greenbrier County, the first of six children. As the oldest, she had the responsibility of caring for younger siblings as well as doing farm tasks like hoeing corn and caring for her mother's flock of turkeys. Her education began in a one-room schoolhouse on Boggs Run and ended in Ohio and West Virginia universities. World War II had created a shortage of teachers in the Mountain State, and Oleta got a teaching certificate by attending West Virginia Wesleyan for two academic years plus two summers. She returned home at the beginning of the 1943–44 school year hoping to find a job in Pocahontas County. But the superintendent said nothing was available, so she applied for a job in Greenbrier County—and got it.

Oleta McMillion Swaney began her teaching career in a one-room schoolhouse in rural West Virginia and ended it in the Jefferson Local District in Ashtabula County. *Photo by Carl E. Feather*

It was a one-room schoolhouse assignment outside Richwood. The school covered grades one through eight, although Oleta had no students in grades four or five the year she taught there. Enrollment stood at twelve students, and Oleta was paid a hundred dollars per month for work that included just about everything except starting the fire in the morning. Oleta boarded with Henry and Tessie Baber. Their three sons were off to war and her extra thirty dollars a month helped the family make ends meet while filling a vacant room. The Baber farm was a mile from the school, easy walking distance for the young teacher. Students walked up to two miles to get to school. The schoolhouse was heated with wood and had no running water or electricity. Three windows on each side of the building provided the only light. Students brought their own lunches and drank water hauled from Junior Mullens's house. "Hot lunches" were unknown unless the students stored their lunch bags near the stove. Biscuits and homemade bread were mainstays. Once in a while a slice of ham would fill the gap between the bread slices, but a filling of cooked, mashed beans was more common.

Oleta looks back on the one-room schoolhouse as an effective educational system. Parents purchased the books and students handed them down to younger siblings as they progressed through the grades. Recitation was done on a bench in front of the teacher while other students worked on their assignments. Oleta believes that the constant presentation of new material, repetition, and review made for an efficient educational method.

However, in Oleta's first assignment, discipline was the greatest challenge. The superintendent neglected to tell her that the previous teacher, a man, had been run out by the rowdy students. "He wouldn't come back, but they never told me this," Oleta said. Of particular concern was Edward Nicely, whose brother was serving time for killing a revenue agent. Just beyond the schoolhouse was the community graveyard, where two of Edward's uncles were buried. They'd gotten into a fight and ended up killing each other. Perhaps as punishment, perhaps for economy, they were buried side-by-side in a double grave. Edward seemed to have inherited his family's short fuse, and a showdown between Oleta and the class troublemaker seemed inevitable. It came during the Lord's Prayer, part of the morning exercises that included a Bible story, Pledge of Allegiance, and singing of the national anthem. Oleta happened to look up during the prayer and saw Edward Nicely dancing in the aisle. And it wasn't because he'd been "moved by the spirit" during prayer. Oleta's father had made her a rough paddle and given it to her as her first line of defense against a room full of rowdy children. But when it came to Edward Nicely, Oleta was outgunned. He pulled a knife on her as she approached him with the paddle. "I hit his hand with the paddle and he dropped the knife," she said. "But he grabbed the paddle." Edward and Oleta scuffled and ended up on the floor in a wrestling match. "I just knew I had to overpower him," she said. "So I hit him in the nose with my fist. When his nose started bleeding, he quit. Then I got a pan of water, helped clean him up and we went on with school."

Oleta's stockings were torn; oil stains from the floor were rubbed so deeply into her wool skirt that dry cleaning couldn't remove them. But her biggest worry was what was going to happen when Edward went home and told his mother about the incident. "I knew I had done something wrong," she said. "I had hit a kid with my fist. . . . I told my father what I had done and he was upset. He said, 'They'll sue you.'" Instead, Edward's mother came to school and begged Oleta not to report her son's misconduct—sufficient was the grief of having one child in prison. Oleta agreed and asked for the family's forgiveness. "I didn't have a bit of trouble with him from then on," she said.

Cass Days

Oleta's second and third years of teaching were in Cass, West Virginia, a booming timber town established in 1901 when the Greenbrier Division of the Chesapeake and Ohio Railroad reached the community. W. E. Blackhurst, a historian, author, and high school teacher Oleta knew during her Cass days, notes in his history of the region that the "entire Greenbrier watershed was clothed in a rich cover of timber. Billions of board feet of the finest trees of a nation were waiting the woodsman's axe. Added to the vast quantity was the fact that here lay the widest variety of wood products to be found in the United States." In the forty years that followed, Cass developed a reputation as a rough, wild town where fights, prostitution, and gambling developed alongside the lumber industry. The mill at Cass could turn out as much as two hundred fifty thousand feet of wood products a day. As many as forty carloads of pulpwood left the town every day bound for mills in Virginia and Maryland. "Every day thousands of feet of dried lumber went through the planing mill to be converted into high grade flooring. Some went to the planers to provide finished lumber. Whatever a buyer wanted in lumber he could find at the Cass mill," noted Blackhurst in *Your Train Ride through History.*

The town was beginning its decline by the time Oleta arrived in Cass. Much of the great timber had been cut and the West Virginia Pulp and Paper Company's holdings had diminished. The mill, town, and timberland were sold in 1942 to Mower Lumber Company, which focused on lumber only. Operations continued for eighteen more years, but on a much reduced scale. Eventually, the mill closed and the mighty Shay engines ceased their labors on the steep grades—at least for three years. On June 15, 1963, the Cass Scenic Railroad began operation as a tourist attraction, a train ride into history and the rugged beauty of the state's second highest peak, Bald Knob. More than one million tourists have taken the Cass excursion since then. The railroad

The Cass, West Virginia, school where Oleta McMillion Swaney taught in the 1940s still stands, although it is no longer used. *Photo by Carl E. Feather*

continues to use Shay, Climax, and Heisler engines, direct-gearing locomotives designed to handle the hairpin curves, frail, temporary tracks, and steep grades on Cheat Mountain. With the help of a switchback, the engine climbs grades of up to 11 percent—eleven feet of altitude gain for every one hundred feet of track. (A 2 percent grade on conventional railroads is considered steep.)

Oleta recalls the Cass of 1943 as a booming town with a big company store where she used her teacher's wages to purchase a bedroom suite for her parents. She roomed with a lumber company manager and his wife in their company house behind the store. She remembers them for their unusual luncheon menu—peanut butter and banana sandwiches. But Oleta and several other teachers usually ate their lunch at the lumbermen's boardinghouse, where a dining room was set aside for the teachers. She doesn't recall the town as being a rough place for a young lady—the only saloon Oleta remembers was across the river from the company store.

Her assignment was teaching math and geography to seventh- and eighth-grade students. The average class had twenty-two students and the teaching environment offered many more comforts and conveniences than the one-room schoolhouse. Nevertheless, local attitudes were somewhat challenging for the young teacher. Oleta said she once told her students that she believed man would one day go to the moon. A student reported the statement to his parents, who called the principal and protested. "Those parents were really worked up because I made that statement," she said. Other parents, it seems, were more willing to accept the possibility of scientific miracles. Among her most memorable students was a girl in the seventh grade who became pregnant. The girl's mother insisted that her daughter had not had sexual relations; rather, she had caught a "germ" during her dunking at the Baptist Church. She was not permitted to come to school, regardless of the virtuous nature of her pregnancy.

The end of the war brought change to Oleta's life as Jim Baber, son of Henry and Tessie Baber, returned home from the fighting. Romance between Oleta and Jim blossomed and they were married in October 1945. The school board granted Oleta two weeks leave for the wedding and honeymoon, after which she returned to complete the school year. Jim searched for work in Pocahontas and Greenbrier Counties and even went to the Adirondack Mountains to work in the lumber camps with his brother for a while. He returned to his parents' farm and an offer from his uncle, Wallace Baber, who needed help on his Denmark Township farm in Ashtabula County. Wallace Baber's father had come to Ohio from Richwood, West Virginia, in the early 1900s and purchased three farms in Denmark Township with money he made logging. But his wife and all but his oldest son refused to come north with him. The elder Baber kept one farm and sold the other two. When his oldest son contracted tuberculosis, he asked Wallace to come north and work the farm. Wallace complied and eventually took over the farm from his father. Later, when Wallace himself needed help, he looked south again and invited his nephew to come work for him. Jim and Oleta headed north in the summer of 1947 and never looked back.

Migrant Teachers

Oleta didn't plan to teach in Ohio—she wanted to raise a family. But she taught for a year at Pierpont and did substitute teaching in Dorset between bearing and raising their four children—David, Stephen, Vivian, and Jerry. They eventually moved off Wallace Baber's farm and rented their own, but a debilitating illness struck Jim and the couple began to drown in bills. Out of financial necessity, Oleta returned to teaching full time. She also returned to college during summer breaks to complete her degree. Her studies took her to Duke University, West Virginia Wesleyan, and Kent State University. But when she applied to KSU for her undergraduate degree, the administration refused to grant it because her first two years had not been taken at that school. After exhausting her avenues of appeal, Oleta reluctantly returned to West Virginia Wesleyan for a summer to complete her degree. All in all, it took her twenty-nine years to get a bachelor's degree.

Liver cancer claimed Jim in 1971; Oleta's father also died that year. The six McMillion children had all moved away from the family farm (Harold migrated to Ashtabula) and Oleta's mother moved to Ohio to live with her.

Oleta remarried in 1979, to Joel Swaney of Kingsville Township. She taught elementary grades for Jefferson Local Schools until her retirement in 1984, after thirty-two years as a teacher. For Oleta, and many other West Virginia young people who graduated from the state's teachers colleges in the 1940s and 1950s, Ohio clearly offered better opportunities. The difference in pay between West Virginia and Ohio was dramatic. In the three years Oleta taught in West Virginia schools, she had paid $90 into the state teacher's retirement system. In her first year at Pierpont, she paid $96 into the Ohio system.

Ron Butcher, a Weston, West Virginia, native who taught at Jefferson High School, said job openings in his home state didn't compare to the number in Ohio. "The people [in teaching positions] wouldn't move," Ron said. "There was just very little turnover. There might be two or three jobs for an entire senior class." Ron had only one job offer in West Virginia when he graduated from Fairmont State in 1956. It carried a starting pay of around $2,800. Another offer, from a rural school in Virginia, paid $2,750 for a full-schedule math teacher, plus filling the head coach position for three sports. The most attractive offer came from Jefferson. Robert McNutt, the district superintendent, came to Fairmont State on a recruiting trip and posted two positions that provided matches for both Ron and his wife Virgie: mathematics for him and girls' physical education for her. The base salary was also a good match, $3,200.

Even West Virginia educators who were not actively looking for a job found Ohio's higher pay scale alluring. George Reed and Mary Ruth Taylor of Wellsburg, West Virginia, were visiting Mary Ruth's sister in Jefferson when the landlord stopped to make some repairs. The landlord was Ralph

Curie, principal at Edgewood High School in Ashtabula Township. "He came over to work on the house and said, 'Do you know where I can find a math teacher?' I said, 'I'm a math teacher.' We just kind of fell into it," G. Reed said. Although they were not looking for a job at the time, the $2,500 annual salary differential made the offer very attractive. "When they started talking about a job, we drove around the Edgewood School District," G. Reed said. "We were quite impressed with the Avon Boulevard area and decided to buy there." G. Reed taught at the junior high school three years, then moved to the new Edgewood Senior High School building in 1962 as assistant principal. He was principal for eight years before being promoted to the central office as director of instruction. He retired from the district in 1982, a highly respected educator.

None of G. Reed's family followed him to Ohio and Mary Ruth's sister moved on from Jefferson to Cleveland Heights. But G. Reed said they have no regrets about moving to Ohio. He echoes the feelings of both migrant blue-collar workers and teachers when he sums it up this way: "We think this area has been good for us."

15 children of thomas

mining town migrants

WESTERN MARYLAND'S rolling farmland and West Virginia's blue-green mountains are delineated only by signs reading "WEST VIRGINIA" and "THOMAS 14" as Route 219 enters the Mountain State. But the highway quickly grows weary of the bucolic scenery and bids farewell to the farms of Preston County. It gives the motorist a last look at relatively flat land as it loops past a pair of '40s tourist attractions: the "Smallest Church in Forty-eight States" and Silver Lake Park, a lily-covered lake surrounded by recreational vehicles and simple cabins. For the next seven miles, the two-lane, concrete highway crawls up Backbone Mountain in a series of tight loops and wide, squiggly curves that slice through the overhanging hardwoods and massive rock outcroppings of the Monongahela National Forest. Just past Leadmine Road, the highway breaks out onto the mountain's first plateau and whips past the Kempton Road and Fairfax Sand and Crushed Stone Company as if tracing a child's scrawling interpretation of "S." A few more miles of climbing, twisting, and descending, and the road enters William, a hollow scarred by an abandoned railroad bed and occupied by a handful of homes. In the depression on the right is a simple, two-story frame house once owned by Ray Cosner. His son, Howard, grew up there, but in the early 1950s left the economic depression of this region for a better life in Ohio.

A half-mile down the road is Sissaboo Hollow—Drunkard's Hollow to the locals. Its five residences don't rate a sign to distinguish the hamlet from William or Thomas; indeed, it seems a part of William. But in the early twentieth century, when a sawmill operated at William, Sissaboo Hollow was home to several company houses. "Sissaboo Mary" was one of the residents, and while the nature of her deeds that gave the hollow its name are lost to local memory, her name remains a part of the hollow's history. Today, there is a mix of old and new housing in the hollow. The last house the motorist passes on the way to Thomas is a white, single-story home with a sprawling garage and washhouse. The house was built in the 1930s by Clayton and Violet Watring from scrap lumber and railroad ties, tar paper and shingles, sweat and faith. Three children were raised there: Robert, Cossette, and Barbara. They were children of Thomas, raised in love and discipline to lead their adult lives not in Sissaboo Hollow, but northern Ohio and Baltimore.

A Time Recalled

From Sissaboo Hollow the highway begins a flirtatious relationship with the abandoned Western Maryland Railroad bed and the North Fork of the Blackwater River. The highway abruptly grows tired of the association just north of Thomas and cuts across the river and railroad bed on a high bridge. In the 1940s Arvin Rumer and his friends swam in the deep dam pond below and played daredevil games from the bridge's apex. They survived more than one hazardous escapade in the murky water, but the perilous game of economic survival in Appalachia was one Arvin could not win, and he, too, headed north.

Route 32 picks up at the sudden departure of 219 and continues through Thomas as East Avenue. Thomas is built on the side of a hill, and streets parallel to East Avenue ascend the steep grade. Square frame houses, brick storefronts with flat, tar roofs, and three churches are stacked on the hillside. East Avenue is a boulevard of retail commerce wide enough to accommodate "head-on" parking on the left and parallel on the right. Weary storefronts in an eclectic mix of architectural styles suggestive of everything from New Orleans to New York line the street's left side. A bank, craft store, coffeehouse, bookstore, and several other tourist-oriented ventures suggest that Thomas is undergoing renewal and has a life apart from coal.

The Cottrill Opera House, formerly the Sutton Theater, dominates the north end of the street with its white lettering on a red facade and large, arching second-story windows. Dave Bennear spent many a long, hot night in the projection booth of that theater during the 1940s. He entertained soldiers and old maids; coal miners and teenagers, including Carl Junior Feather, who came over the mountain from Eglon to court Cossette Watring. But the escapism of Hollywood ended when the house lights came up and Dave, Cossette, and Carl stepped out onto East Avenue after the show. There they faced the dingy future of an Appalachian town fading to black. With little prospect of a happy ending in Thomas, they watched their last picture show in the Sutton Theater and headed north for Ashtabula County's prosperity.

Built and Slain by Coal

Ironically, the first settler in the Thomas corporation was from Ohio—John William Bonnifield, who took his family there from Muskingum County in 1883. Development came quickly after the West Virginia Central & Pittsburgh Railway reached Thomas August 10, 1884. A coal mine had opened the previous winter and was ready to ship its product as soon as the railroad arrived. A post office, hotel, bakery, and two stores also appeared in that short span. The town exploded in population and prosperity in the next two decades, with coal fueling the growth. But on the morning of November 12, 1901, it was wood fueling the fire that consumed eighty-three buildings within two hours. Among the casualties: the Catholic church, town hall, six saloons, twenty stores, a hotel, and many of the better residences.

Most of the owners did not have fire insurance, but within a year they had rebuilt the town and prosperity returned. The Davis Coal & Coke Company, which had a monopoly on a hundred thousand acres of coal lands in six counties, built more than four hundred company tenements in Thomas. Davis Coal & Coke was one of the largest and best-known coal companies in the world and Thomas was its hub. In its golden age, the company employed nearly 1,600 people in Tucker County. It supplied the town with its own electric power plant, water system, and telephone connections. At the peak of operation, 1910 to 1912, nine producing mines and nearly a thousand coke ovens were operating within a one-mile radius of the Thomas office. The ovens, which burned coal day and night, produced so much light that the sky was illuminated for miles around. The glow was compared to the aurora borealis. The Buxton & Landstreet Company followed in the footsteps of the Davis Coal & Coke Company, setting up a company store wherever a mine opened. Many private shop owners started businesses in Thomas and cashed in on the good fortune.

It was a fragile, fleeting prosperity. A new, less wasteful, process for producing coke was developed, closing the beehive ovens that remain standing to this day along the abandoned railroad bed near what used to be Coketon. The mines closed one by one in the ensuing years; the Kempton Mine was one of the last to go, in 1950. The Buxton & Landstreet store in Thomas closed May 27, 1950, and King Coal's reign in Thomas ended. Census figures tell the story: in 1910, Thomas had 2,354 residents; by 1950, only 1,146 called the city home.

Ghost Town Memories

Cossette Roselean Watring was among those 1,146 souls enumerated in 1950. She was named for the character Cosette in *Les Misérables*, but both her first and middle names were disregarded by her family after her grandmother saw in the 1932 Christmas toy catalog a Tickle-Toes doll she thought looked like baby Cossette and nicknamed her "Tickle." Most of her friends and family abbreviated it to "Tick." She was born August 3, 1932, on the Maryland side of Henry, a hamlet between Thomas and Bayard. A river divided the community, which is now only a memory in gray-haired heads. Clayton worked the track on the Western Maryland Railroad, when there was work, which was not very often. Violet, who had grown up helping her mother Cora Keiper operate boardinghouses in Shaw and Valleyhead, was accustomed to the hard work that comes with being poor in Appalachia. Nevertheless, they gave Cossette and her brother Robert a wealth of memories.

The house at Henry was along the Western Maryland Railroad line that serviced the coal mining towns of Wilson, Dobbin, and Bayard. The kitchen was the first room entered from the front porch. A wood-burning stove warmed the frame structure and cooked the meals. Bedrooms branched from one side of the kitchen; a parlor from the other. Quilting frames dominated the parlor and provided the center of family activity on many a long winter night. "Bobby and I got into a fight and we knocked the kerosene lamp over on the quilt that Mom was quilting on," Cossette recalled. "That did not go over too good with her." Clayton read to the children at night and there was a battery-powered radio to listen to, but only when there was money for batteries. But even without power, the large cabinet provided amusement for the children as they crawled behind the radio and produced their own shows to entertain their mother and themselves.

The demands of daily living left little time for horseplay, however. There was no running water nor an indoor bathroom in the house, and the chore of hauling water for cooking and bathing fell to the children. "We carried the water from a spring . . . on Sunday night, that was our job," she said. "At that time you could buy lard in five-pound buckets, and Bobby and I had one that fit each hand and we'd carry water from that spring in those buckets."

Cossette attended first grade at Bayard, but first had to walk a mile up the railroad track to catch a bus at Wilson. Their older cousin, Okarita Keiper, came to live with them during this time so that she could accompany them on the long walk and help with household chores. "If Okarita was sick and she couldn't go to school, none of us would go," she said.

Clayton worked only one or two days a month during the Depression. Money was so tight that broken shoelaces were sewn back together and each child had only two pairs of underwear: one to wear and one to wash. When there was a paycheck, it warranted a trip to Bob Shoemaker's store at Wilson, or, on special occasions, to the larger community of Bayard, which had a gas station, school, and stores. Cossette recalls the purchase of an "Imp," an ice cream treat on a wooden stick, as one of the few childhood treats she knew.

Most of the family's meals came from a large garden that supplied them with food year-round. Clayton dug a large hole in the fall, lined it with roofing paper, and filled it with the harvest: "Turnips, hanovers [rutabagas], cabbage, onions, potatoes, and apples," Cossette said. "On a bad day, Dad would open up that hole it would be just like Christmas because you would have all this stuff you wouldn't have other times."

The community provided a richness of memorable characters. "There at Dobbin, there was a man, Helmicks, who lived up on a hill and they had a bear that they kept out in a cage," she said. "The bear would get out and his wife would take the wheelbarrow out and get after the thing and it would go right back in its cage. When her husband died, she buried him right in the backyard. She could sit right at the kitchen table, or just about anywhere in that house, and look right out at her husband's grave."

Among the handful of homes at Henry was a boardinghouse run by "Maggie." Maggie was so poor she made shoes out of cardboard. Cossette recalls eating corn cakes there one day when one of Maggie's sons walked in. "He was so ugly, I took one look at him and I fainted," she said. Also traumatic for the young girl was the wake for a male suicide victim at a neighbor's house. "We had to sit there night after night," she said. "His girlfriend came in and started crying and went over and pulled him out of that coffin."

The Cassidys were the Watrings' neighbors, and Cossette believes that the family's uncivilized behavior eventually drove her parents from Henry to Thomas. "They were such mean people," she said. "They were going to kill Dad one night. This Bill Cassidy, he was terrible. He hit Dad on the head with this board, just split his head wide open. They took him to court and everything. They just were terrible, mean people. Every time we would go out, and then come back, they had done something to the house. I can remember we were coming by the old mines down there. There was snow on the ground, and there were these big balls of snow they had rolled onto the road—we and the Cassidys were the only ones who used the road. So Dad speeded up in that old Model A Ford and Mom screamed 'No, Clayton, no! It's not snowballs!' And it's a good thing he didn't hit them, because they were cinder."

Going to Town

The summer after Cossette completed first grade, Clayton moved his family to an old house on Railroad Hill in Thomas. Cossette recalls the house as cold and conducive to illness. Both she and Robert failed to pass their grades that year due to illness-related absences. "I had the croup the whole time I was there," she said. "Mom and Dad would get up with me in the middle of the night and work with me. I'd turn blue. They'd give me sugar and salt. It was a big old house. I can remember it was so cold in that house that winter we didn't even use the upstairs. Mom and Dad had a daybed and they just used that daybed at night."

Clayton dismantled the house in Henry and, using the timber from that structure, built their house in Sissaboo Hollow. The home was built on land leased from the Western Maryland Railroad for five dollars a year. It was across the road from the railroad tracks and tool shed. Behind the house, the mountain rose sharply into a deep forest that was home to wildflowers,

berries, beaver, and deer. Springs flowed on both sides of the house and provided a source of fresh water and greens.

Opportunities for work improved for Clayton in the late 1930s and '40s,
and he advanced in his position on the railroad to track foreman. A third
child, Barbara, was added to the family in 1944. "I spent an awful lot of time
taking care of that bratty kid," Cossette said. "She was such a brat when she'd
get her hair washed. She was really nasty about getting her hair washed and
I still remind her of that." Cossette recalls her teen years as ones of hard work
around the home and training for a domestic lifestyle. When she ran out of
things to do for her mother, she was sent to her grandparents' house in Davis
to work. One summer, she worked in Thomas with Rosie Landsberry cleaning rooms at the Thomas Hotel. She also worked as a waitress at Joe Grecco's
Restaurant in Thomas. But there was seldom time for work outside the home.
"My mother kept me very busy. She seemed to find all kinds of jobs for me
to do," she said. She graduated from Thomas High School in 1951, with a desire to stay close to home and a dream that would go unfulfilled. "My biggest
thing was I wanted to be a nurse," she said. "I would have liked to have been
a nurse, but it takes that stuff called money."

The Link North

Down in William, Howard Cosner was also growing up the son of a railroad
man. He was born June 26, 1932, the second son of Leona and Ray Cosner.
His brother, Gilbert, was born July 26, 1930; a younger sister, Darlene Ruth,
died in infancy. Howard was born in Elizabeth, Pennsylvania, where Leona's
father, an itinerant preacher, made his home. Originally from William, Ray
moved to Elizabeth after marrying Leona. He went to work for a steel mill
there, but when the mill went on strike he refused either to cross the picket
line or to be without work. So he packed up his family and returned to
William, where he purchased his house from Frank Cosner, an uncle. "He
bought it for seventy dollars, but he sold the pump organ that came with it
for ten, so he only paid sixty dollars for the house," Howard said. Howard's
grandfather, Oliver Cosner, operated a store that stood across the road.
Oliver's store supplied food, pots and pans, penny candy, and gasoline to the
few families who lived in Sissaboo Hollow, William, and the environs. Oliver

ran the store until the early 1950s. The building still stands, but as a private residence.

Ray found steady work on the Western Maryland Railroad. The land around the house provided a garden for the family and hay for a couple of cows. Electricity and indoor plumbing did not come to the hollow until after Howard left home. Yet he recalls his childhood as a good one, filled with simple pleasures like ice-skating, playing ball, and singing with his family's impromptu band. "My dad played the banjo; brother played the accordion, guitar, and violin; and mother played the piano," he said. They traveled to the homes of neighbors who shared their interest and played music together.

What made Howard's childhood different from that of the Watring children or other youngsters growing up in Tucker County was the Cosner family's annual summer vacation to Ashtabula County. Howard's uncle, Charles VanKirk—his mother's baby brother—had followed his father Norman, a missionary, to Kingsville in 1936. This established a kin link that provided employment not only for Howard but for several other Thomas friends. But in Howard's childhood and adolescent years, Ashtabula County was just a place to escape the chores of making hay, tending to animals, and carrying water. "I liked it," Howard said. "It was different than them hills. There wasn't much down around that Thomas, but it's pretty."

Howard didn't give much thought to his future until his senior year, when he began to recognize how limited his options were in William. "There wasn't any jobs down there at that time. Mines, and I wouldn't work in the mines. I had a great-uncle killed in one and I said I'd never go in one," he said. Charles VanKirk assured Howard that there was plenty of work in Ashtabula if he wanted to head north. Charles worked at Electromet and promised to help Howard get a job there, with any luck not in the furnace room, where most southern recruits started.

"I graduated the twenty-third of May, 1950, and came up here the following weekend," Howard said. He was not alone in his exodus. Of the thirty-five youngsters in his graduating class, he counts only ten who stayed in Thomas—mostly offspring of shop or business owners who had a modicum of security in the faltering Thomas economy. "The majority went to Washington, D.C.," he said. "And there were four or five who went into the service after a couple years."

Howard's parents took him and Dave Bennear, a distant cousin, to

Ashtabula County to apply for Electromet jobs. But Howard hadn't turned eighteen yet, so he waited a couple of weeks until he was of age. He took his physical the day after his birthday and started work the next day as a laborer in the traffic department. He rented a room at Flat Iron Park, a rooming house at the junction of Center Street and Route 20 in Ashtabula. Rent was six dollars a week, leaving a fair amount left over from his $1.20-an-hour wage.

But a call to the army in September 1952 interrupted his new life in Ashtabula for two years. Howard was stationed at Fort Knox, Kentucky, where he met Virginia Lanham. When he left Fort Knox for Ashtabula in September 1954, he brought a bride with him. "I was so in love," Virginia said. "He said, 'We're going to Ohio.' I said, 'I'm going where you go.' I wasn't going to let that West Virginia hillbilly get away. I packed my things and left and never went back. Moved right here to Kingsville and I've never been sorry." Howard and Virginia were married in Louisville on September 10, 1954, just four days after his discharge from the army. Howard made a side trip to Georgia to check out a job lead at a Lockheed plant, but they weren't hiring at the time. So he headed back to Ashtabula County, where he got his old job back with Union Carbide. After staying with friends for a short while, they found an apartment in Kingsville, on the second story of the post office/service station building.

Mechanic's Son

Back in Thomas, times were rough for the class of 1952, which included Arvin Rumer. He was born in Eglon, Preston County, West Virginia, April 4, 1933, to Gilbert A. and Idella (Harsh) Rumer. The family moved the thirteen miles to Thomas when Arvin was twelve. His father, a mechanic, worked for a garage in Eglon, but business soured and Gilbert saw a better opportunity in Thomas, where he worked for the Milkint Brothers, Charles and Pete.

The Rumer family lived on Fourth Street, a narrow residential street overlooking the unadorned back of Thomas's retail section. Behind the Rumer's house was a pasture where Ruby Rubenstein, the owner of the meat market, kept four milking cows. One of Arvin's jobs when he was in the sixth grade was to lead the four cows from Fourth Street each morning to an alley on First Street, where Annie Cooper milked them. Then Arvin led them back up the hill to pasture and headed off to school. "I got paid a dollar a week for that—and a ten-cent lunch pie, that was my bonus," he said. "I never had trouble with those cows, but the first time I did that I was nervous. I didn't know what the hell I was doing."

In 1945 Arvin got a job at the Sutton Theater. The part-time job paid him seven dollars a week; when he left seven years later, he was up to twenty-two dollars a week and working full-time. The economy in Thomas was fading as the coal mines closed and, with them, the small businesses that depended upon the miners' money. "In '51, it was pretty well dead," Arvin said. "That's why Dad had to leave."

His father found work in Moorefield, and after graduating from Thomas High School in 1952, Arvin got a job at Moorefield Motors as a mechanic's trainee. A draft notice in 1953 sent him to the army for a year in Louisiana followed by a year in Kansas. After his discharge, Arvin returned to West Virginia, but his father had moved again, this time to Franklin. His father told him not even to bother looking for work. There simply were no jobs to be found. "But I didn't give up," Arvin said. "And the second place I stopped, I got a job with a chicken contractor." He worked eight to fifteen hours a day hauling chicken feed to farmers and chickens to market. He made five dollars a day. "There were no jobs there that paid anything," he said.

The Projectionist

That was a fact David Bennear had discovered in 1950 when, at the age of twenty-five, he quit his job at the Sutton Theater and headed for Ohio. The son of Roy William and Anna Mae (Cosner) Bennear, Dave was born November 10, 1925, on Bunker Hill, Thomas. His father was a custodian for Tucker County Schools, a job that required Roy Bennear's frugality and resourcefulness. "The school board was so poor that if he had to fix a broken window, Dad would fix it and pay for the glass, then have to wait until the end of the year to be reimbursed," Dave said. "He worked for the school board in the summer, but he didn't get paid until in the fall, after the taxes had been collected."

Despite the school board's poverty, Dave recalls Thomas as a "lively little town" that bustled with the business and excitement of miners coming into town on a Saturday night to purchase clothes, food, beverage, and a seat in the Sutton Theater. As a child, Dave was hired by its owner, Lee Sutton, to distribute show bills to homes in the surrounding communities. The theater operated every day of the week in the early 1940s. There were three changes of program each week: Sunday, Monday, and Tuesday; Wednesday and Thursday; and Friday and Saturday. The best films ran Wednesday and Thursday, to attract audiences on what would otherwise be slow nights. Westerns were shown on Saturday nights. "He didn't have to worry about Saturday," Dave said. "They'd always come to town, no matter what the movie was. The house was usually just about full on Saturday night." A cartoon, short subject, newsreel, and feature were a part of every program. Admission was fifteen cents for a child, a quarter for an adult.

The theater was the center of the community's entertainment in the 1940s. Buses ran from Thomas to surrounding communities to bring people to the Sutton Theater. Dave said the movie house was usually filled; Monday and Tuesday nights, it overflowed. Those were "bank nights," when the theater's management threw another $50 into the jackpot and patrons had the chance to win it by purchasing a lottery ticket. He recalls the prize going as high as $800. "Sometimes there were more ticket holders than building to put them in," he said. "Sometimes, people would buy a ticket and take their chance on seeing the show."

Soldiers provided the Sutton Theater with another steady source of business during the Second World War years. The army used the mountainous terrain around Thomas for training troops because it was comparable to Italy. At night, or when the weather was too inclement for training, the troops piled into the Sutton. "I remember getting out of school to go down there to run the movies for the soldiers," he said. Hired on as an usher in 1942, Dave quickly moved into the job of projectionist when a twenty-two-year veteran at the post died suddenly. Dave still recalls the title of the last film the projectionist showed before he collapsed with a heart attack—*Dead Man's Gulch*. After a short training period under another projectionist, Dave had the job. He held the position for the next eight years. There were no vacations or other benefits, just plenty of overtime without pay and an occasional bag of popcorn.

Dave started his workday at 4:30 P.M., right after school. It ended about 11:30 P.M., when he delivered the film to the post office. "That's why I did so much sleeping in school," he said. "I was up too late at night to go to school." Things didn't improve after he graduated and had more time to devote to his job. "I remember one time I worked night and day, every day—seven days a week—for eight months straight," he said. "I got so mad, I went out in the woods and told him somebody else could run it." But it was a job no one wanted—at least not for long.

The projection room was on the top floor of the three-story brick opera house. There was no air conditioning in the theater or projection room. The heat from the six-hundred-seat house hugged the ceiling and projection booth. Crammed into the twelve-by-eight-foot booth were two Simplex thirty-five millimeter film projectors with carbon arcs for a light source. The exhaust pipes for the projectors and a small fan provided the only ventilation. There were no windows. "Those projectors would be just like two big stoves," Dave said. "The temperature in that place would be unbelievable at times. It had to go to at least 115 degrees."

With two shows on weekday nights, three on Saturdays and Sundays, Dave was assured a steady diet of heat and hard work. But his duties exceeded threading and running the projectors. He also cleaned the theater at the start of each day, a job that paid an extra dollar a day but could take up to eight hours some days. "I sure did sweep up a lot of popcorn," he said. Another duty was re-upholstering the theater seats. The job paid well, fifty cents a seat, but, like the other theater jobs, had its drawback: the stuffing was often infested with bugs. Dave said many patrons went away from the theater scratching bites received from vermin in the folding seats. And yet another job that fell to the projectionist was the task of removing the ashes from the basement. The theater burned ninety tons of coal a year. At the end of the heating season, Dave had to shovel the ashes up to street level and haul them away. It was an all-day, back-breaking job. Nevertheless, Dave has a few good memories of his eight years as a projectionist. "I'll never forget this one film, *Rhapsody in Blue*," he said. "My sister came home from college at Christmas. It just happened to be playing at that particular time and she was going back to college and wanted to see it. So I ran that picture one night after the regular show just for her, the whole movie."

By 1950 it was evident there was no future in either the theater or Thomas. "I just stayed there until they cut it down to two or three nights a week," he said. "I knew I had to do something. . . . There just weren't any jobs there. There was nothing to do." When Howard Cosner announced that he was going to go to Ashtabula to get a job at Electromet, Dave decided to quit the theater and head north. "[Howard] said, 'How about going up to Ashtabula with me?'" Dave said. "We came up that same night in my Jeep." Howard's father rode with Dave to show him the way to Ohio. Howard, Dave's father and grandmother, and Howard's mother went in a separate car. Howard and Dave stayed in a small building on the VanKirk property until they could find jobs and get settled into apartments.

Dave felt no mountain roots holding him back. "I was ready for a change of scenery," he said. "I thought [northeast Ohio] was all right. There was lots of work here. . . . It was a nice little job. You could get a job here without having to know somebody." Three weeks after arriving in Ashtabula, Dave had his job—not at Electromet, but in the finishing department of Lake City Malleable. Dave said he was too small at 120 pounds to get a job at Electromet or National Distillers, both of which told him the work would be too hard for his small frame. Dave stayed at Lake City Malleable eighteen months, then set sail on the Great Lakes as a coal passer, shoveling coal out of the steamship's bunkers. Dave said the ship he worked on, the *Howard M. Hannah Jr.,* burned one and a half tons of coal an hour. For the coal at the rear of the bunker, Dave would have to shovel twice to get it in position for the fireman to feed into the firebox. That worked out to shoveling three tons of coal an hour, four hours straight. But that wasn't the end of the job. Dave also had to shovel the ashes into a box that emptied into the lake. "One and a half tons of coal an hour made a lot of ashes," Dave pointed out. "They shot them out into the lake. There was a lot of pollution back then."

"I didn't like sailing," Dave said. "I stayed with it during the season, but I didn't care to go back the next year." Instead, Dave returned to West Virginia, where he spent a year helping his father build a new home in Canaan Valley. But the employment situation in Tucker County had not changed, and Dave eventually came back to Ashtabula in search of work. He heard through his landlord's daughter that Lake Shore Gas was hiring, and he got a job in the meter repair shop there November 9, 1953.

A Registered Letter

Two years later, Dave wrote back to West Virginia and told Arvin Rumer about a job opening at Lake Shore Gas. Arvin knew Dave from working at the Sutton Theater and had kept in touch with him after Dave went to Ohio. While still in high school, Arvin had gone to Ohio with Dave in the summer of 1951 so he could work at Lake City Malleable. The dollar-an-hour wage tempted Arvin to stay in Ashtabula at the end of the summer rather than return to Thomas and finish high school. But his Thomas High buddies talked him into returning so they could play football together. He returned, played football, and graduated in 1952. Then he went back to Ashtabula and his job in the foundry. But after several weeks, Arvin became discouraged and homesick. "I wasn't making it," he said. "The room and eating out all the time were eating it up. I didn't have any money." He hitched a ride back home with Howard Cosner's mother and father and went to work for a farmer.

But after several months of hauling chickens twelve hours a day, Arvin was ready for new opportunities. When he received the registered letter from Dave, he settled his affairs and headed north to apply. "He told me if I was interested in a good job, East Ohio Gas was looking for a mechanically inclined person to work in the shop as a meter repairman," Arvin said. "They interviewed me and hired me on." Arvin worked long enough to get an apartment and money for a trip back home. Then he returned to get his bride, Lucy Porter, a Petersburg, West Virginia, native, whom he married May 20, 1955. It was the first time she had ever been away from home.

Life in Ashtabula was a bag of mixed blessings. Making friends was difficult at first, especially for Lucy, who was stuck at home while Arvin worked. Their first home, on West Forty-fourth Street, was near Ashtabula Bow Socket and the railroad tracks. The noise of the hammers and trains was maddening to a young woman who had grown up in a small town. "I just slept all the time, just to pass the time. I just slept and waited for the weekends," she said. The weekends were set aside for going home to visit her parents and seven siblings. Only one of them, Shelby Jean, who married Arvin's brother Alvin "Bub," followed them north. But they stayed only one year, 1956, then returned to West Virginia. The familial pressure for Arvin and Lucy to do the same was great—Arvin said his father-in-law tried to talk him into coming back and getting a tannery job. Arvin felt there was a better life in Ohio and stayed.

But the weekly trips became a severe drain on the couple's finances and 1951 Chevy. They left for "home" as soon as Arvin got off second shift Saturday night, arrived in West Virginia around six in the morning on Sunday, and left in time for Arvin to report to work Monday afternoon. Finally, when Lucy was seven months pregnant with their daughter, Diane, Arvin put their future on the line. "I told [Lucy] one weekend, if we go home this weekend, we'll stay and not come back. I came home from work that night, and the suitcase was unpacked," he said. "It was hard for us. You don't leave your roots easily."

Culture and Bluegrass

Arvin said making friends outside of work was difficult because many locals had a prejudice against mountain people. "I wasn't known and it wasn't easy to make friends," he said. "Once they found out you were from West Virginia, they didn't want to make buddies with you. They figured you were up here taking their jobs. But jobs were plentiful, all you had to do was open your mouth and you had a job." One of the best pieces of advice Arvin received on surviving in the northern culture came from Dick Sayers, another Thomas-area native, who had followed Dave Bennear to Ashtabula in 1951. "He told me, 'From now on, when they ask you where you're from, tell them Indiana or Illinois,'" Arvin said. "When you said you were a hillbilly, they tied you in with the very uneducated, low-energy people." Co-workers at the gas company provided the core group of friends for the couple. "Gordon Bovee, Tom Bancroft, Bill Allds, Don and Gatha Hill, Donald Dunne, Ralph and Pat Diemer," Arvin said, naming some of the locals who befriended them. "They were our main friends. I guess you'd call them an anchor."

Bluegrass music also became an anchor for Arvin. He learned to play the mandolin while living in Moorefield. "I was bored and couldn't make friends in that town," he said. "So I saw this mandolin in the Sears catalog and I ordered it. My brother-in-law, George Montgomery, was a good musician and he helped me learn to play it." In 1963, while working a second job at a service station, Arvin struck up a conversation with a customer who was on his way to play bluegrass music in Conneaut. Arvin said he had to ask what bluegrass was, but it wasn't long before he was picking tunes with Bill Adams and John Stump in Conneaut. "They taught me the bluegrass style of music," he said.

Working in bands like the Frontier Bluegrass Boys and Johnny Stump and the Flatlanders, Arvin played throughout Pennsylvania and Ohio for the next seventeen years. One of the bands he played in was invited to go to England and perform. Their largest audience, eight hundred, was in Butler, Pennsylvania. A car accident in 1980 resulted in disabilities that prevented

Arvin from playing the mandolin for any extended period. The accident also forced his retirement from the East Ohio Gas Company. But every New Year's Eve, Arvin takes his mandolin back to Bill Adams's house and jams into the early morning hours with Adams, Stump, and other northeast Ohio bluegrass artists. Their mountain strains rise above the frosty flat lands, mountain hearts and tunes united hundreds of miles away from the land that gave them and their music birth.

Eglon Childhood

Howard Cosner's recruitment efforts did not end with Dave Bennear and Arvin Rumer. There was still one more Thomas family to be transplanted: Carl Junior and Cossette Feather. Carl Junior (his name reflects the widespread mountaineer partiality for the name "Junior," without regard for whether there is a "Senior") was born in Eglon September 5, 1932, to Russel and Maud Feather. As third cousins, Carl Junior and Arvin Rumer grew up together and worked on their grandfathers' farms, which were on opposite sides of the road. Eglon was not as rustic or remote as many of the more southern West Virginia farming communities of the 1930s. The Feather farmhouse, birthplace of Carl Junior, had been built in the early 1930s and wired for electricity at the time of construction. Even so, lights were the only appliance running on electric power.

Cooking was done on a wood stove, which also heated water for household use. A wood stove in the living room heated the house. Refrigeration consisted of spring water running through a concrete trough in the basement. Milk and cheese were kept in the running water. Meat preservation was accomplished by sugar curing the hams and shoulders. The cured meat hung in the smokehouse until it was needed. "That meat was so salty, it was a wonder we didn't die from it," Carl said.

The community, located along Route 24, was entirely agricultural in its economy. Its only businesses were the Fike and Judy General Store, post office, and gristmill. An elementary school provided education until eighth grade, after which students had to go to Aurora High School. Russel Feather worked for Blands Lumber Yard in Aurora, driving a log truck. As the family grew—to a total of four children, Arnold, Carl Junior, Dorothy, and Shirley—so did the need for cash income. In the early 1940s, a barn raising

Eglon, West Virginia, the hometown of Carl Junior Feather, ca. 1978. The barn and farmhouse in the foreground belonged to Carl Junior's parents, Russel and Maud Feather. *Photo by Carl E. Feather*

was held. The first farm animal owned by the family, a pony, was used to excavate the foundation. A fine structure made from rough-sawed chestnut was built there. Chickens, pigs, and dairy cows were acquired to supply the staples of the family diet. "We used to have a big kettle of milk on the sink all the time," Carl said. "Mom would put vanilla and sugar in it. We had to drink that milk all the time and eat that homemade cheese. That's all we had." The steady diet of milk, butter, and cottage and other homemade cheeses during childhood alienated Carl from dairy products for the rest of his life. After he left home, he would never again spread butter on his bread or eat anything with cheese in it. Another family staple did not produce the same lifelong distaste. Both he and his father started their days with "coffee soup," homemade bread with coffee poured over it. "Dad lived off that," he said.

Nothing went to waste in the household. Fat rendered from meat by cooking was poured from the frying pan into a jar and saved for the next meal. The fat was substituted for margarine, creating a high-cholesterol, high-fat diet. "Everything we ate had grease on it," he said. Surplus milk was sold to Carnation Milk in Oakland, Maryland. Carl's job was to milk the four cows before and after school. "Saturday's we'd clean out the barn," he said. His uncle Guy Feather drove a truck for Carnation and stopped at the farm every day to pick up the milk. Farm work was done with a team of horses borrowed from his grandfather and grandmother, James and Estella Feather. It was not until after both boys had left the farm that Russel had his first tractor, an Allis-Chalmers, to help with the farm work. The farm was not totally unmechanized as they were growing up, however. A 1936 Ford with a rope attached to it was used to operate the hay fork that raised the hay from the wagons to the haymow, the loft area of the barn where the loose hay was stored.

Carl's first paying job was working for his uncle, Clifford Feather, who owned a hay baler. He contracted with farmers to bale their hay, and Carl worked for him on Saturdays, pitching, stacking, and tying bales. A Jeep pulled the baler, which was driven by a power take off, a belt that ran from the engine of the Jeep to a shaft with pulleys on it. His second paying job was at the Ford garage in Oakland. He started there in the summer of 1949, washing cars and doing detail work. He advanced to pumping gas and by the summer of his senior year was working in the garage as a mechanic. He graduated from high school in the spring of 1951 and went to work at the garage full time. Six months later, he followed his brother's lead and entered the navy. A train took him from Cumberland, Maryland, to boot camp at Bainbridge, Maryland. He recalls boot camp as being particularly hard on the men in his company. Of the thirty or so who entered with him, only seven graduated. "There was so much sickness, they dropped out," he said. His entire four years were spent aboard the U.S.S. *Tutulia* AR64, a repair ship that sailed out of Portsmouth, Virginia.

He and Cossette, sweethearts from high school days, were married at Red House, Maryland, April 20, 1952. They set up housekeeping in an attic apartment in Portsmouth. Their son, Carl Eugene, was born at the Portsmouth Naval Hospital in 1954.

A Tenacious Transplant

Carl Junior was discharged from the navy in 1956. "I could have gone right back to work at the Ford garage—probably should have," he said. "But Howard said Union Carbide was hiring, so we came up and I got a job." Carl recalls his mother being very angry with him for leaving for Ohio. He was the only one of the four children to go to Ohio. His older sister married and headed south with her career navy husband; his brother and younger sister moved across the state line to Oakland, Maryland.

Cossette remembers it as being late January or early February when they first came to Ashtabula County. They stayed with the Cosners, who were renting the upstairs of a house on Main Street in Kingsville. The next day Carl applied at Electromet and was given a job. Then they went looking for a place to live. They stopped at Bob Swanson's store and were referred to Fox's apartment house on Priest Street. They paid their forty-dollar first month's rent and returned to West Virginia to pack their belongings—a sofa, two chairs, blond bedroom suite, baby bed, and miscellaneous tables Carl had made while aboard ship. His uncle, Artenis Harsh, moved them in his milk delivery truck. "We left down there at midnight and got here at six in the morning," Cossette said. Carl reported for work and got one of the worst surprises of his life. "They gave me another hearing test and told me I had perforated ear drums," he said. "They told me my hearing wouldn't last a year with all the noise that was at Union Carbide. I should have gotten in the car and gone back the other way."

Stuck in a strange town with no jobs and only a couple of acquaintances, Carl began driving the streets of Ashtabula in his '49 Ford looking for work. He found a job installing windows and doors for Peter A. Bodnar, Ashtabula Aluminum Products. The family stayed, but it was a tenacious, uncomfortable transplant that was repeatedly tugged from its loose soil and replanted with every trip back home. "This was one of the most unfriendly places I ever lived in my life," Cossette recalled. "It seemed like the people were so snotty. They acted like you had some kind of disease, like they didn't want someone from West Virginia living around them. These people here were so unfriendly, I just stayed in and made two quilts when we lived in Fox's apartment—a little fishing boy quilt and a red rose applique quilt." But Carl and Cossette put down roots into the community, regardless of the reception. In 1958 they moved from their Priest Street apartment and purchased "the little house on the hill" on Wright Street. One of the modifications they made to the property was to erect a rail fence along the property line, a singular reminder of the rural life they knew in West Virginia.

Carl lost his job with Bodnar the same month, another omen that the transplant still might not take. He went to the unemployment office, how-

Children of Thomas (left to right): Howard and Virginia Cosner; Carl Junior and Cossette Feather; Arvin and Lucy Rumer. *Photo by Carl E. Feather*

ever, and found a job with Niven Hoefert, Weather Rite Manufacturing, an aluminum storm window contractor. Carl learned how to custom build aluminum storm windows and doors by day; at night and on weekends he gutted and remodeled the old house.

But the storm window business was not steady work, and Carl continued to apply for factory jobs around the city. The economy was slowing, however, and the job market was not what it had been ten or even five years before. Arvin Rumer and Dave Bennear had both gone to work for Lake Shore Gas by that time, and they kept Carl posted on job openings there. In early 1962 an opening came up in the maintenance garage and Carl applied for it. Weeks passed without any word on the opening, then one of the mechanics died suddenly. Arvin saw Rolland B. Pinkston, superintendent of operations, in the lunchroom one day and asked him if they'd found someone for the position. "I told him I had a cousin who was looking for a job," Arvin said. "I told him he was a religious man, didn't drink, didn't smoke, and was a good family man. And he said, 'Sounds like the man we could use.'" Carl started at the gas company on Washington's Birthday 1962 and worked there thirty years. He was hired to gas and wash the fleet, but quickly advanced to mechanic and eventually fleet mechanic in charge of the entire garage. His hard work, conscientiousness, and excellence as a mechanic became legendary at the Ashtabula plant and won him awards from the corporation and the respect of all who worked with him.

Cossette also got a job, working at Kingsville Elementary School as a playground aide from 1968 to 1981. They transformed their Wright Street home into a showcase of carpentry and landscaping. Their flower gardens, Cossette's collections of glassware, dolls, and figurines, and Carl's mechanical and woodworking skills make the home an attraction for acquaintances, who stop in frequently. Most of all, it is a home where mountain hospitality is still practiced forty years after the Feathers left Thomas.

During the 1960s the home was a gathering place for Dave, Lucy, Arvin and their children. Thanksgiving, Christmas, and Easter dinners as well as weekend visits around a pot of coffee and stacks of homemade cookies were rituals. With time, the roots of each migrant family grew deeper into Kingsville and Ashtabula and the trips back home became less and less frequent.

Home, the Price of Success

Four decades have passed since the children of Thomas came to Ohio. Howard Cosner retired from Union Carbide in 1988, after working his way up the ladder from the furnace room to paymaster, administrative assistant, and shipping coordinator. One of his retirement projects was co-ownership of a furniture store, D&G Furniture, in Kingsville, and he maintains a fine home and good-sized garden. A large woodworking shop keeps him busy in the winter. Virginia is well known around the community for her excellence as a quilt maker and waitress. "I've poured coffee and bull-crapped all over town," she quips. Their two children, Donnie and Darlene, pursued careers in Texas.

Arvin Rumer spends his summers fishing with other mountaineer outdoorsmen like Dave Alley, Red Herron, and Glenn Gatrell. Several times a year, he returns to West Virginia to visit relatives and in-laws and to hunt and fish. He and Lucy have three children, Diane, Kevin, and Greg, all of whom live in Ashtabula County.

These migrants have proven themselves by their works and friendships, as all migrants must do. Their houses and yards are neat, well maintained, and comfortable; they speak of material success and pride of ownership. Yet they are split on their affections for the new land. Howard Cosner and Dave Bennear have found all they wanted in Ohio. "This Ashtabula treated us a lot better than Thomas, West Virginia, ever could have," Dave said. There is no reason or desire to return to the mountains. But there is a sense of deep longing, sometimes regret, in the words of Carl and Cossette, Arvin and Lucy.

Perhaps more so for the women than their husbands, for they spent their prime years often staying at home in a strange land without transportation, family, or childhood acquaintances. Their initial mistrust of northern, urban culture and its accompanying unfriendliness has changed little from that night in the late 1950s when they were motoring through North Kingsville on Lake Road. Lucy, Cossette, Carl Eugene, and Diane were in the back seat of the Feathers' car; Carl Junior was driving; Arvin was a passenger in the front seat. They came upon a stranded motorist, and Carl stopped and got out of the car to offer help. He misunderstood what the man said to him— "Do you want to make something of it?" is what the women thought the motorist asked. "We thought the guy wanted fight," Cossette said. "So we started shouting 'Go Junior, go. Get us out of here!'" He jumped in the car and sped away, no doubt leaving the stranded motorist wondering about the supposed southern hospitality of Appalachia's latest arrivals.

The migrants still get together to talk about former days. They dip Cossette's homemade peanut butter and molasses cookies into cups of hot coffee, although not as frequently and excessively as they did thirty years ago. The men talk of their gas company days; the women of the bleak weather, the latest rash of Ashtabula crime, the cold strangers, and strange attitudes they've encountered in the flatlands. Cossette and Lucy still feel unwelcome in the north and often long to go back to the Henry, Thomas, or Petersburg of their childhood and youth. They see the North as a clique into which one is born but never grafted. They would go back to their mountains, but things have changed there, too. Mothers, fathers gone; sisters, brothers scattered; childhood homes sold and neglected. Today, there is no trace of their families left on the mountain. The children of Thomas have gone north.

But the mountains remain, and the memories created there just a few days past yesterday. Some days, most days, these transplanted mountain folk believe that those memories and mountains would be enough to sustain them until they migrate to an eternal home. Regardless of the material wealth earned and accumulated in the North, there remains in these mountaineer women's hearts a huge, empty chamber that longs for the company of kin and homeplace.

"I wanted to stay there so bad, I just loved being there," Cossette says. "We made our big mistake by staying here."

So why did they leave? "I don't know," Carl says, looking out his kitchen window at the dreary, wintry Ashtabula County sky.

16 montani semper liberi

daniel gillespie: trading freedom for work

From Scotland to Greenbrier Mountain

Daniel Gillespie is a mountain man. Standing six feet plus a few inches with his leather boots on, Dan is comfortable in his brown and tan plaid shirt and blue jeans. He is dressed for the outdoors and its freedoms. His silver and black hair is pulled back in a short ponytail; his mostly gray, short beard is neatly trimmed. He is muscular, yet softspoken, with a hint of West Virginian heritage in his deep voice.

An unfinished western paperback lies on the stand next to his tan easy chair. The large living room with its blue carpet and dark paneling is heated with an airtight wood stove, vented to a stone fireplace painted black. Sparse woods surround his house, which Dan reckons to be more than 140 years old. He has remodeled it with vinyl siding and a large natural wood front porch. One might imagine Dan sitting on that porch with a hunting dog at one side and rifle on the other, relaxing after a day of tramping through the hills.

But Dan's home is on Lake Road in North Kingsville, not Greenbrier Mountain, West Virginia. He has not lived in the mountains since 1956, when he came to Ashtabula County to visit an uncle and ended up getting a job. A wife, children, and a house followed. Obligations, Dan calls them. They have kept him from going back.

Dan is a smart man. The words he speaks belie his tenth-grade education, and Dan can strike up a conversation on just about any subject. He reads a lot—history books, mostly. He is fascinated with the history of his family, which originated in Scotland. He's been told some of his ancestors were knights in the Crusades. He is more certain of his family's history in the New World. Hugh Gillespie surveyed the Greenbrier, West Virginia, area in 1735; Hugh's brother, Jacob, came in 1745 through Philadelphia. Dan traces his lineage through Jacob, although there are gaps in the first hundred years or so after he came to Greenbrier County.

This he knows for sure: his great-grandfather, James, served in Virginia's Seventeenth Cavalry. Prior to the Civil War, the Gillespie family was prosperous. They raised horses and had more than two hundred of them on the Wild Meadows area in present-day Greenbrier County. But frequent raids on the herd, including by James, whose horses kept getting shot out from under him, obliterated the herd and destined the family to a century of subsistence farming. James was shot in the knee and spent more than two and a half years in a Union prison near Columbus, Ohio. Nine decades later, his great-grandson returned to Ohio as a free man in search of work. North and South were reconciled in Dan's family tree: although Dan's maternal ancestors had fought for the Union, love and marriage brought the Gillespies and Perrys, Confederate and Union, together.

His maternal grandparents, Tipsy Ned and Minerva Lee (Coulter) Perry, had a 250-acre farm atop Greenbrier Mountain. Dan was born on that mountain, January 14, 1935, to John Daniel and Hazel Irene (Perry) Gillespie. He had two siblings, George and Gloria Ann (Withrow).

"The Happiest Time of My Life"

Dan's first fourteen years were divided between his family's farm in White Sulphur Springs District and his grandparents' farm. The 250-acre farm owned by his parents provided the family with vegetables, grains, and meat needed to survive the Depression and war years. There were two house on the property, the one Dan's family lived in and his uncle's. There was no electricity or running water. Dan didn't get those conveniences until he left Greenbrier County. It didn't matter; the mountains more than compensated. "We really didn't have any money," Dan said. "But we ate better than we do now. We ate healthier, too."

School was five and a half miles away in White Sulphur Springs, a health resort area with a population of about 2,500, well known for its luxury resort, The Greenbrier. Just about everyone in Greenbrier County worked there. "To most families around there, The Greenbrier meant the difference between hard times and making it," Dan said. It was no different for the Gillespies. Dan, his brother-in-law, father, and cousins worked at The Greenbrier at one time or another. But Dan learned how to work on the farm—chores that build muscle and character, feed the stomach, and fuel the will for a better life. "I largely took care of the garden," Dan said. "Back then, I thought it was drudgery, now I wish I could go back and do it again." His grandfather's cornfield was a mile long. It would take a half day to hoe one row, but at the end was a dip in the swimming hole and a hearty meal. "It was the happiest time of my life," he said.

The Gillespie family found both spiritual and social life at church. "We kids went to church all the time," Dan said. "That was more or less our social hall. We had two churches, Episcopal and Methodist. But there wasn't any denominational ties. We'd switch back and forth. A lot of times, the crowd would go to the Episcopal church and then walk up the street to the Methodist church."

Recreation was simple and healthful in Greenbrier County. "We had the whole mountain for recreation," he said. "On a farm like that, you could always find something to do. The neighbor kids would get together and play football, baseball. Not through school, just in the neighborhood. And we'd play cowboys and Indians. We pretty much had the run of the hills around there when we were kids. We learned early in life how to watch for snakes and not to do the things we were told not to do." Once a year, Dan left his mountain home and traveled to church camp in Romney in West Virginia's eastern panhandle. That was as far away from home as Dan ever ventured until he left for Ohio.

As a teenager Dan spent Saturday evenings at the theater in White Sulphur Springs—if he cared to walk the eleven-mile round trip. He earned his spending money helping a friend cut pulpwood on Saturdays. "I earned four or five dollars a day," he said. "One summer, I made enough to buy a bicycle."

Changing Times

John Gillespie sold his farm in the late 1940s and moved his family to an eight-acre homestead. He was working for The Greenbrier, and there was neither the need nor the time to manage a large farm. Two years later Dan hired on with the groundskeeping crew at The Greenbrier. It was hard, outdoor work, enjoyable to Dan, as enjoyable as any job he's had. "I wish I could go back to that job and make the money I make today," he said.

He completed one more year of high school, then on an overcast morning in November he and his dad boarded the Greyhound bus for Ashtabula. Two of his father's brothers and their wives were already in Ashtabula: Harry and Ruby and Joe and Euna. Joe opened his home to their kin. Joe's son, Bob, a supervisor at Ashtabula Hide and Leather, arranged jobs for them. Dan's first impression of Ashtabula was "dark, gloomy." "I was very homesick," he said. Nevertheless, on Monday morning the two men reported to their jobs at the tannery. "At seventeen, I could care less where I worked," he said. "To me, it was just an adventure." The tannery was a foul, dirty place frequently cited as one of the major polluters of the Ashtabula River. Dan's job was in the shipping department and consisted of driving a truck to the railroad depot where raw hides were loaded and hauled back to the tannery. "It was hard, stinking work," he said. "The first time I walked in there, I wanted to vomit. But you'd get where you could climb up on top of that stack of hides and sit down and eat your lunch."

The $1.25-an-hour wage was not a big improvement over The Greenbrier, and the working conditions were definitely worse. After six weeks in Ashtabula, Dan and his father bid farewell to Ohio. His father never returned. "My dad was one of those people who couldn't give West Virginia up," he said. "He never liked Ohio. He used to say he never lost anything in Ohio."

John Gillespie went back to his job at The Greenbrier. Dan enlisted in the army. The Korean Conflict was raging and two of his buddies had already been claimed by the Communists: one killed and the other a prisoner of war. That was enough to stir the fighting spirit in Dan. He trained in the airborne division to replace the 187th Combat Team. After graduation from jump school, the men got their orders to go to Korea. But the war ended before Dan could get there, and he finished his stint at Fort Bragg in the 82nd Airborne.

An army friend promised Dan a job driving truck for his father's company in Seattle if he could wait just six months after being discharged. Dan passed the time working at The Greenbrier, then headed back to Ashtabula to visit with his uncles before moving west. "The visit lasted and lasted," Dan said. "Pretty soon, I had too many obligations and I couldn't leave." Dan stayed at his Uncle Joe's house on Lake Avenue, Ashtabula, and applied for

Daniel Gillespie in his North Kingsville, Ohio, home. *Photo by Carl E. Feather*

a job at Union Carbide. The firm had recently opened a titanium plant and was looking for workers, lots of them. Three days after arriving in Ashtabula, October 18, 1956, Dan went to work there, along with several hundred other new employees. A year later, they were furloughed. "We were all at the bottom of the seniority list and were out the door," he said.

Going back to West Virginia didn't occur to Dan. He had obligations in Ashtabula now, and he had met the woman who would become his wife, Juanita Andrego. Born in Gary, West Virginia, the daughter of a second-generation Russian/Austrian immigrant, Juanita had migrated to Ohio with her parents and grandparents as a young girl. Her family had lived in Cleveland a while, then moved to West Virginia to work in the coal fields during the Depression. She grew up on a farm in Plymouth Township.

Dan said it was tough finding steady work in Ashtabula in the late 1950s. He plowed snow for Plymouth Township and worked construction in Erie, Pennsylvania. But he quit when the firm wanted him to move to Kentucky to work on a big church job. In 1962 he found work with Inland Container on Benefit Avenue. Two years later, Dan and Juanita purchased their home in North Kingsville. It was a bank repossession, so badly neglected that Dan had to cut two years' worth of overgrowth from the yard. He's made a fine country home of it.

Dan figured he'd have a job for life at Inland, but the factory closed in the late 1970s. Three years later he got steady work with Stone Container in Jefferson. He plans to retire from there. Will he go back to West Virginia then? No, he says. Too many obligations, too many things to hold him down. But he will return every summer for a couple of weeks, to hike in the woods and maybe shoot a squirrel or two, and every November, for hunting season. Mostly, he just hikes around the woods. Dan doesn't believe in shooting a deer unless its rack is eight points or more. It's been a few years since Dan shot a buck.

Sometimes Dan wonders what his life would have been if he'd stayed in West Virginia, gone to Seattle, or become an army career man. This he knows: life in West Virginia would have offered more freedom than he's experienced in Ashtabula County. In Ohio he can't walk out his door and enter a world of mountains, deer, forests, rattlesnakes, solitude, and childhood memories. Like his great-grandfather who was incarcerated in the Union prison there more than a century ago, Dan doesn't feel like a free man in Ohio. He's a prisoner of obligations, no trespassing signs, and the busy highway that passes just a few yards from his front porch.

"If I could live my life over again, I probably never would have left," he muses, sitting on the edge of a large, upholstered chair in his living room. "You had so much freedom there that you don't have here."

As the West Virginia state motto says: *Montani semper liberi*—Mountaineers are always free.

17 going home for good

mountain retirement home

Homesickness

EMMA BONHAM greeted garage-sale shoppers and tallied their purchases while her husband Ralph answered questions about the golf clubs spread across the driveway of their Saybrook Township bungalow. Boxes containing the couple's seven decades of material acquisitions were stacked in the living room, kitchen, and garage, awaiting the rental truck's arrival. Out front, a "For Sale" sign with a big "SOLD" notice completed the story: the Bonhams, after forty-two years of living in Ashtabula County, were selling out and moving back to West Virginia.

"I never did really think about going back," Ralph said. "I didn't think I could do it financially, and so forth. But I had an aunt die . . . and I wasn't able to get back for the funeral. And I just got to thinking, 'How many more are going to die without me being able to go back?'" Another sad event confirmed their decision. The Bonhams' oldest son, Ralph Jackson "Jack," died suddenly in January 1997. Jack had always wanted to return to West Virginia, where he was born and spent much of his childhood. But after a career in the navy, he and his wife decided to make Florida their retirement home. Jack was buried in West Virginia, however. And for Ralph and Emma, to be in their home state, near the soil where their son rests, was just one more reason for leaving Ohio on July 25, 1997.

They first arrived in Ashtabula on Labor Day weekend 1955—in an Archway Cookies truck. Ralph became a sub-distributor of cookies in 1954, following a layoff from DuPont and a short run as a produce delivery man for his friend Tom Moore. "The store owners kept telling me I was going to get a good job," Ralph said. "And one day, this man come to my home and offered me this cookie route. I said I only got a station wagon, and he said I'd have to have a truck—and he'd sell me one. I paid for it a penny for every package of cookies I sold." Ralph said he paid off that truck, a three-quarter-ton International panel truck, and purchased a one-ton Chevrolet with a bank loan. He took the larger truck to Akron and had the Archway logo painted on it.

But business began to slow after a year on the route, which covered three southern West Virginia counties. Ralph paid twenty-three cents for a package of cookies and sold them for twenty-eight. After deducting his gas, truck payments, maintenance, and returned products, Ralph figured he wasn't getting ahead on a nickel a package. So he came up with the idea of selling candy and potato chips as well. "I told [the distributor] I was going to put candy bars on that truck," Ralph said. "And he said, 'No, you're not putting nothing on that truck with my cookies.' But I told him it was my truck and I was going to do it. He told me no again, but I went ahead and got some potato chips and stuff, and the next thing I knew, he was doing the same thing."

But the extra product lines didn't make the business profitable, and Ralph began looking at other options. His brother-in-law, Leroy Young, had come home from Ashtabula and told him about job opportunities up north. "He'd come down to visit us and said they were hiring over to the Electromet," Ralph said. "I told him when he got back up there to find out if there were any jobs open. He let me know there were, and I loaded my cookie truck up with my family and they hired me the next day after I came." Ralph brought his wife, three children—Jack, Pauletta Ann, and Jenny Lynn—and two dogs to Ohio in the three-quarter-ton truck. "I put a rod across the back of the truck and hung our clothes on there," he said. He told the distributor, whom Ralph describes as one of the happiest men he's ever known, that he was quitting the route and moving to Ohio. "I had three thousand packages of cookies to sell back to him," Ralph said. "He just whistled and paid me for them."

Ralph didn't tell his mother he was going to Ohio. Family members who knew about his plans tried to discourage him from going. On the way to Ashtabula Ralph and Emma passed one of his brothers, who was returning to the Mountain State after a visit in Ohio. Ralph and his brother turned off,

Ken Lewis checking his oil before a trip back to Greenbrier County, West Virginia. *Photo by Carl E. Feather*

pulled onto the berm, and talked for a while. Ralph was tempted to just turn around and go back with his brother—but he continued north. When his brother got home, he told his mother where Ralph had gone and predicted he'd be back in about a month. Ralph came back, all right, but it was to fill the one-ton truck with furniture and belongings. Another man followed him north in his station wagon. Ralph said he had only one set of license plates between the two trucks, and he swapped them back and forth, depending on which truck he was driving. When all possessions were finally in Ohio, he sold the Chevy to pay off his loan and traded the International to the gas company man for a cooking stove. That was the end of Ralph's cookie business, and for the next forty-two years, he and Emma made their home in Ashtabula.

A second son, David Kenneth, was born in Ohio in 1960. "Jack never did adjust too well here," Emma said. "The kids didn't like it here." The relatives who served as the Ashtabula link for the Bonhams, Leroy and Margaret Young (one of Emma's sisters), had come in the late 1940s. Two other sisters followed, Rachael Massey and Laura Mae Garrett, both of whom married local men—Tony Callipair and Steve Esposito, respectively. But Ralph's family could not be coaxed northward. Ralph said his brothers and sister often visited them and made the lakeshore a vacation spot. But living in the Charleston area provided sufficient employment opportunities for Ralph's brothers. The lure of the North Coast was limited to its good fishing.

The couple purchased and remodeled a series of residences and investment homes. Ralph, who started in the carbide packing department at Electromet, became a pipe fitter and worked on the maintenance gang at Union Carbide Metals. He gave the Electromet twenty-eight years of his life and a river of sweat. The children grew up, went to college, married, and moved away from Ashtabula County, which could no longer offer the job opportunities their father had found.

Leroy and Margaret Young left the area; Rachael and Tony passed away. Only Laura Mae and Steve—and the couple's church family at Ashtabula's First Baptist Church—remained for them. "I guess the main thing that kept us up here was the church," Ralph said, as they planned their move. "They're the best," Emma added, surveying all the households goods that would soon be on a truck—this time a Ryder rental—and on their way to Belle, West Virginia.

In the spring of 1997 packing was also on the minds of Herschel Blevins, the Kentucky migrant who brought the gift of mountain music to Ashtabula County. Herschel and his wife Linda moved to Olga Hollow, McDowell, Kentucky, near the Floyd County homeplace where Herschel grew up. Linda said they decided to give it a try after visiting the mountains for a week and noting an improvement in their health and dispositions. "I like it pretty well down there," Linda said. "The people are so nice."

Herschel is much more emphatic about his move. "I feel better now than I've felt since I was working for the railroad back in '62," said Herschel as he sprinted across a field at a July 1997 northeast Ohio bluegrass gathering. "You get me down in those mountains and I'm just like a young goat, all over them."

Herschel said he felt called back to Kentucky by a force, and once he got there he realized that God had a mission for him in Kentucky: to help a dying friend through his last days. Herschel found his friend in a restaurant shortly after arriving in Pike County, and for the next two months he provided his ministry of prayer, companionship, and song. Although that friend is gone, there are many more childhood buddies and distant family members in those hills. Herschel's having the time of his life rediscovering them and the countryside.

"Now my family is raised, they have their home and families," Herschel said. "I feel my work is done, so I'm heading back to Kentucky once more."

Maurice Osburn, the brother of Kedron native Jean Hornbeck, made the move back to West Virginia in 1971, after spending twenty years at Union Carbide. "I guess I just got to the point where I couldn't take so much dust in that plant and all the work," he said. Maurice, who was the highest-paid hourly employee in the plant at the time he left, said he was working forty hours plus getting ten to fifteen call-outs on overtime every week. He also operated a radio and television repair shop as a service to older people. Maurice, his wife Norma Jean, and two sons moved back to Buckhannon, and he found a job there on the construction crew of a plastic pipe plant. He said the electrician skills he learned in Ohio made him employable in West Virginia. "I was really fortunate at Electromet," he said. "I got to work with guys who showed me how to do anything I wanted to learn."

While finding work was not a problem, creating a new life after being gone for twenty years was. "We got back and all our friends had gone too," he said. "It was a hard decision to make and I regretted it several times. And other times I didn't know if I had made a mistake or not." The fact that his wife's family still lived around Buckhannon and that the Osburns had two children at home helped make the transition smoother. "We decided to stick it out," he said. "Now, it's home again. I just love to hunt and fish here and get out in the country and roam the hillsides."

The Magnet: Mountains and Kin

Herschel, Linda, Ralph, Emma, Maurice, and Norma Jean are exceptions for the generation that moved from the mountains to the flatlands in the 1940s and 1950s. Most of the migrants, with family transplanted and new friends established in northeast Ohio, remain even though the economic necessity that drew them to Ohio is no longer a requisite for staying. Philip J. Obermiller, in his introduction to *Down Home, Downtown: Urban Appalachians Today*, notes that the most of the Appalachian families succeeded in overcoming the social and economic barriers they found in the northern cities and were either assimilated or became bicultural. Many of the families became anchored to the cities by their descendants, who also found jobs in the strong economies. The authors of *Mountain Families in Transition* noted that the Kentucky migrants had exhibited a pattern of gradual upward mobility over the years and had done well for themselves. Most of them were employed and at reasonably high wages.[1] The overwhelming majority of the men surveyed said they were "satisfied" with their jobs. But that does not mean that the nostalgic tug of home and the mountains on the migrants' hearts has been severed. "Nostalgia, it seems, is something most migrants have learned to cope with and perhaps have internalized into a dimension of their personality. Although they may be unable to overcome the nagging feeling of being more at home in the mountains, that aspect of deprivation is more than compensated for by the material advantages they have attained and enjoy in the area of destination."[2] But John D. Photiadis, in his study of Cleveland migrants, discovered that 59 percent of the Appalachian study group and 42 percent of the suburban migrants wanted to retire to West Virginia, despite their satisfaction with economic achievement in Ohio.[3]

O. Norman Simpkins notes in *Mountain Heritage* that the mountaineers' love of homeplace and kin is what drew them back on weekends and holidays. "They love the hills and every holiday is marked by the number of cars with out-of-state license plates back in the community returning to visit home

Emma and Ralph Bonham sold their Saybrook Township home in the summer of 1997 and moved to Belle, West Virginia, after living in Ohio more than four decades. *Photo by Carl E. Feather*

and kin. They just get lonesome for home. They gotta go back and see the old 'homeplace.' They seem to be tied to the hills long after they leave the area."[4]

Most migrants without the means to purchase and maintain a mountain vacation home must be content with a couple of nights in a mountain cabin or motel several times a year, or a standing invitation from a sibling, cousin, or elderly parent. Many have standing dates for a reunion, deer or turkey hunting, or community festival. Increasingly, trips back home are for a family medical emergency or funeral. Regardless of the itinerary, the underlying reason for every trip taken can be summed up in two words: home and kin. "It's a magnet," Arvin Rumer said. "It almost brings tears to my eyes." Like most transplanted mountaineers Arvin frequently returns to the mountains to camp, hunt, fish, and relax. The West Virginia he returns home to has changed dramatically—many of his relatives have passed away and child-hood friends found lives beyond the ragged boundaries of the state. But one thing remains unchanged—the matchless scenery and serenity of the mountains. "It's just like the song says," according to Ken Lewis, the migrant from White Sulphur Springs: "It's 'almost heaven.'"

"I always will say I enjoy the scenery down there," Dave Bennear said. "I like the hills." But Dave has no reason to return to Thomas. "I haven't been back since 1991," he said. "I don't have a reason to go back. I don't know hardly anybody there. My Dad died and that made a difference."

Della Forinash, who is well into her eighties, still tries to get back to West Virginia once a year to attend the Forinash reunion. Despite the hard times she had there, Della retains a deep appreciation for the beauty of that country and for family members who once roamed the hills with her. "I like to go back to visit, but to live there—no," she said.

Lester and Mabel Herron have established good lives for themselves in Ashtabula County. Lester is retired from Union Carbide and raises one of the biggest retail crops of pumpkins to be found in this area. "My family all lives here. I don't even think about moving there," Lester said. But he still returns to the mountains around Buckhannon to do much of his hunting and fishing. "I own a trailer down there," he said. "We go back there all the time to hunt and fish. . . . I have a lot of friends that go down there with me."

Glenn Gatrell owns forty-five acres in his native Tyler County, West Virginia. He goes back as often as every two weeks in fair weather. It's a place for him to get away and camp, to appreciate the present and recall his past. But it is increasingly difficult to find any physical mementoes of the childhood he knew there. The family farm and those around it are neglected and covered with undergrowth. Except for a cousin, there's no one down there from his family—they all moved to Ohio or died. "I guess it's the wide open spaces I miss down there," he said. "The peace and quiet. But I wouldn't want to go back there and live. All my children are here."

Don and Opal Booth used to go back to Elkins, West Virginia, every four weeks during their first few years in Ohio. But now he makes just a couple of trips each summer to check on his land. His father left him thirty-three acres of Don's grandfather's farm. It's hardwood forest, near the large timber operation of the former Moore and Kepple Company (chapter 7) that turned out twenty-five thousand board feet of lumber every eight hours. Men worked two shifts on that sawmill, the largest hardwood mill east of the Mississippi. But today the land is a place for Don to walk around and remember. He's had offers to cut the timber; Don could make a lot of money if he did that. But Don says he doesn't need the money, so he leaves the trees for another generation.

Greenbrier County migrant Robert Viers calculates that he has made at least a hundred trips back to West Virginia since coming to Ohio in 1945.

Two trips a year, guaranteed—Easter and state fair time. Funerals, reunions, and vacations add to the count. A handful of relatives, including two aunts, an uncle, and a half sister, keep him in touch with the mountains. Although he has no plans to move there, he also has no plans to stop going back as long as he is able.

"I have a feeling of being mothered by the mountains," Bob says. "They protect me when I get in them. I feel great security in the mountains."

Notes

1. For a thorough discussion of how migrants fared in Ohio Valley towns, see Harry K. Schwarzweller, James S. Brown, and J. J. Mangalam, *Families in Transition: A Case Study of Appalachian Migration* (University Park: The Pennsylvania State University Press, 1971). It is significant that the researchers found that, of the Beech Creek migrants studied, about 18 percent achieved skilled, clerical, or professional status and 60 percent were semi-skilled workers. Only 19.2 percent were working in unskilled labor. Very few of the migrants ended up on welfare or other public assistance, dispelling a popular stereotype of migrant mountaineers.

2. Ibid., 130–31. The authors noted that Beech Creek families made 3.4 visits per year, or excluding the 23 percent who did not return to visit, 4.5 visits were made per family per year. A survey of the migrants showed that 23 percent of them were "chronically homesick."

3. John D. Photiadis, *Selected Social and Sociopsychological Characteristics of West Virginians in Their Own State and in Cleveland* (Morgantown: West Virginia University and Office of Manpower Research, U.S. Department of Labor, 1975), 91.

4. O. Norman Simpkins, "Culture," in *Mountain Heritage,* ed. B. B. Mauer (Parsons, W. Va.: McClain Printing, 1980), 44. Simpkins, who was chairman of the Department of Sociology and Anthropology at Marshall University, also notes that many of the migrants live out their retirement years in the north, but arrange to be buried in West Virginia. This pattern is represented in the Ashtabula County migrants, as a regular reading of the local obituaries will bear out. However, many of the migrants interviewed for this book indicated that they had already made burial arrangements in northeast Ohio cemeteries.

18 "god love you"

bittersweet homecoming

WE'RE GOING HOME. When I was growing up in Kingsville Township, Ohio, those words spoken at the dinner table meant that we would be traveling to a magical place three hundred miles and eight hours away—West Virginia. Although my parents had made a good living for themselves in Ohio with a job, a house, and several acres of suburban land, our hearts' home remained in the mountains of Tucker and Preston Counties where my grandparents, aunts, and uncles lived. Ohio was never "home."

In my earliest recollections of conversations between my parents and other migrant mountaineers, "going home" was the most frequent topic. Every weekend, holiday, or vacation, we or other migrant families we knew were beating that long path back to the mountains. This was before the days of Interstates 79, 77, and 68, which have cut travel time from northeast Ohio to West Virginia to three or four hours. In the 1950s and '60s, the trip home was an eight-hour adventure made on a thread of two-lane state and federal highways, except for about sixty-five miles on the Pennsylvania Turnpike, which was always under construction.

Many of the trips were brief: down on Friday night, back on Sunday afternoon. We left as soon as Dad got home from work, five or six in the evening. The suitcases were packed and waiting at the door. There were bags filled with freshly baked peanut butter cookies, my maternal grandfather's favorite, and the shopping we'd done for relatives back home. Prices were lower and selection greater in Ashtabula than in Thomas.

I slept off and on as the yellow sunset gave way to a silver moonrise that illuminated the highway markers flying past Dad's black '63 Ford Falcon. Our first stop was usually to get a cup of coffee or chocolate milk at a Howard Johnson's on the turnpike. Somewhere along U.S. 40, we'd stop for our late-night dinner. The Hopwood Restaurant at the foot of Uniontown Mountain in southern Pennsylvania had won our trade for their burgers and fries. A sign over the serving counter, "Cows may come and cows may go, but in this place, the BULL goes on forever," fascinated me long before I understood its meaning.

If the Hopwood was closed, we'd continue over Uniontown Mountain and stop at the Lone Star Restaurant near the Pennsylvania/Maryland border. It catered to the truck traffic along the lonely National Road and was open all night. I was usually asleep by the time we reached the Lone Star. Dad roused me to "get a bite to eat," and I crawled out of my backseat lair into the cool, foggy night air of the mountains. The mist was exhilarating— an ethereal brew of dew, diesel fumes, frying burgers, and semi-truck exhaust that I still associate with those childhood pilgrimages. "Four Walls" played on the jukebox as we slid into the puffy, red-upholstered seats sticky from the mountain air and pancake syrup. A blur of semis and migrant traffic heading south zoomed past the plateglass windows while we waited for our hot roast beef sandwiches, hamburgers, and toast. The final bite of my sandwich was always reserved for my friend back in the car, my dog Snowball, our faithful traveling companion who seemed to enjoy our trips south as much as we did.

We were more than halfway home now, but slow going lay ahead as the curves got sharper and the grades steeper. The sound of Dad downshifting the Ford's transmission from third to second and second to first set a new rhythm for our journey. Excitement built as the flatlands of Ohio were left farther and farther behind. We were in the mountains, and each mile took us a few feet higher, a few minutes closer to home.

Oakland, Maryland, was our last checkpoint. From there, it was less than an hour to home. We slipped through the sleepy town past midnight and soon encountered thick fog as we headed up the mountain. The going was slow and tedious; the final fourteen miles from Red House, Maryland, to Thomas were filled with sharp curves, steep grades, and edge-of-seat expectation. The Fairfax Sand and Crushed Stone plant, with its huge hills of sand perched on the mountainside, was the final landmark before Sissaboo Hollow, where my maternal grandparents lived. The fog thinned as the highway

Carl Junior and Cossette Feather stand along West Virginia Route 219 where it
snakes through Sissaboo Hollow, where Cossette's parents, Clayton and Violet Watring, built their home in the late 1930s. *Photo by Carl E. Feather*

followed the ridge of the mountain; the moon and stars reappeared. In
Ashtabula, the incandescent glow of the city and round-the-clock fires spewing from Electromet's stacks obscured all but the brightest stars. But in the
mountains the stars burned with a wonderful clarity. They were all we needed
to light our way home.

Just past the Pierce Road, we descended the hill by Ray Cosner's house,
bounced over the Western Maryland Railroad tracks, and slipped past the
"William, Unincorporated" sign in third gear. We noted whether the Lands-
berrys still had their lights burning and started looking for the lights of my
grandparents' house as we crested the hill from William. The yellow turn
signal cut through the fog as Dad swung the Ford into the gray ballast-stone
driveway. Shivering and brrr-ing, we scurried up the rubber walkway to the
back porch. The wooden screen door rattled under our knocking and Penny,
my grandfather's dog, announced our arrival. Lights came on—bedroom,

kitchen, pantry, porch. The door opened. "God love you, honey, we thought you'd never get here," Grandma said.

The late hour, one or two in the morning, didn't prevent us from sitting around the Formica and steel kitchen table and catching up on Thomas gossip over plates of homemade cookies. A pot of coffee perked in the background and the cuckoo clock in the living room announced the passing of each precious quarter hour. Grandmother entertained me with stories of life in Sissaboo and Grandpa stoked the Warm Morning coal stove in the living room. The coal stove's accepted place as centerpiece was a convention in the mountain home, as typical as the established position of televisions in the living rooms of our Kingsville neighbors (Mother insisted our television be kept in the TV room, so the living room could be kept quiet for quilting and visiting). Indeed, the Warm Morning stove pre-empted the console television, and just as well, for television reception in the mountains was an irritating display of lines and snow interspersed with an occasional picture, usually the commercial message. But while television frustrated and distracted, the stove encouraged the gathering of kin and friends around its portly belly. Its dry warmth was an Appalachian sauna that relaxed and soothed our travel-weary muscles and drew us into the spirit of the mountains, from which the fuel had been harvested. Hauled a bucket at a time from a bin next to the garage—a short but nuisance of a walk in a downpour or blizzard—the coal gave off a slightly acidic, sulfurous smell that was one more assurance we had safely arrived home.

Eventually, sleep replaced that initial rush of excitement and we turned back the covers on our waiting beds. Outside my window, a mountain stream gurgled its timeless folksong, while logging trucks whined at the grade and cars screamed on the curve. Images and memories of the trip flashed through my mind. The flatlands of Ohio and the childhood fears born there seemed a million miles away.

I woke to the sound of Grandpa shaking down the ashes and Grandma talking to her canaries and finches as she uncovered their cages. "God love them," she whispered as they sang their morning mantra. She looked in on me and I pretended to be asleep. Like a fisherman baiting his hook, I stuck my bare foot out from underneath the covers. Grandma stepped in and covered it up. "God love him, she said.

Saturdays were for visiting kin. Dad usually went "up home" to the farm in Eglon to visit his parents, and I accompanied him. The best treat I could hope for from a trip to Eglon was a bottle of orange Nehi pulled from the chest cooler at the feed mill, where my Uncle Edeburn worked. Dad, Edeburn, Grandpa, and my uncle talked farm machinery, jobs, and cars while I looked for snakes in the creek or made small talk with my grandmother. A trip to Thomas with my Grandfather Watring was usually materially more productive—a stop at Cooper's Haberdashery, which had started selling toys during World War II when fine suits got hard to come by and miners couldn't afford them anyway, usually resulted in a sale at my grandfather's expense.

Grandfather Feather was, with the exception of my father, the kindest, humblest, most sincere man I have ever known. He was the epitome of a gentleman farmer whose massive, strong right hand was always outstretched with a simple "How do?" His barn was a major source of entertainment, where the mousing cats eluded my determined efforts to catch them and the sunlight projected abstract patterns on the dusty floor. A tractor ride at his side along the steep hill provided more thrills than any amusement park back in Ohio.

Evenings were spent at my paternal grandparents' farmhouse watching Lawrence Welk polluted by poor reception. Grandpa played with the TV antenna rotor while Grandma served ice cream in plastic bowls that imitated white hobnob milk glass. As dusk settled over the farming community, Dad and I headed back to Thomas on the twisting highway. Fog enveloped our car as we crawled up Backbone Mountain and Dad tuned the radio to a gospel music show. The Acorn Sisters wailed the question "Where Will I Shelter My Sheep Tonight?" and the Ford's transmission seemed to sing along as it downshifted and groaned at the change in topography.

Back in Sissaboo Hollow we sat around the stove or kitchen table and swapped tales of mountain and flatland life. Our sides ached from laughter by the end of the evening, a pain encouraged by the ample servings of homemade donuts and German chocolate cake smothered in my grandmother's caramel frosting. The cuckoo clock kept track of our mortality in mocking tones as the fog enveloped the mountain and sleep overtook our minds.

Dad made a final trip back to the farm Sunday morning while Mom stayed home with Grandmother and helped prepare the send-off meal. Grandfather Watring was a Sunday school teacher and pillar of the Thomas Methodist Church. "Gotta hustle," he'd say as we headed off for church in his aqua and white '57 Chevy. The sanctuary was upstairs, a cold, cavernous room that echoed and amplified the slightest sound. Mrs. Duncan, the funeral direc-

Sissaboo Hollow, West Virginia, as it appears today. The white house is the former Clayton Watring residence. *Photo by Carl E. Feather*

tor's wife, was organist; a sincere soul, she nevertheless lacked the talent for the job. "JESUS SAVES, JESUS SAVES," bellowed my grandfather as the service got under way and the congregation, organist, and song leader each rendered a different version of the hymn. Then a verse or two of "NEARER MY GOD TO THEE, MY DOG HAS FLEAS" . . . "That's what Grandma taught me," I whispered as Grandpa glared, trying not to smile. I snickered.

After church we stopped at the Erhard Jewelry Shop on Front Street, which also sold comic books spread across a large library table in the center of the store. My selection would be my entertainment for the long trip home, a trip that always seemed ten times longer than the one coming. After a lunch of tomato sandwiches, beans, cucumbers, Jello salads, and cake, we piled in the Ford and began the ritual of departure. There were farewells and tears that flowed into Ohio and the next week. Grandmother begged us to stay, but sent us on our way with her blessings. There still were no jobs in Tucker County. "I can't believe you kids are leaving already," she'd say. "It seems like you just got here. Time flies so quickly when you kids are home." Dad slipped the car into gear and started down the driveway. My grandparents followed alongside. He'd stop and there would be more conversation, then another few feet of departure, and more conversation, until we had exhausted the driveway and it was time to leave Sissaboo Hollow for another four or six weeks.

The hollow faded quickly in the rearview mirror as we headed north on Route 219, our image of home blurred by tears, our hearts aching from the fresh re-opening of departing's scar. But there were no opportunities in this hollow, no Ford plants, natural gas company garages, or bustling railroad yards to feed the children, pay the mortgage, and heat the house with fuels conveniently delivered to concealed furnaces. Thomas was a place of inconvenience, depression, and stagnation, so we bought our ticket and hopped on the ride to prosperity, a winding, nauseating rush down the mountain, across two state lines, and far from the warmth of a Warm Morning stove permeating every crevice of a modest house that will always be "home."

Thirty-five years later Clayton and Violet are gone. The house is rental property owned by Barbara and Lowell Long. Dad's homeplace was sold after his father died and his mother went into a nursing home. She died in June 1997, the last of my immediate connections to the mountains. The almost unbearable sense of anticipation and coming home that I experienced whenever we crested that hill above Clayton and Violet's house is gone. Yet every time I pass that house at night in search of a motel, I long to pull into the driveway, bang on that wooden screen door, and hear the sweetest words this side of heaven's mountain: *God love you, honey, we thought you'd never get here.*

references

No mention of references can be made without thanking the scores of mountaineer migrants who shared their stories with me during many long winter nights. This book is primarily based upon their recollections and experiences. The following documents were used for fact checking and background material.

Introduction

Charleston Daily Mail, as cited in notes to the Introduction.

Fowler, Gary. *Appalachian Migration: A Review and Assessment of the Research.* Washington, D.C.: Appalachian Regional Commission, 1980.

Kunkin, Dorothy and Michael Bryne. *Appalachians in Cleveland.* Cleveland: Cleveland State University Institute of Urban Studies, 1973.

Maurer, B. B., ed. *Mountain Heritage.* 4th ed. Parsons, W.Va.: McClain Printing, 1980.

Obermiller, Phillip J., ed. *Down Home, Downtown: Urban Appalachians Today.* Dubuque: Kendall/Hunt Publishing Company, 1996.

Photiadis, John D. *Selected Social and Sociopsychological Characteristics of West Virginians in Their Own State and in Cleveland, Ohio.* Rev. ed. Morgantown: West Virginia University Division of Personal and Family Development; and U.S. Department of Labor, Office of Manpower Research, 1975.

Rico-Velasco, Jesus Antonio. "Immigrants from the Appalachian Region to the City of Columbus, Ohio: A Case Study." Master's thesis, Ohio State University, 1969.

Schwarzweller, Harry K., James S. Brown, and J. J. Mangalam. *Mountain Families in Transition: A Case Study in Appalachian Migration.* University Park: The Pennsylvania State University Press, 1971.

Chapter 1

Ashtabula Star Beacon, Industrial Review Section, 11–15 November 1951, and other issues as cited in the notes to chapter 1.

Colyer, Dale. *West Virginia Employment by Industry Category.* Morgantown: West Virginia University College of Agriculture and Forestry, Division of Resource Management, Agricultural Experiment Station, June 1973.

Explorer: The West Virginia History Database Timeline Module (CD ROM). Charleston: The West Virginia Division of Culture and History, Archives and History section, 1995.

History of Ashtabula County. Jefferson: Ashtabula County Genealogical Society, 1985.

Holden, Jean. "Mountain folk's role important." *Star Beacon,* 15 April 1994.

Kirby, Jack Temple. *Rural Worlds Lost: The American South, 1920–1960.* Baton Rouge: Louisiana State University Press, 1987.

Large, Moina W. *History of Ashtabula County,* 2 volumes. Topeka-Indianapolis: Historical Publishing Company, 1924.

Littell, William Adams. "The Great Chemical Shore." *Inside Ohio* 3 (April 1954): 15–17.

Schweiker, William F. *Some Facts and a Theory of Migration.* Morgantown: West Virginia University Office of Research and Development, Appalachian Center, 1968.

U.S. Bureau of the Census. *U.S. Census of Population: 1950, Vol. 1, Number of Inhabitants.* Washington, D.C.: U.S. Government Printing Office, 1952

U.S. Bureau of the Census. *U.S. Census of Population: 1960, Vol. 1, Characteristics of the Population, Part A, Number of Inhabitants.* Washington, D.C.: U.S. Government Printing Office, 1961.

Weller, Jack E. *Yesterday's People: Life in Contemporary Appalachia.* Lexington: University of Kentucky Press, 1965.

Chapter 3

Anderson, Stanley J. *Tales of Northern Webster County.* Utica, Ky.: McDowell Publications, 1978.

Foster, Elaine Morrison. "'Big Andy' Boggs." *Goldenseal Magazine* [Charleston: West Virginia Division of Culture and History] (January–March 1978).

Miller, Sampson Newton. *Annals of Webster County, West Virginia.* Buckhannon: West Virginia Wesleyan College, 1969.

Chapter 7

Norvell, Artie J., and Ruth Spiker. "Ten Mile." (1927) In *History of West Virginia Communities*. Morgantown: Agricultural Extension Division, College of Agriculture, West Virginia University, 1924–28.

Chapter 10

Fansler, Homer Floyd. *History of Tucker County, West Virginia*. Parsons, W. Va.: McClain Printing, 1962

Knepper, George W. *Ohio and Its People*. Kent: The Kent State University Press, 1989.

Chapter 11

Miller, Sampson Newton. *Annals of Webster County, West Virginia*. Buckhannon: West Virginia Wesleyan College, 1969.

Chapter 12

Fansler, Homer Floyd. *History of Tucker County, West Virginia*. Parsons, W. Va.: McClain Printing, 1962

Chapter 14

Blackhurst, W. E. *Your Train Ride through History*. Parsons, W. Va.: McClain Printing Co., 1968.

Chapter 15

Fansler, Homer Floyd. *History of Tucker County, West Virginia*. Parsons, W. Va.: McClain Printing, 1962.

Chapter 17

Obermiller, Phillip J., ed. *Down Home, Downtown: Urban Appalachians Today*. Dubuque: Kendall/Hunt Publishing Company, 1996.

Photiadis, John D. *Selected Social and Sociopsychological Characteristics of West Virginians in Their Own State and in Cleveland, Ohio*. Rev. ed. Morgantown: West Virginia University Division of Personal and Family Development; and U.S. Department of Labor, Office of Manpower Research, 1975.

Schwarzweller, Harry K., James S. Brown, and J. J. Mangalam. *Mountain Families in Transition: A Case Study in Appalachian Migration.* University Park: The Pennsylvania State University Press, 1971.

Simpkins, O. Norman. "Culture." In *Mountain Heritage,* ed. B. B. Maurer. Parsons, W.Va.: McClain Printing, 1980.

Also consulted to verify residences of sources interviewed: *Ashtabula City Directories, 1939-1960, Ashtabula County Farm and Business Directory,* 1950–52 and 1955 editions. R. L. Polk Publishing. For dates of migration and other matters of record for deceased migrants, I consulted Ashtabula *Star Beacon* obituaries.

index